THE PEOPLE
vs
THE BANKS

'Our financial services industry is a crime scene and Michael Roddan is the forensic pathologist. He has written a compelling account of what happened—it is a page-turner in the great tradition of true crime, but also a cautionary account of how a service industry forgot how to serve.'
ALAN KOHLER

THE PEOPLE vs THE BANKS

MICHAEL RODDAN

MELBOURNE
UNIVERSITY
PRESS

MELBOURNE UNIVERSITY PRESS
An imprint of Melbourne University Publishing Limited
Level 1, 715 Swanston Street, Carlton, Victoria 3053, Australia
mup-contact@unimelb.edu.au
www.mup.com.au

First published 2019
Text © Michael Roddan, 2019
Design and typography © Melbourne University Publishing Limited, 2019

Cover design by Peter Long
Typeset in 11/16pt Sabon by Cannon Typesetting

A catalogue record for this book is available from the National Library of Australia

9780522875188 (paperback)
9780522875195 (ebook)

CONTENTS

ABBREVIATIONS

ABA	Australian Banking Association
ACBF	Aboriginal Community Benefit Fund
ACCC	Australian Competition & Consumer Commission
ACTU	Australian Council of Trade Unions
AEC	Australian Electoral Commission
APRA	Australian Prudential Regulation Authority
ASFA	Association of Superannuation Funds of Australia
ASIC	Australian Securities & Investments Commission
ASX	Australian Securities Exchange
AUSTRAC	Australian Transaction Reports and Analysis Centre
BBSW rate	bank bill swap rate
CBA	Commonwealth Bank of Australia
CDPP	Commonwealth Director of Public Prosecutions
CFMEU	Construction, Forestry, Maritime, Mining and Energy Union
CFR	Council of Financial Regulators
FOFA	Future of Financial Advice
FOS	Financial Ombudsman Service
FPA	Financial Planning Association
FSC	Financial Services Council
FSU	Finance Sector Union
GFC	global financial crisis
ICAC	Independent Commission Against Corruption
ICAN	Indigenous Consumer Assistance Network
ISA	Industry Super Australia
NAB	National Australia Bank
PC	Productivity Commission
RBA	Reserve Bank of Australia
SMSF	self-managed super fund
UAP	United Australia Party

1

BARBARIANS AT THE GATE

'Things have changed,' Scott Morrison told the guardians of the financial system.

It was Wednesday night, 29 November 2017, and Wayne Byres, the head of Australia's banking regulator, APRA, and Philip Lowe, the Reserve Bank governor, were hooked up on a call to Morrison, urging the treasurer to take control of the situation at the eleventh hour. It would be 'the least worst option', they said.

Frustrated by the Coalition's refusal to set up a royal commission into the banks, a cabal of rogue backbenchers led by Nationals MP Barry O'Sullivan were on the brink of clinching enough votes to launch their own unwieldy financial services inquiry. The proposed commission of inquiry, which would be instilled with all the powers of a royal commission but set up outside of the hands of the government, was finally within reach. Tomorrow, the bill was sure to pass parliament.

It couldn't be allowed to happen, Byres and Lowe warned Morrison. O'Sullivan's commission could do irreparable damage to the financial system. Everybody's job, everybody's mortgage, every loan to every business in the country was dependent on the strength and credibility of the financial system, they said, and O'Sullivan was about to lift the lid on Pandora's box.

With the help of a few of his Nationals colleagues, Labor, the Greens and a handful of crossbench MPs, O'Sullivan had just secured the numbers to blow open the casket. On the numbers, Morrison had lost control, and the executives of the major banks were terrified. For two years, they had claimed the sky would fall in should they be subjected to the glare of a royal commission. Recessions, spiralling interest rates and housing market implosions were all forecast by a sector desperate to avoid scrutiny. Now, it was all but certain at the hands of the uncontrollable O'Sullivan bill.

Lines of urgent communication were opened up between the banking sector and the Reserve Bank of Australia (RBA) and the Australian Prudential Regulation Authority (APRA), the two regulators charged with protecting the stability of the financial system.

For Lowe and Byres, the national economic interest dictated that the government would have to take a different course from the one it had charted. A royal commission was 'regrettably necessary', the pair told Morrison.

'We had to deal with the maths in the Parliament,' Morrison later said. 'And the maths in the parliament was going to lead to an unwieldy and directionless and haphazard commission of inquiry which would have done far greater damage—and that was not something that we believed should be allowed to happen.' Things had changed.

There are decades where nothing happens. And then there are weeks where decades happen. Over that last week of November, everything happened.

Just seven days earlier, O'Sullivan had released his private member's bill for the commission of inquiry into the banking sector. It had sprung from a seldom-used piece of legislation that allows the parliament to hold the government to account. When the government of the day will not launch a royal commission into a particular case, a separate Act allows the parliament to establish a commission of inquiry that reports to parliament rather than the governor-general. Any such inquiry can be given whatever powers a parliament sees fit to give it, as long as they are constitutional.

Greens senator Peter Whish-Wilson had floated the idea of a financial services commission of inquiry a year before, borrowing from the unusual parliamentary manoeuvre that had been used to investigate High Court justice and former Labor attorney-general Lionel Murphy in the 1980s.

Despite the pace of events in the last week of November, momentum for the commission of inquiry had been building for some time.

In late October, the High Court's decision to disqualify former deputy prime minister Barnaby Joyce on the basis of his dual citizenship had shaved down the government's wafer-thin parliamentary majority. In the aftermath, Queensland independent Bob Katter and Nick Xenophon Team MP Rebekha Sharkie had given support to a push by Queensland Nationals MP George Christensen to trigger a commission into the banks. Christensen had only recently backed down from his threat to cross the floor to support the Greens' own bill for a commission of inquiry, which was co-sponsored by the Senate crossbench and passed the upper house.

Fast-forward a few months, and now O'Sullivan was releasing his own draft bill for a commission of inquiry. This time, it had the numbers to pass. O'Sullivan had opened the door to his office and invited input from any other politician on Capital Hill. The bill would hit the floor in a week's time, and all he needed was seventy-six votes on the floor of the House of Representatives. With a few concessions here and a few amendments there, he was virtually assured of the numbers.

The horsetrading resulted in dramatically expanding the terms of reference for the mooted inquiry as input from various MPs who stormed into his office dragged them wider. But O'Sullivan was happy to be accommodative.

The breadth of what the commission would be investigating sent shivers down the spines of the banks. It proposed to test whether behaviour in the financial sector was 'unethical'—a seemingly absurd hurdle to clear for a financial services firm, let alone any business. A 'fairness and propriety' test would have implications well beyond the banking sector, while an investigation into whether banks had acted fairly when impairing sinking borrowers would directly fall foul of prudential laws requiring banks to do so. The ragtag parties across the Senate would also be given the power to nominate three commissioners—a former judge, a community representative and a financial expert. The banks feared a circus where they'd be forced to swallow the sword.

All sorts of MPs were walking into O'Sullivan's office, across party lines, with every idea being written into the draft bill. One of them was Labor senator Sam Dastyari, who had eventually persuaded his leader, Bill Shorten, to take up a proposal for a banking royal commission in the party's election platform.

The Nationals MPs were determined to launch the inquiry. Liberal government MPs were aghast at their Coalition partners. Prime Minister Malcolm Turnbull had been calling O'Sullivan repeatedly over the week. A former merchant banker himself, he believed O'Sullivan had little comprehension of what he was about to unleash and, like a dog chasing a garbage truck, little idea of what he wanted. It would be a political disaster if Labor and the Greens could anoint the commissioner overseeing the inquiry, but it was an own goal O'Sullivan didn't seem to comprehend.

Financial Services Minister Kelly O'Dwyer was told to try to sort the mess out. She called O'Sullivan into her office on that Wednesday morning as he was wrapping up the draft bill. While O'Dwyer kept her composure at the meeting, she was privately horrified about the extent of control the Greens and Labor would have over the inquiry. She told O'Sullivan the government needed more time to consider the draft bill and urged him to hold off on his threat to introduce it at least until the next day, which would give Morrison enough time to work out a plan.

The delaying tactic worked, and pushed the treasurer and prime minister into crisis mode. As her meeting with O'Sullivan ended, O'Dwyer strode across parliament and into Morrison's office. He was sitting with Nationals MP Llew O'Brien, who had threatened to cross the floor to support the O'Sullivan bill. O'Brien pleaded with

Morrison to back the inquiry. He was under pressure from constituents in his regional Queensland electorate over recent sackings of local bank employees.

As O'Brien left, O'Dwyer and Morrison came to the reluctant conclusion that the Nationals would not be for turning. They didn't understand the consequences of the O'Sullivan bill, nor did they care. As things stood, the parliament would in about twenty-four hours' time be voting for the commission of inquiry.

It was clear Morrison's Plan B had not worked. Under the threat of the O'Sullivan plan, the treasurer had been rushing together a new compensation scheme for victims of financial scandals in a bid to soothe the Nationals revolt. A week prior, he had called the chief executives and chairs of the major banks to discuss his plan to resolve 'legacy issues' attached to historical misconduct. Under the proposal, a panel would mediate and review cases and award compensation.

The mini-royal commission looked promising. Warren Entsch, a Liberal MP who had long been agitating against the banking sector, was involved in the negotiations. But the banks were circumspect about the plan's ability to derail O'Sullivan.

The discussions with the bank bosses brought all the executives together. National Australia Bank chairman Ken Henry and Westpac chairman Lindsay Maxsted met with Morrison on 23 November, and Commonwealth Bank chairman Catherine Livingstone and ANZ chairman David Gonski met with him the next day. The bankers were supportive of the move, but didn't think it would kill the political football O'Sullivan was handballing around parliament.

They were proven correct. Come Monday, the nation's politicians had once again descended on Canberra and O'Sullivan was able to gather the numbers for his commission of inquiry bill. Tuesday's newspaper headlines told the bankers all they needed to know. Time was up.

The bank chairs discussed the imminent threat over a phone hook-up and decided they needed to come up with a contingency plan. They tapped their chief executives to get together on the Wednesday, at the same time as O'Dwyer was winning her brief reprieve from O'Sullivan in his office.

By early evening on Wednesday 29 November, the bankers had all agreed it was desperate times. The desperate measure, then, would be to rip off the bandaid. A letter signed by the four chairmen and the chief executives was sent to the treasurer in which they told him that the next morning they would call for a royal commission into themselves—one with properly instituted terms of reference—and hoped the government would fall behind the plan. The letter would be lodged with the Australian Securities Exchange (ASX) on the Thursday morning at 8.30 a.m., which would make it a public document. It would be game over.

Unbeknown to the bankers, Morrison had been preparing a grudging Plan C. The wheels had already been in motion as the government was not oblivious to reality. A small circle of Cabinet ministers had been working fast and hard behind the scenes to prepare the ground for their own banking royal commission. After opposing such a move for two years, in the panicky week Turnbull had decided he was now open to such a measure.

In a Cabinet meeting earlier in November, the prime minister had raised the prospect that the government might be forced to hold a royal commission. Morrison had been furious at the suggestion. Back-flipping would make him look utterly foolish for arguing so stridently against such an inquiry for so long, he told the meeting. But it was clear the ground was already shifting beneath him.

On Tuesday 21 November, a second small Cabinet meeting was called. In that meeting of crestfallen MPs, all too aware that they had their backs against the ropes, Turnbull raised again the possibility of the government holding its own royal commission. If it was inevitable, they might as well control it. They could even broaden the inquiry beyond the big four banks to the places they wanted it to go, while keeping it on a tight leash so it didn't look where they didn't want it to look.

After that meeting, the pointy heads in the Department of Treasury were asked to start designing the government's own royal commission, just in case. Treasury dutifully came back to Morrison with advice and a draft terms of reference, and held discussions with Attorney-General George Brandis about the potential inquiry's content and scope.

The government's key economic advisory department basically already had everything ready to go. Treasury deputy secretary John Lonsdale had spent quite a lot of time in the year leading up to this moment thinking about a royal commission and advising the government on what it might look like.

After the Cabinet meeting, Morrison used the next two days talking to the banking chiefs and the rest of his parliamentary colleagues. The treasurer would become a late convert, changing his mind on the royal commission given the threat of a much more uncontrollable commission of inquiry. As he received the signed letter from the bank bosses, everything had fallen into place. A late-night phone call soon after with the APRA and RBA bosses, warning of the price of inaction, was enough to seal the deal.

Turnbull called a Cabinet meeting for early on the Thursday morning, just before the ASX would publish the signed letter from Commonwealth Bank, Westpac, National Australia Bank and ANZ.

At 8.31 a.m., the statement hit the market: 'Major banks unite to call for certainty and stability'. David Gonski and his ANZ chief Shayne Elliott, Catherine Livingstone and CBA boss Ian Narev, Ken Henry and head of NAB Andrew Thorburn, and Lindsay Maxsted and his chief Brian Hartzer said it was time for the government to 'act decisively'. Writing to the treasurer 'as the leaders of Australia's major banks', they gave the government all it needed to backflip on its own reticence regarding a royal commission. 'Our banks have consistently argued the view that further inquiries into the sector, including a royal commission, are unwarranted,' the letter said. 'However, it is now in the national interest for the political uncertainty to end.'

As financial market traders digested the document, the meeting of Cabinet ministers endorsed a decision to set up a royal commission. Less than half an hour after the bank statement went live, Turnbull and Morrison walked out into the prime minister's courtyard for a press conference to announce the commission. What had once been unthinkable was apparently now the only way to restore confidence in the financial sector.

'Since the financial crisis there have been examples of misconduct by financial institutions, some of them extremely serious. And that's demanded a response from the institutions themselves and from government,' Turnbull said. 'The only way we can give all Australians a greater degree of assurance is a royal commission into misconduct in the financial services industry.'

The prime minister gave one stern warning: 'This will not be an open-ended commission. It will not put capitalism on trial.'

In Sydney, Australian Banking Association (ABA) chief executive Anna Bligh was caught unawares.

Bligh, the chief lobbyist for the banking sector, had been forewarned that the letter from the major banks would be sent to the treasurer, but she was shocked at the pace of events. As the statement went live, the former Queensland premier was on stage at the national conference of the Association of Superannuation Funds of Australia (ASFA) partaking in a discussion about the diminishing trust in the financial sector. On one side of her was ASFA chief Dr Martin Fahy, and on the other, the chairman of the superannuation fund Cbus, Steve Bracks.

In the final minutes of the hour-long session at the Sydney Convention Centre, a hand arose in the crowd, begging to interject. The room was informed that a banking royal commission had just been announced by the government, and the tenor of the discussion took a turn.

'The thing about commissions of inquiry,' Bligh said, 'I've called them. I've given evidence in them. And they don't always go the way that people think they might when they go out.'

As the discussion drew to a close, Bligh slipped out the back door of the conference room. She stopped for a quick discussion with two reporters but, not having been forewarned of the immediate launch of the royal commission by the government, was whisked away to catch up on the news.

I was one of those reporters, and the pace with which the government had turned around its opposition to a royal commission had taken me by surprise, too. I'd had little reason to believe the O'Sullivan bill would be successful. I had been with *The Australian* newspaper writing about the banking and financial sector for a few years by this point, and there had been a lot of posturing but little in the way of delivering a royal commission.

I had been watching in parliament in Canberra just a few months earlier, in June, when George Christensen had backed down from his threat to cross the floor for the Greens commission of inquiry bill. Despite Christensen talking a big game about how he wanted an inquiry into the lenders, when the Damocles sword was dangled over Turnbull's head the rogue Nationals MP failed to swing. It had seemed to me that rhetoric would be taking precedence over action against the banks for some time to come.

And there had been little sign from the banking community that they would buckle to the pressure. The day before the royal commission was called, Westpac head of business banking David Lindberg, one of the most senior executives at the nation's second-largest bank, had told a gathering of industry figures that an inquiry into the banking system could bring the nation closer to a recession and 'economic collapse' if it deterred global investors from operating in the local financial sector. Little did he realise that his boss was part of the industry coup organising a royal commission into themselves.

While it seemed few people inside the industry were aware of the plan, Bligh was by now used to being the last to be told of the government's intentions. The Coalition had already sucked dry its account of political capital in defending the banking sector from a royal commission, but as it did so, Morrison had been intent on proving he was not a lackey for the financial industry. Indeed, the appointment of Bligh to the banking sector's top post just six months earlier had caused more bad blood between the financial industry and the Turnbull Government than could have been predicted. The appointment of a former Labor premier to be the new chief negotiator for the banks in Canberra? It was clear what the banks thought of the chances of a Turnbull re-election.

When Bligh was announced as the new ABA boss in February, relations instantly broke down between the sector and Morrison. NAB boss Andrew Thorburn, the then-chairman of the ABA, rang Morrison to give him the news of the appointment, but the treasurer was already fully aware: his chief of communications, Sasha Grebe, had applied for the job too.

In a late-night phone call before the announcement of the choice of Bligh, NAB had got in touch with Grebe to arrange for Thorburn to call the treasurer the next morning. Grebe had that day been contacted by headhunting firm Heidrick & Struggles to let him know he hadn't got the job. It was a blow for Grebe—and for Morrison's ego.

When former ABA chief Steve Münchenberg had announced his resignation, Morrison had personally supported Grebe's attempt to relocate to Sydney for the job, where his young family was based. ANZ chairman David Gonski, Business Council chief Jennifer Westacott and Westpac board member Craig Dunn had all given endorsements for Grebe in the role. So when the chief executives of the big four banks signed off on Bligh's nomination, it caused quite the stir. Financial-rag gossip columns were devoted to it for a week. On the news, Morrison at short notice cancelled a string of meetings with the bank executives that had been scheduled over the coming fortnight. And by Sunday, Grebe had resigned from the treasurer's office. The situation between the government and the banks would only deteriorate from there.

The treasurer responded in kind just an hour before he handed down the May federal budget three months later. A courtesy call from Treasury Secretary John Fraser told the chief executives that Morrison would, in forty-five minutes time, be announcing a new $6.2 billion tax on the big four banks. It was the centrepiece of the budget, the treasurer's big day.

The banks could hardly contain their rage. They had been given no forewarning of the measure. On budget night, having learned of the new law while trapped in the budget lock-up with other industry groups, Bligh went on the attack, claiming it could undermine the stability of the financial system. However, as ANZ chief Shayne Elliott believed, it seemed the price tag to avoid a royal commission was just a little over $6 billion.

When Fraser had finished calling the executives, the major banks had already lost $14 billion in market capitalisation as their stock prices were heavily sold off. Eyebrows around Canberra were raised. Boardrooms across Sydney and Melbourne scratched their heads at the sudden imposition of the major bank tax and a raft of other measures targeting the sector, brought in by a Liberal government that had been defending the banks against calls for a royal commission. Was this what it was going to be like from now on?

Sniffing a conspiracy, several industry figures suggested Morrison had foisted harsh new rules on the sector because of the shafting of Grebe. The politically astute ANZ, chaired by Turnbull's close friend Gonski, had even warned Thorburn against the selection of Bligh, although ANZ eventually signed off on the decision. The ABA appointment had clearly been an attempt to soften Labor's hostility to the industry, but Labor MPs saw Bligh transformed into a persona non grata as her appointment stoked resentment of the banks among Coalition members.

Having been hammered day in, day out by Shorten with his calls for a royal commission during the previous election, the banks repaid Turnbull and Morrison with a slap in the face, naming Bligh, a political enemy, as the face of the industry. Adding further to the insult, the banks had just months earlier ended their political donations to the Liberal Party when the party's finances were at their weakest.

Under questioning at parliament in the lead-up to the election, Elliott had revealed that his bank was debating whether it should end donations to both Labor and the Coalition amid rising public disquiet regarding corporate donations to political parties. ANZ's decision followed a move by NAB to quietly ban all political donations from May 2016, bringing it into line with Westpac and CBA, which had banned donations earlier.

The donations ban stoked fear within Liberal Party ranks because it meant the party's coffers were being squeezed of an important source of financing for campaigns. Labor, on the other hand, was able to rely on funds from the union movement.

The knife-edge 2016 federal election had revealed the sorry state of the party's finances. Turnbull, in the weeks leading to the vote, had to donate $1.75 million of his personal savings to the party. At the same time as the huge donation, the financially troubled New South Wales division of the Liberal Party was sending out urgent letters to members asking them to 'step up' and donate as little as $10. 'Even $5 would make a difference,' finance director and former federal MP Peter McGauran wrote to the party faithful.

For months, the Coalition had had to defend what would have otherwise been indefensible behaviour from the banking sector. All the while, the government was muttering that the business community and the banks were missing in action from its campaign to lower the corporate tax rate to 25 per cent. Labor's campaign against that '$50 billion handout' to big corporations and the banks had the Coalition on the back foot at the same time it was doing big business a favour by trying to shut down momentum for a royal commission.

The alliance between the biggest businesses in town and the Liberal Party had begun to fracture.

Just as Turnbull was heading to the polls in the 2016 election, he was the guest of honour at a Westpac event celebrating the bank's 199th birthday. Like rain on its wedding day, just twenty-four hours before Westpac's big bash, the Australian Securities & Investments Commission (ASIC) had served the bank with a lawsuit in the Federal Court over claims it had rigged a key interest-rate benchmark, relied on to price billions of dollars of loans every day. It was a sensational move in which the corporate regulator had expanded its concurrent action against rival lender ANZ over similar claims.

Turnbull had already been scheduled to deliver an address to the Westpac event, and in a speech that went down like a lead balloon with the cream of Australia's corporate scene, he claimed the banks were 'unlike any other' business and were failing the community.

'We have to acknowledge there have been too many troubling incidents over recent times for them simply to be dismissed,' Turnbull said. 'We expect our banks to have high standards, we expect them always rigorously to put their customers' interests first, to deal with their depositors and their borrowers, those they advise and those with whom they transact, in precisely the same way they would have them deal with themselves. This is not idealism, this is what we expect. The singular pursuit of an extra dollar of profit at the expense of those values is not simply wrong, but places at risk the whole social licence, the good name and reputation upon which great institutions depend.'

It wasn't capitalism on trial just yet, but the political mood was edging closer to it.

The deluge of corporate scandals had been piling up for a decade. In the months before the Westpac rate-rigging scandal became public, CBA's mistreatment of life insurance customers—including using outdated medical definitions to deny payouts for heart attack survivors—had been splashed across the media.

The CommInsure life insurance scandal had been a game changer. Despite the grave allegations made about CommInsure riding rough-shod over its customers, CBA said nothing was wrong. It would maintain its indignation about the scandal for another two years. But it was the final straw for Bill Shorten. At this point, he made the decision to back his colleague Sam Dastyari and broaden Labor's electoral platform with a promise to hold a royal commission into the banking sector.

As Turnbull urged the banks to shore up their standards, the bodies continued to pile up. Not long later, ASIC would serve a rate-rigging suit against NAB in allegations it also, following the Westpac and ANZ cases, was manipulating the so-called bank bill swap rate. CBA would be dragged into the scandal post-haste.

The banking industry was yet to cotton on to just how fast its stocks with the community were sliding. Worse still, the problems did not seem contained to one part of the financial sector. New financial advice scandals continued to drip out of the major wealth managers. The insurance industry was pilloried for reaping billions from high-pressure sales of useless 'add-on' products sold through car yards, but it resisted ASIC's demands to curtail the practice. Life insurers were found to be funnelling customers into poor-quality policies at the same time as huge kickbacks were being paid to the advisers who were hocking the products. Superannuation funds were being gifted trillions in savings and then siphoning out as much as possible in profits and fees from the nest eggs of millions of Australians.

CBA was then hammered over breaching anti-money-laundering regulations more than 50,000 times, allowing terrorist financiers and criminal syndicates to wash money through the nation's largest lender unchecked. It was the third major scandal to tarnish the country's biggest bank in as many years.

It looked as though the warnings of the head of ASIC, Greg Medcraft, had been right all along.

The deliberate sidelining of Bligh by the government in its rush to call a commission was a sign of terse relations between the Turnbull Government and the banks. The same could be said of what it thought of ASIC.

While Morrison had spent the evening before announcing the inquiry on the phone to APRA and the RBA, the last member of the esteemed Council of Financial Regulators (CFR), ASIC, had been left in the dark.

The corporate watchdog, whose job it was to police misconduct throughout the financial sector, had not been notified of the government's imminent decision to launch a royal commission into the sector. The government's terms of reference even included an examination of the 'effectiveness and ability of regulators' to address financial misconduct—putting the track record of ASIC squarely in the firing line of the commission. At the same time, the terms specifically excluded an inquiry into 'macro-prudential policy and regulation', which appeared to exempt the RBA and APRA from the inquiry.

ASIC had long been a kicking bag of critics of inaction against corporate crime, and now the government was keen to stick the boot in too.

Like the banks, ASIC had long fallen out of favour with the government. In 2014, the then chairman of ASIC, Greg Medcraft, had used an incendiary speech to label Australia a 'paradise' for white-collar criminals. Existing penalties for white-collar crime, particularly civil penalties, were a 'slap on the wrist' that failed to instil sufficient fear in executives to deter offences, he had said.

It was a direct shot across the bows of the Abbott Government, and Medcraft said ASIC was underfunded and lacked the resources to tackle corporate crime. Tony Abbott had just sliced $120 million from ASIC's budget.

Medcraft's remarks enraged government ministers. Finance Minister Mathias Cormann immediately phoned him and told him to back-pedal his comments. He didn't, but he slightly refined them. What he'd meant to say, Medcraft said the next day, was that ASIC wanted to ensure Australia never became a paradise for white-collar criminals.

The damage was already done. The day after making the comments, Medcraft appeared before a Senate committee. As he walked into the hearing room, Nationals senator John 'Wacka' Williams greeted him with 'Mr Medcraft, welcome to paradise. I've said for five-and-a-half years we should have a royal commission into white-collar crime, because I believe Australia is, today, a paradise for white-collar crime.' Cormann was forced to sit through a humiliating hearing where ASIC's funding cuts took centre stage. It would be another two years until, under Turnbull, the government reversed the Abbott funding cuts—in a decision that was announced the week after Bill Shorten formalised Labor's call for a royal commission, in the wake of the Westpac birthday party.

When the royal commission was finally announced, it looked as if the government was about to get its revenge on ASIC for its intransigence. ASIC had already been subjected to a gruelling 'capability review' in 2015 that shone a light on the regulator's weaknesses. However, that review revealed, too, how poorly ASIC was funded compared to its counterparts.

Senior executives at ASIC were concerned about what the exclusion from Morrison's phone call with the regulators revealed about ASIC's relationship with the government. The government had already been reluctant to reappoint Medcraft, a Labor appointee, to the chairman's role. 'We were not consulted,' ASIC acting chair Peter Kell told a parliamentary committee the day after the commission was announced. 'The royal commission and the terms of reference are ones for government. We haven't had any input.'

Labor was furious at the admission, but the inquiry it had fought so hard for was quickly escaping its control. It was no longer the domain of the Opposition party. Indeed, the Turnbull Government had turned the royal commission on the Labor Party. Having been forced to launch an inquiry it never wanted to hold, the government now saw an opportunity to pay back Labor for its part in whipping up community support for the commission.

In the draft terms of reference for the inquiry, the government included an investigation into the superannuation sector. This would inevitably point to a closer examination of industry funds, which were the hallmark of former Labor prime minister Paul Keating's legacy and one of the crown jewels of the Labor Party. Superannuation was a fully-fledged $700 billion sector composed of super fund managers controlled by union-appointed board directors aligned with Labor.

While many of the largest industry funds, such as AustralianSuper and the CFMEU-backed Cbus, were among the best financial firms in the country, delivering significant investment returns for their members while keeping their beaks clean of scandals, the inclusion of super funds in the royal commission was a direct smack at Labor. Government backbenchers had been hyping up a conspiracy that industry funds were stealing members' savings and handing over the money to unions. The unions would then donate the funds to Labor, to the tune of $50 million over a decade—or so went the claim.

Government legislation to remove union appointees from director boards—an attempt to crack down on the alleged behaviour—had been stuck in the Senate and unable to pass. A fierce advertising campaign by the industry funds against the legislation accused the government of letting foxes into the henhouses where Australians' nest eggs were safe, and had convinced the crossbench to withhold support for the bill.

Painted into a corner by Labor, the government had now snuck into the terms that the commission must inquire into the use of superannuation members' retirement savings 'for any purpose that does not meet community standards and expectations or is otherwise not in the best interest of members'. It was clear the government wanted to investigate the way industry funds distributed money to unions for marketing and other services.

'The government's made a decision,' Home Affairs Minister Peter Dutton said the day after the announcement of the royal commission. 'So hopefully for some people they can present their cases and there can be some closure around what's been a difficult situation.

'But there's also another element to it,' Dutton went on, 'that is, to have a look at some aspects within the industry super funds which have union members and whatnot on the board. People lose a lot of their super through fees and through donations and all sorts of support for unions. So I think it's a good opportunity in that sense.'

If the government was going to go down for protecting the banking sector, it was going to try to drag Labor down with it. After two years of campaigning for a wide-ranging investigation into the banking sector, Labor appeared to have been outplayed by the government. For it would not just be capitalism that was put on trial, it would also be organised labour.

2

CAPITAL IN THE TWENTIETH CENTURY

The day after the government announced the royal commission, Anna Bligh phoned the treasurer's office and pleaded with Scott Morrison's staff to limit how far back in time the commission could investigate bad behaviour.

Bligh, a former Queensland Labor premier, also tried to twist the arm of Treasury to ensure the government expanded the terms of reference for the commission to ensure it was not just the misdeeds of the major banks and their various divisions that were going to be aired. She wanted it to investigate misconduct in rival firms, mortgage brokers and unregulated 'shadow' banks.

We know this because at 5 p.m. the day after the inquiry was announced, one of the treasurer's staffers passed on the ABA's concerns, made through Bligh, to senior Treasury officials. Her wishes were passed on to government mandarins including Treasury Secretary John Fraser and Morrison's own chief of staff, Phil Gaetjens—who would later replace Fraser to become secretary himself. Bligh's 'preference' was to limit the terms of reference 'as to how far back' the commissioner could venture.

In documents unearthed using freedom of information laws, Bligh also wanted to make sure the inquiry had the ability to disregard some scandals thought to be superfluous to the process: 'i.e. has the discretion not to inquire and can exercise this discretion where cases are too far back/too long ago', the Treasury official dutifully explained to Morrison.

While the terms never explicitly restricted the time frame able to be investigated, the first order of the inquiry's business was to demand from the financial companies extensive lists of any possible misconduct going back ten years. A lot can go wrong in a decade—but for some, including Nationals senator John 'Wacka' Williams, it didn't go back far enough.

Whenever Wacka calls you, he has invariably just finished hammering in steel posts on his property, rounding up sheep, cutting firewood, or warning that his reception is about to cut out as he drives through a black spot between two regional towns with unfamiliar names.

This time, the former sheep shearer had just finished mending a fence down the back paddock on his 160-hectare farm, Rob Roy, near Inverell in northern NSW, when he picked up the phone. 'I just sat down for a cup of tea,' Wacka told me. 'I had the iPad out to read the news and I've seen your story.' My article detailing Bligh's attempts to limit the royal commission had just been published, and Wacka wanted to share his thoughts.

The outspoken senator burst onto the political scene in 2008 and made his name as a fearless critic of white-collar crime and corporate malfeasance, whether dodgy bankers, ruthless liquidators or parasitic financial planners. With the help of Commonwealth Bank whistle-blower Jeff Morris, he helped unearth the multimillion-dollar financial planning scandal that had festered in the nation's biggest lender for years and was broken to the public by Fairfax reporter Adele Ferguson. Wacka's ambition to drive hard-hitting investigations through Senate committees had made him a sworn enemy of CBA.

He even had firsthand experience of the damage that could be wrought by unruly financial institutions. The senator had lost a previous property, along with a marriage, after his family fell victim to a bad foreign-exchange loan spruiked to him—and many other farmers—by CBA in the 1980s.

But Wacka didn't let his own history get in the way of looking to mend fences with the banks. He had maintained a good relationship with the ABA's previous boss, Steve Münchenberg, and when Bligh was announced as the association's new chief executive in early 2017 he stuck out his hand across the ideological divide. However, Bligh had never returned Wacka's phone call or accepted his invitation to have a meeting. So be it, he'd thought.

Now, the idea that Bligh had pressured the government to restrict the royal commission he'd fought hard to establish incensed him.

'The last time we had a royal commission was in 1936 when the Country Party leader, Sir Earle Page, forced one,' Wacka said. 'We haven't had a royal commission into the banks ever since. As far as I am concerned, it's a long time from 1936 to now, and I don't care how far you have to go back to bring out the wrongdoing, clean out the dirty laundry and set us in the right direction.'

At the end of 1935, Prime Minister Joe Lyons was just a year and a bit into leading the country. He was soon forced to announce that the government would hold a royal commission into the behaviour of the banks.

Lyons, the leader of the United Australia Party, had promised such an inquiry as part of a deal to form a coalition government with the Country Party, led by Sir Earle Page, following the 1934 election. Much like in 2018, the majority government party had fiercely resisted the establishment of a banking inquiry, which was forced on it by its minority coalition partner. Lyons didn't want to upset the financial interests that had backed his rise to leader of the UAP, but after a year of fruitlessly resisting, he buckled. The wide-ranging banking inquiry was established and would leave its mark on the financial system for decades.

It leaves one thinking that corporate boards should perhaps have at least one director with an interest in history. Directors are sought out for their corporate memory of institutions, economic cycles and markets. However, while this knowledge has been built up from decades of following the market in financial institutions, there are far longer cycles of economic and political upheaval, and the ramifications of these slow-moving social cycles are much less understood at the corporate executive level.

The public discontent that had driven the establishment of what was until very recently Australia's only royal commission into banking was resuscitated eighty years after Lyon's banking royal commission handed down its report.

The 1936–37 Royal Commission on Monetary and Banking Systems aimed at putting the banks on trial, because they were seen to have played a role in dragging out the Great Depression in the late 1920s and early 30s. The banks, Page's Country Party argued, had sharpened the pain during the economic downturn by restricting credit and calling in teetering loans.

There may have been some intergenerational antagonism behind the Country Party's push for the commission. Page's own father had been bankrupted during the 1893 Australian financial crisis, the deepest and most severe in the country's history.

While the 1936 royal commission did take a close look at the commercial banks, the hearings ended up being dominated by a focus on the regulatory architecture of the financial system, and whether central banks could have done more to stave off the Depression. The then government-owned Commonwealth Bank, which from the 1920s onward had been given some responsibilities for central banking, had refused to lend with gusto during the economic downturn, in direct conflict with what Treasurer Edward Theodore in the Scullin Labor government had urged them to do.

Many in the Labor government saw this as an act of political betrayal by the 'people's bank', and CBA was accused of succumbing to the financial interests it had been created to counter. Fallout from the dispute between the bank and the Scullin Government would ultimately cause the government to fall, resulting in Labor honing its political message at the next election to call for greater government control over banking and monetary policy.

After calling the commission under pressure from the Country Party, Lyon's treasurer, Richard Casey, made its terms of reference extremely broad and, unlike the contemporary royal commission, without any input from the banks. He gave a team of six commissioners instructions to 'inquire into the monetary and banking systems at present in operation in Australia, and to report whether any, and if so what, alterations are desirable in the interests of the people of Australia as a whole, and the manner in which any such alterations should be effected'.

Casey was sceptical as to whether anything would be gained from the exercise. Privately, he told former prime minister Stanley Bruce he was initially 'horrified' by the prospect of the commission. Publicly, Casey told a church congregation that the royal commission would be useful, even if it showed only how the present system could be improved.

It did just that. The commission attracted a bevy of pointy-headed experts who wanted to reshape the country's financial system. Leslie Melville, a renowned Australian economist, took a whole day's hearing just to read out his statement, while Professor Torleiv Hytten was in the witness stand for five days to answer questions based on his own lengthy submission. The inquiry coincided with the publication of Maynard Keynes' landmark economic tome, *The General Theory of Employment, Interest and Money*, which heavily influenced the economists who gave evidence. Their evidence was better informed and thought through than the evidence put forward by the other banking witnesses, especially Commonwealth Bank officials, who gave tepid responses as they were filled with dread about where the royal commission could go.

One of the major causes of the Depression in Australia had been the nation's unwavering faith in sticking to the 'gold standard' of a fixed exchange rate for the currency. The trouble with holding the foreign exchange rate steady when a country's exports are crashing, as the value of wool did just before the Depression, is that governments need to respond by devaluing the currency. But CBA employees argued that maintaining the country's exchange rate was paramount.

This was dismissed by the economists giving evidence, who generally agreed that the exchange rate should play second fiddle to ensuring the stability of the domestic economy, meaning that rather than cutting off borrowers and refraining from lending vigorously during a crisis—as CBA was accused of doing during the Depression—the banks needed to sell loans and stimulate the economy. The CBA central bank had managed to stave off inflation during the downturn, but it had done so by crushing the economy.

The 1936–37 royal commission led to a strengthening and clarification of CBA's powers and recommended decimal coinage, among other proposals. However, it specifically said the government shouldn't step in and nationalise the private trading banks, as Labor had wanted it to.

Ben Chifley, who was at this point an ambitious junior minister in the Scullin Government still years away from taking the prime ministership, had been appointed as one of the commissioners on the inquiry to appease Labor. In a three-page dissenting addendum to the royal commission, he put forward the case for bank nationalisation. Although he had an interest in economics and banking, he wrote his report without citing any of the evidence presented before the commission while arguing that none of the evidence he had heard convinced him to accept the continuation of private banking.

In his now-infamous dissent, Chifley said there was 'no possibility of well-ordered progress being made in the community under a system in which there are privately owned trading banks'. 'Banks differ from any other form of business because any action, good or bad, by a banking system affects almost every phase of national life,' he said. 'The effect on the community of the action of most companies is of little moment compared with the effects of the actions of banking companies.'

Chifley proposed limiting profits on the banks at a cap of 5 per cent because of 'their privileged position of semi-monopolistic public utilities': 'In the public interest, there should be some restriction on the profit which they are able to make from the supply of necessary services that the community is unable to obtain from other sources.'

It wasn't until Chifley, a former train driver with four years' high school education, actually became PM that he, albeit unsuccessfully, attempted to nationalise the banks, in 1948. But as the collapse of the government-owned State Bank of Victoria in 1990 showed, Australia may consider itself lucky to have missed out on Chifley's government takeover of commercial lenders. The public antagonism to highly profitable banks and the role the lenders play in the fortunes or demise of the economy is still pervasive today.

Perhaps if we listened more closely to history, it might not have to repeat itself.

Looking at the establishment of the 2018 royal commission is like holding a mirror to the establishment of the banking inquiry launched by Lyons. In both cases, the underlying drivers of disenchantment with the economy and the financial system follow remarkably similar arcs.

Take, for example, the fact that at the start of the Great Depression there were just ten trading banks in Australia following a decade of mergers and takeovers among private lenders. Because of this concentration, the banking system had become far less competitive than in previous generations.

The financial crisis of 1893 had been sparked in part by incredibly loose lending. But over the next few decades, the banks changed their habits and became stiflingly conservative. By the 1920s, banks in Sydney and Melbourne were acting like a cartel, pricing their products at remarkably similar points.

Although no private bank in Australia collapsed during the Depression, the public was not assuaged by the relative stability of the local financial system compared to offshore economies. The financial strength of the sector did nothing to prevent the banks from being used as a political lightning rod for the apparent damage wrought on the Australian economy during the downturn. About a month before the 1934 election, Labor opposition leader James Scullin delivered his policy speech at the Richmond Town Hall, and most of it focused on reforming the financial system.

Lyons, standing under the UAP banner, exhausted his political capital by continuing to defend the private banks. He claimed the conservative lending standards of the banks had saved the country from the brink of collapse during the recession. Meanwhile, Page's Country Party was still hung up on the tightened availability of credit during the early years of the Depression, which had a huge impact on farmers attempting to get loans.

In the elections of both 1934 and 2016, Australians were suffering a hangover from a global banking crisis, pushed along by a financial system that was seen as not acting in their interests.

The early twentieth century was beset by a marked trend towards higher inequality, one that the Great Depression disrupted because it destroyed the massive amounts of wealth collected by the top echelons of society. But as the accumulated wealth held by the rich was demolished during the Wall Street crash of 1929, which quickly infected Australia's own wealthy, the country's broader population acutely felt the sting of the downturn. Unemployment in Australia hit a record-high 20 per cent in 1930, and workers suffered low wages and lost opportunities for economic growth for years afterwards.

Today, the massive amounts of wealth collected among elite circles is yet to be destroyed by a similar crash, but it is also not being filtered back through society by some sort of post-world-war redistribution program, as happened across the developed world following the 1939–45 war. Because of this, inequality across the developed world has now risen to its highest point since just before the Depression.

Shortly after the election of Kevin Rudd's Labor government in 2007, the largest financial crisis since the Great Depression took the world, in Rudd's own words, by 'economic shitstorm'.

Inequality had barely rated a mention in the lead-up to the change in government. Australia was at the end of a decade-long economic boom, and the windfalls were being scattered around the country in the form of massive wage increases, huge spending programs fuelled by healthy tax revenue, and skyrocketing property prices. Neither Rudd nor Opposition treasurer Wayne Swan carved out financial sector reform as a key part of his election platform.

The global financial crisis (GFC) changed everything. Although it was never as severe or prolonged as the Great Depression, it brought with it ramifications that fundamentally altered the way in which the economy enriched different parts of society.

The crisis was essentially triggered by a housing-market crash in the US after banks sold unfathomable numbers of dodgy loans to borrowers who could never have afforded to repay them. Major global financial institutions found themselves at risk of collapse because the financial system had become so intertwined. Huge investment bonds, packed full of 'subprime' home loans, were sold to investors and institutions across the world. Overly relaxed regulation played a huge part in the crash, and private financial firms had become blind to the risks they were taking on, all in the pursuit of super-large profits.

The Australian banks were well insulated from the US subprime housing crash, but the Reserve Bank was still forced to dramatically lower interest rates in a bid to rescue the faltering economy. As workers were laid off, and as investment and business activity dried up as the global financial system raced towards the precipice, lowering the RBA's interest rates was designed to fuel borrowing and lift spending across the economy. Central banks around the world slashed official interest rates in concert, sometimes to zero per cent, in a bid to entice borrowers and businesses to take out loans in the hope they would create jobs and stimulate the economy. In the years after the GFC some central banks, such as the European Central Bank, even lowered their interest rates below zero, into negative territory, where a borrower would essentially be paid to take out a loan.

While it narrowly avoided economic disaster, Australia was still forced to face the end of the mining boom. The economy was spluttering, and unemployment rose from 4 to 6 per cent and stayed there.

Underemployment, where workers couldn't get as many hours as they wanted, shot close to 15 per cent and refused to come down. Businesses were not investing and growing jobs, which made it harder for workers to find better-paying jobs or jump ship to a more lucrative offer.

It all left people feeling ripped off by the system. The animosity was shared across the developed world in the decade after the GFC, and the crisis's ramifications were still being felt ten years later. Europe had sunk into a rolling sovereign debt crisis, and nearly ten million jobs had been destroyed in the US.

As the smoke began to clear and the public sifted through the rubble at GFC ground zero, the finger of blame, rightly or wrongly, pointed squarely at the greed of the banks that dominated the financial system. People were enraged by the failure of authorities to jail any executives for the misdemeanours that had contributed to the GFC, and the Occupy Wall Street movement was born in 2011.

At first it was just a motley crew of protesters in Manhattan, the heart of global capitalism, angry about the wealth amassed by the top 1 per cent. But the Occupy protests soon turned global. That year, activists turned up on the doorstep of Sydney's cosmopolitan financial district in Martin Place, just up the road from the head office of the 'millionaires' factory', Macquarie Bank.

Within a fortnight of the protestors setting up ramshackle lodgings outside the RBA office, police had evicted them. Operation Goulding, as the police action was termed, would evict the Occupy Sydney protesters again in February the next year, and a further five times in mid-2013, only for the activists to regroup and re-establish their tent city within hours. It was at first a rallying cry against corporate greed and regulatory failure, but it morphed into a wide-ranging outpouring of grievances on everything from growing inequality to civil liberties and social injustice.

Occupy Sydney, much smaller than its US counterpart, achieved little immediately, and may have achieved nothing substantial at all. By the end it was largely a collection of homeless people looking for a safe place to sleep and regularly being visited by charity workers.

However, the symbolism couldn't be missed. Scrawled on one of the tarpaulins in the Martin Place tent city was a message: 'For many, this is what affordable housing in Sydney looks like.' For the Reserve Bank employees who traipsed past it on their way to work every day, it was a reminder of the lasting damage wrought by the financial crisis and the ultimate result of the RBA's own response to the downturn.

'The home is the foundation of sanity and sobriety; it is the indispensable condition of continuity; its health determines the health of society as a whole.'

So said opposition backbencher Robert Menzies in his landmark 1942 speech, 'The Forgotten People'. For the conservative MP, who would later reclaim the prime ministership after he had been ousted a few years prior to making the speech, home ownership, and increasing the number of people who owned their own home, was the best way to guard against the revolutionary tendencies of a society.

As the spectre of communism and the tentacles of the Soviet Union started to reach into the crevices of the developing world by the end of the Second World War, Menzies believed that if all Australians had a stake in society, they would not seek to overthrow it. Homes—material, human and spiritual—were the foundation of this bulwark against communism, he said: 'Your advanced socialist may rave against private property even while he acquires it; but one of the best instincts in us is that which induces us to have one little piece of earth with a house and a garden which is ours; to which we can withdraw, in which we can be among our friends, into which no stranger may come against our will.'

After he become PM for a second time, Menzies helped introduce all kinds of federal and state housing schemes to make home ownership more accessible and affordable. In the early 1950s, at the start of his prime ministership, about 50 per cent of Australia's homes were either owned or being purchased by the people who lived in them. By 1966 that number had risen to almost 75 per cent.

Encouraging young people to lock themselves into affordable 25-year mortgages meant that they were more likely to go to work, work harder, pay their bills and vote the conservative government back into power. In this way, the middle class would keep the fundamental structures of society in place.

But the movement was far from permanent, and as the threat of revolution subsided, so too did home ownership. By 2011 it had fallen to its lowest level in half a century, at 67 per cent. Five years later it had tumbled again, to 65 per cent, and by 2016, one in every two loans sold by the banks was being sold to a landlord, not an owner-occupier. Young Australians were most affected by the slide in ownership. In 1981, more than 60 per cent of 25- to 34-year-olds owned their home. That number had fallen to 45 per cent by 2016, and the drop had been particularly steep in the immediate past decade. Only one demographic increased its levels of home ownership over the same period—baby boomers aged over sixty-five.

When the socialist Labour leader Jeremy Corbyn almost trounced the British Conservatives in the 2017 UK election, he was aided by a strong protest vote from young voters and those who didn't own their home. Voter turnout for those who were renting private properties jumped 10 per cent, while public housing tenant turnout increased by 6 per cent. Almost all of these voters, who had decided not to vote in the previous election in 2015, voted for Labour in 2017 when they were given the chance to vote for someone who wanted to dramatically reshape society. Among renters who voted in both elections, the Tories lost a staggering 29 per cent of their 2015 vote, with about three-quarters of it switching to Labour.

The UK election came against a backdrop of home ownership rates across the UK falling to their lowest point in thirty years. In London, house prices had soared from costing five times the median income to more than sixteen times that income over two decades. The driver of the surging house prices, which had locked large slices of the public out of affording their own home, was in large part the response of central banks to the GFC.

While the Australian experience of the GFC was different from that of other developed countries, the Reserve Bank's actions were largely the same as those of offshore central banks: slashing official interest rates rapidly and significantly. In 2008, the official cash rate in Australia was 7.25 per cent. A decade later, the rate had plummeted to—and was stuck at—a record low of 1.5 per cent.

One of the reasons the RBA had to keep lowering rates over the decade following the crisis was because it took so long for the economy to recover from the GFC. After the initial fright, there was a lingering reluctance for people to spend or invest out of fear the global economy could tip over again at any point. In cutting interest rates as low as possible, RBA governor Glenn Stevens was attempting to lure borrowers off the sidelines to drive the housing construction boom in place of the dwindling mining boom, which by 2015 had turned into a mining bust.

However, lower interest rates—the only policy tool at the RBA's disposal—were a Faustian pact. Lowering interest rates triggers near-identical declines in the interest rates paid on term deposits and government bonds. These are considered the safest form of investment because it is unlikely a sovereign country will collapse without paying back your money.

In search of better investment returns, the massive pools of money sloshing around the globe had to be funnelled into riskier investments with better investment yields. Thus, the global 'search for yield' was born. This search for yield resulted in money managers pumping up the price of riskier assets, such as stock prices on the share market, which was great if you had your wealth tied up in the stock market, but for most people living pay cheque to pay cheque, it was a bull market they weren't a part of. It delivered little in the way of investment in the 'real' economy outside of financial markets.

House prices were also dramatically inflated by the low interest rates. With the commercial banks cutting mortgage rates in the wake of the RBA rate cuts, borrowers were able to gain approval for larger loans than ever before. Property buyers no longer had to prove to a bank that they could afford to repay monthly mortgage bills for supersized loans, like they'd had to when the official interest rate was 7.25 per cent. With the RBA cash rate at 1.5 per cent, borrowers could hit up the bank for more and more cash as they'd be able to afford larger monthly repayments.

All this did was arm prospective home buyers and property investors with more ammunition to throw at auctions, bidding up the prices of properties to sky-high levels.

When the RBA cash rate was 7.25 per cent, the median house price in Sydney was a touch above $400,000. By early 2018, when the cash rate had been stuck at 1.5 per cent for nearly two years, median house prices had surged to $1 million. This was great if you owned a house, but for many people in the large capital cities, home ownership rates were falling. Those renting and dependent on wage rises for better living standards were missing out on the so-called 'wealth effect' of these surging asset prices. Since the mid-1970s, real earnings for the top 10 per cent of wealthy Australians had risen by 60 per cent, but for the bottom 10 per cent, earnings rose by just 15 per cent.

Thomas Piketty, who carried out a study of long-running inequality in his home country of France, found that those who already had wealth were likely to experience greater growth in their riches than someone who was dependent on wages and economic growth. In his book *Capital in the Twenty-first Century*, Piketty found that if the rise in the value of capital—the value of all land, houses, vehicles, jewellery and so on—owned by a person was greater than the rate of economic growth, then the gap between rich and poor would increase. He argued that if wealth accumulates faster than output and wages, the 'entrepreneur inevitably tends to become a rentier, more and more dominant over those who own nothing but their labour'.

According to Labor MP Andrew Leigh, who ran Piketty's theory over the Australian experience, the data matched the hypothesis only from 1980 onwards. Over this period, the wealth of the top 1 per cent of Australians doubled, and as asset prices and household wealth rose, wages for the lower end of workers stalled.

The jitters of the financial crash were hovering over the shoulders of businesspeople. They pulled investments and scrapped plans for expansion that would have fed through to wage gains for workers. Instead of spending on expanding their operations, many of Australia's largest companies followed a global movement to spend significant amounts of their cash buying shares in their own groups, in a financial move known as 'stock buybacks'.

Over the past decade, the 500 largest companies listed on the US stock markets have bought back US$4.4 trillion of their own shares. This money could have been used for investment in research and development, wage rises for workers, or creating newer or better products. Rather than having an impact on the real economy or growing the revenue or profit of a business, stock buybacks were simply being used to help keep share prices high and shareholders happy. Buybacks also helped executives hit their earnings-per-share targets, which in a roundabout way trigger long-term incentive payments for bonuses.

Meanwhile, corporate Australia was arguing for Malcolm Turnbull to slash the corporate tax rate for the country's biggest companies, which would see $65 billion lost from budget revenue. At the same time, the local business community was on a spending strike. They had bucketloads of cash: they just didn't want to spend it. Cash holdings for the 200 biggest Australian companies—money that was sitting idly in accounts owned by a corporation—had reached $110 billion by the end of 2016, but rather than investing this money into the economy, corporate Australia was sitting on its hands.

As the calls were growing louder to launch a royal commission into the financial sector in early 2017, Australia's largest wealth management company, AMP, and largest insurance group, QBE, announced that they would be buying back a collective $1.5 billion of their own shares. They chose to do this rather than make their products cheaper for customers or reward their employees with salary increases. In fact, tens of billions were being spent each year by Australia's largest corporations across all sectors in purchasing back their own shares.

At an industry lunch in early 2017 hosted by the Financial Services Council (FSC)—the lobby group that represents the biggest banks and wealth managers—Westpac's chief economist, Bill Evans, gave a firm warning to the executives gathered. Sitting on a panel with FSC chief executive Sally Loane, he was asked to speak about the most pressing political, regulatory and economic issues facing the financial services industry.

'One of the issues with cutting the corporate tax rate is that it really only helps the economy if improved cash flow gets invested and used for employment,' Evans told the luncheon. 'If it just gets accumulated in cash or goes out the back in dividends or the buyback of shares, it doesn't really help the economy. We need a policy stance that provides people with an expectation that growth is going to be lifting.'

His warning fell on deaf ears.

As with the Great Depression, Australia's banks survived the GFC relatively unscathed. According to the banks, this was because of their prudent management, diligent executives and robust financial strength. Following the GFC, it was a claim repeated ad nauseam by the sector as reason enough to leave them alone. They were already regulated enough, they said.

Overseas, the experience was markedly different, and authorities clamped down on their respective financial systems with vigour. In Britain, chairman of the Financial Services Authority Lord Adair Turner pinned the crisis on overly complex investment products that were sold irresponsibly after a huge binge on debt. UK authorities responded to the GFC by launching a massive bank levy, putting badly behaved executives on a register, and increasing powers for watch-dogs. 'We failed to constrain the financial system's creation of private credit and money,' Turner said.

In the US, Lehman Brothers collapsed after it took too many bad punts on subprime mortgage bonds, which triggered a widespread credit crunch. The Dodd-Frank bill passed by Congress overhauled the country's financial regulation architecture, while the Volcker Rule banned retail banks from using the financial system like a casino.

Australian banks were largely missing from the global regulatory reform movement. Local banks were not invested in toxic products, such as subprime mortgage bonds, but only because they had been prevented from doing so by the banking regulator. If APRA hadn't had its eye on the ball, who can say whether or not Australia's banks would have ended up in the same implosion.

For all the banks' posturing over their success in the downturn, the sector gave little credit to the regulators and the government that steered them through the GFC.

In July 2007, just as investors lost faith in the value of US subprime mortgages, APRA started making emergency calls to the treasury departments of the major Australian banks. They wanted clear daily updates on the funding position of the country's biggest financial institutions. The Reserve Bank joined in: almost every day for the next fifteen months they would call the big four banks to see how they were faring.

The concerns culminated in Prime Minister Kevin Rudd, fearing a widespread run on the banks in October 2008, announcing that the government would guarantee all customer deposits and would step in and fund the banks if they couldn't source funds from overseas.

It was a massive intervention, and the major banks still reject the notion that they needed it. Rudd needed to calm the nerves of not just the customers of the big banks, but particularly the customers of smaller regional banks, who would have caused dramatic problems if there had been a bank run on less resilient lenders.

Amid the crisis, these more vulnerable lenders were encouraged to be swallowed up by the major banks. Westpac took over a shaky St George, which was then the country's fifth pillar, and CBA was tapped on the shoulder to buy Bankwest after its British owner sailed into distress.

By September 2008, ASIC was having to intervene in financial markets to ban traders from short-selling the shares of the banks.

In this way, financial markets couldn't bet against the companies and encourage their stock prices to fall further. The short-selling ban was put in place as Macquarie Group stared into the abyss, with its shares heading towards zero after they had been heavily targeted during the crunch.

A few days after the ban, the government announced it would step in and start buying residential mortgage-backed bonds, as all the other lenders had stepped away and funding markets had frozen. Then, a month later, Rudd was forced to launch the first stage of the government's economic stimulus package, shelling out $10 billion to households before Christmas in order to keep the economy moving. Early the next year, in 2009, the government spent another $3 billion to support the commercial property industry, which was at risk of crashing. Rudd then announced a further $42 billion stimulus plan, which ended up aiding the economic recovery but put the government under severe political pressure amid accusations of profligate spending levelled by the Liberal Opposition.

The major banks took serious advantage of the government funding guarantee. They sourced more than $150 billion of funding through the plan and paid back only around $5 billion in interest for the free kick, with little in the way of thanks. After narrowly avoiding catastrophe, Macquarie Group went on to use the taxpayer-backed funding to plough billions of dollars into high-earning but risky corporate debt across the globe. Macquarie's so-called Corporate and Asset Finance Division, which houses these risky junk bonds, tripled its profit in the year after the taxpayer guarantee was introduced. It appeared that reforms designed to protect the financial giants from collapse were being used to make questionable investments, all on the taxpayer dime.

But the hubris would leave the banks exposed. By cruising through the GFC, all the while arguing down the role the government had played in saving the financial system, the banks were soon stung by their own arrogance.

'In the aftermath, some of these bankers started to believe it was due to their genius, they should take the rewards, and they took the eye off the ball, which was the customer,' former treasurer Peter Costello told a lunch a decade after the crisis. 'I think in 2008 the financial system performed beautifully under stress. Financial systems are designed to make sure that our institutions are strong in a time of stress, and they were. Many of the things you are now seeing are the consequence really of bankers becoming complacent. They thought that sharing in the benefits of a system that had performed well was more important than keeping customers first. Whoever was in charge of keeping an eye on reputational risk on these boards did not do a very good job.'

Following the crisis, the bank chief executives were clouded by their own egos, ignorant of the growing economic and social discontent pulsing through society. It had been brewing for some time. Indeed, NAB chairman Ken Henry, who had been the treasury secretary under the Rudd Government during the GFC, had a more intimate knowledge of the economic landscape than any other bank executive.

Australian society had been drifting towards a more unequal footing since the 1980s. Although the banks were not the cause of the GFC in Australia, they still had to be backstopped by the taxpayer.

The public got little in return for guaranteeing the sector's survival. As wages and incomes stalled during the years after the downturn, financial executives seemed immune from the hardship. Bonuses and multimillion-dollar salaries continued to flow, while at the same time the number and severity of financial scandals began to mount.

Then the banks had the temerity to demand a $65 billion corporate tax cut. The public were no longer buying it, and they certainly weren't going to pay for it. They demanded that the banks pay.

3

THE IMPECCABLE SYSTEM

The top brass at National Australia Bank had the paperwork all ready to go.

It was early September 2018, and a steady stream of embarrassments unveiled by the royal commission over the past six months had kept pressure on the banks to keep their home loan rates as low as possible—for as long as was needed to help repair their reputations.

There was no way they could once again hit the hip pockets of their long-suffering customers at the same time as they were fending off accusations that they had been stealing from the dead. But the sector was feeling the squeeze. The cost of funding on the international money markets was rising and beginning to eat away at their profit margins.

The big Australian banks get much of their lifeblood from tapping into international funding markets. There they are lent money, which in turn allows them to lend money out to local borrowers. Since the ascension of Donald Trump to the White House in late 2016, the cost of sourcing those funds had dramatically increased. Under the strain of a determined march by the US Federal Reserve towards higher official interest rates, the price of money was rising the world over, and Australia was not immune.

In the balancing act of the price NAB paid for money coming into the company versus the cost at which it chose to lend it out, the short straw was going to be drawn by local home-loan borrowers. Customers would have to pay more.

Luckily for NAB, Westpac had already done the hard yards. Just weeks earlier, Westpac boss Brian Hartzer had bitten the bullet and fronted the nightly TV news bulletins to tell borrowers they'd have to pay more for their monthly home loan lest the bank's profits be impacted. 'That started going up in February,' he said, pointing to the bank's funding costs. 'We were hoping that it would go back down, but it hasn't and, after six months at a sustained level, we've reluctantly concluded that it's going to stay at that more elevated rate. Therefore we came to the conclusion that that needed to be reflected in the price of our loans.'

While customers groaned, the rest of the major-bank chief executives sighed with relief. When one institution breaks ranks and foists higher interest rates on customers, it provides cover for the rest to follow. Rod Sims, the chairman of the competition watchdog, calls it 'synchronised swimming'—behaviour more suited to lemmings than Australia's most powerful corporations. It's a pool routine well known to Australian borrowers. For decades the big four have waited for one lender to stick its head out and raise rates, only to then follow in quick succession.

By midday on Thursday 6 September, a week after Westpac had first hiked its rates, ANZ and Commonwealth Bank had announced within hours of one another that they'd be swimming the same stroke. Thus the stage was set for NAB, and instructions had been sent out internally to bring together the paperwork to make a rates announcement of their own.

The Melbourne-based bank, the smallest of the big four, was always going to wait until last. The month before, it had been dragged through a torturous round of public hearings at the royal commission, where it was accused of deliberately misleading regulators over the size of its $100 million fees-for-no-service scandal, and its executives were singled out for acting in contempt of the law. NAB boss Andrew Thorburn had already been forced to publicly apologise for the behaviour of the bank's most senior executives, whose attempts to run circles around the corporate watchdog had been painfully aired at the public hearings.

With the blame for rising mortgage rates now squarely on the shoulders of Westpac, NAB was readying itself to sneak out its own mortgage hikes and salvage its threatened profitability. However, just hours after the CBA and ANZ rate hike announcements, a Federal Court lawsuit over the fees-for-no-service scandal landed in NAB's mailbox, sent by ASIC, which was accusing it of having broken the law no fewer than seventy-seven times.

As he digested the statement of claim, which accused the bank of sucking out $35 million and $67 million in differently labelled but inherently useless fees from savers' retirement nest eggs, Thorburn second-guessed his plans to immediately hike interest rates. The next day, he came into the office and told staff members and executives the bank would not be hiking its rates. They had to repair the damaged brand of the lender.

Deciding not to hit customers with higher fees during a public relations crisis may seem the obvious path to take for a company in search of redemption. But perhaps unsurprisingly, the plan incensed some of Thorburn's subordinates. Relaying the story, one insider said they were gobsmacked when other bankers lobbied Thorburn to stick with the plan to hike rates. 'Think of the shareholders!' one of the bankers said, without a hint of irony.

The chief executive was convinced to go home and use the weekend to think over the plan. Many in the upper ranks were hopeful he would come to his senses and put the bank's balance sheet ahead of some bleeding-heart plan to put its reputation before its profits.

It was of no use. Come 9 a.m. on Monday, NAB announced it would be holding rates steady. 'We are listening and acting differently,' Thorburn announced to the public.

The message was replete with a hastily filmed video of the chief standing in front of a few ATMs explaining why the bank, for once, wasn't following its rivals: 'We need to rebuild the trust of our customers, and by holding our NAB standard variable rate longer, we help our customers for longer.'

It may seem like a small moment in the long history of one of the country's biggest institutions, but the tale is more than a room full of NAB bankers preparing and then scuppering a plan to raise rates when the heat got turned on. Even though the spin doctors had managed to recast the story of a bank cowed into submission into one of a company embarking on a journey towards redemption, the moment marked an important juncture in the behaviour of the most dominant players in the financial system.

The industry had, until now, been used to getting its own way, whenever it wanted, because it went unchallenged in its practice. For so long there had been such little heat applied to the finance sector that it had settled under a permafrost as bankers rode roughshod over customers. Then had come the glare and the blowtorch and the sheer attention, and the old world began to melt before the bankers' eyes.

The mundane world of interest rate movements may seem incidental to the more salacious scandals perpetrated by the banks over the years. Compared to laundering cash for terrorists, concocting fraudulent reasons to deny insurance claims for heart-attack survivors and stealing money from the dead, the charging of unfavourable mortgage interest rates barely registers on the scandal-Richter scale. But interest rates, and the way banks have acted in open collusion to pass on all of their costs to customers, played a pivotal role in turning public mood against the sector.

While the sizeable few Australians were the victims of shoddy financial advice, callous life insurance claim rejections and ruthless fire sales of intergenerational farming land, the majority were turned against the banks by the slow but systemic heist that is uncompetitive interest rates. Whatever the product was—home loan rates, credit card rates or term deposit rates relied on by retirees—Australians knew they were getting a raw deal. This was served up fresh each time the board of the RBA met and decided to change the country's official interest rate.

With every cut or hike by the RBA, the focus inevitably turns to which of the nation's largest banks pass on the higher costs, or the savings from a lower rate, to home loan borrowers.

At any time, one-third of all Australians are paying down a mortgage. Thanks to the great Australian dream of home ownership, interest rate changes are a unique point of tension between the public and the financial sector. Banks are, after all, meant to be just an intermediary for money flowing around the economy. Their job is to be the pipes of the financial system.

But Australia's banks, playing as if they were the dodgiest plumber *A Current Affair* could find, decided they would take the biggest cut possible of every dollar that flushed through one of their pipes, and in the process undermined the trust that is paramount to the banking business model.

When customers put money in a bank, they trust that when they want to withdraw money, the bank will have it. In return, the bank pays the customer a small interest payment as a thank-you. The bank is then free to lend the money out to borrowers, and trusts that the money will be repaid. As borrowers repay the bank, they also pay fees in the form of interest rates. Shareholders, who also fund the bank, trust that the company will pay them a return. It's a money-go-round based on trusting that no one will act in bad faith.

It should be simple. But somewhere along the way, Australia's biggest banks became powerhouses in turning out supersized profits. Year after year, they would announce another record-high annual profit. Commonwealth Bank, the country's biggest, in 2018 produced a profit of almost $10 billion—after tax. The big four combined have reached a combined profit of about $30 billion a year.

Senior bankers, regulators and politicians laud the strength of the financial sector and wear it as a badge of pride. It makes sense when you look at the rolling banking crises that European and US taxpayers are beset by.

For a country with a relatively small population, the big four banks are incredibly successful. Their sales, profits, assets and market value have them ranked among the largest 100 companies in the world. But their size is also one of their biggest problems. Mergers and take-overs that were waved through by weak regulators over the past three decades—think Commonwealth Bank's takeover of Bankwest, or Westpac's swallowing up of St George—have resulted in a system now dominated by just four companies. With 80 per cent of the housing market under their control, the lenders wield significant pricing power. Rather than competing for customers with lower prices, as more combative industries are forced to do, the major banks engage in a permanent truce where no lender will rock the boat.

The situation got so bad that the competition watchdog was forced to investigate mortgage pricing between the major banks. 'The pricing behaviour of each of the inquiry banks appears more consistent with "accommodating" a shared interest in avoiding the disruption of mutually beneficial pricing outcomes, rather than consistently vying for market share by offering the lowest interest rates,' the Australian Competition & Consumer Commission (ACCC) found in 2018 after trawling through thousands of documents and emails at the top ranks of the banks.

As consumers lose out, the cosy situation has made Australia's banks the most profitable in the world. On the basis of the banks' return on equity—a key measurement of profitability that shows how much money an investor will get back every year for a dollar invested—Australia is a world-beater. The return on equity for the major Australian banks of roughly 15 per cent a year is 50 per cent higher than that of US or Scandinavian banks and eight times more lucrative than that of the UK banks.

The bankers of Macquarie and Collins streets are not gifted with the touch of Midas. Rather, the penchant for profit comes from the banks' 'pricing power'—the ability for the lenders to charge what they like without the threat of a challenger coming along and offering better products at a better price. While it's great for shareholders, it's financially bruising for customers. The higher the return on equity, the more money is being charged to borrowers and the less interest is being paid to savers. It also strips money out of the economy that could be spent at local shops or on other projects.

If customers picked up stumps and shopped around it would benefit the economy as much as individuals and force the banks to offer better rates. The problem is that Australians are more likely to divorce their partner than change their bank. From Dollarmites to death, Australians are unflinchingly monogamous with their bank, even when they are treated terribly for their faithfulness.

The Productivity Commission (PC) has found bank customers are penalised by remaining loyal to the tune of $87 a month on the average home loan balance. According to the PC study, the banks offered discounts only to new or angry customers, unbeknown to the loyal borrowers who were taken for granted.

For many financial watchdogs, the most frustrating manifestation of the lack of competition in the banking sector is the lock-step behaviour of the major banks when they set interest rates. Despite having changed the rates on standard variable loans multiple times a year for decades, the rates charged by the lenders track remarkably similar patterns, and always fall within a range of a few percentage points.

Stockbroking industry veteran Brian Johnson, who advises international clients on the Australian banking sector, labels the big four banks a 'cartel' in his investment research notes. If you're an investor, you'll take it as a compliment for the sector. 'When you speak to overseas investors, the one thing Australia is known for is for having these real oligopolies,' Johnson said.

Think of the biggest companies in the department store sector, newspapers, supermarkets, airlines, baby food or beer. Just like the financial sector, Australia's business sectors are plagued by at best a 'big four' oligopoly, and at worst a duopoly. It's common currency that the banks have been happy with this situation, protecting their profits at the expense of customers and putting the interests of their shareholders before borrowers.

The research backs this up. A 2013 paper from the *Journal of International Financial Markets, Institutions & Money* found that the three largest Australian banks passed on RBA rate hikes much faster than they did for rate cuts. For every day a bank postponed passing on a 25-basis-point rate cut, they would draw in an extra $6.2 million in profit, according to the research.

After examining the interest rate movements of twenty-three banks over a period of more than a decade through the GFC, Swinburne University business professor Abbas Valadkhani concluded that the banks dropped their standard variable rates like 'feathers' but increased them like 'rockets' whenever the RBA changed rates. They waited a long time to pass on RBA rate cuts, but acted immediately to hike rates. Up like a rocket, down like a feather.

Banks were also more likely to pass on less of a rate change when the RBA cut rates, lowering their rates by a margin smaller than the official rate cut. Conversely, they would over-egg a rate rise when the central bank hiked rates. On average over the same period, the big four banks gave their customers only 85 per cent of every RBA rate cut but immediately passed on 120 per cent of any rate rise.

Exactly how the banks set their interest rates, who makes these decisions and the excuses deployed to justify them is quite opaque. The Rudd and Gillard governments introduced laws aimed at limiting 'price signalling'—the sector's lead-and-follow behaviour—but the plan was met with private and public hostility by the industry.

Politicians were worried because Australians are rather vulnerable to interest-rate gouging, where banks charge fees well above what a reasonable person would expect. The country is a global anomaly in that most home loan borrowers take out a loan with a 'variable' rate. This gives the bank the ability to re-price the interest rate at will, with very few rules regarding when, or how often, the rates are changed. Overseas, borrowers are far more likely to have fixed-rate loans, or rates that automatically track changes in the official interest rate with no mark-up or gouging.

According to internal data from the ABA, public perceptions of local banks fell rapidly to their lowest point since the GFC when, in 2012, the lenders stopped passing on the entire reduction in the cash rate announced by the RBA. Prior to the GFC, it took exactly one week for each and every bank to respond to the RBA's official rate cuts; in the post-GFC world, that average blew out to 2.4 weeks. The failure of banks to pass on these rate cuts stoked disaffection with the sector.

'The speed and accuracy with which rate cuts and increases are passed on to borrowers, especially among highly indebted households, impacts significantly upon their financial wellbeing,' Valadkhani said. Since the year 2000, there had been nineteen occasions on which bank rates changed when the RBA did not do anything, as lenders responded to higher or lower funding costs or changes in financial markets. As luck would have it, on eighteen of those nineteen occasions the rate changes were to the detriment of the consumer and left borrowers with rates around 2 per cent higher than they would have otherwise been if variable rates simply tracked changes in the RBA cash rate.

According to former ASIC chairman Greg Medcraft, it was these out-of-cycle rate changes that chipped away trust in the banking oligopoly. As borrowers became increasingly frustrated with their treatment by lenders, they were unable to get a better deal elsewhere as the entire industry was in cahoots. 'International investors used to say to me with incredulity: "The banks can just charge whatever they want?" Yep, that's the way it works in Australia,' Medcraft said.

It was this behaviour that slowly fermented in the minds of consumers, making them question what little trust in the big end of town they had left. And locked away in their corner offices, the bankers believed themselves shielded from the turning tide of public opinion, safe in the knowledge that they, not the central bank, would control the price of money in the economy.

When the longest federal election campaign in Australian history ended in early July 2016, it did so with a near-defeat for Prime Minister Malcolm Turnbull.

Voters gifted Turnbull a hostile Senate that had the numbers to set up an expensive and lengthy royal commission into the banking sector. Labor was intent on casting Turnbull as the protector of the scandal-prone corporations and had campaigned relentlessly in favour of setting up the banking inquiry.

It was in this eggshell environment, over the months in the lead-up to election day, that Australia's big four banks were on their best behaviour.

In May, just two months before the election, the RBA had cut the official interest rate by 25 basis points to 1.75 per cent. Conscious of the growing tide of public resentment, all the chief executives of the big four banks raced to announce within hours that they would be passing on the entire 25-basis-point RBA rate cut to customers.

Just a few months later, in August, and with Turnbull back in the prime minister's office, the banks were faced with another RBA rate cut, this time to a record-low 1.5 per cent. This time, however, the big four banks did not pass the savings onto customers.

CBA was first out of the gate, announcing it would reduce rates by 13 basis points—half the RBA rate cut. NAB moved second, moments later promising to reduce mortgage rates by just 10 basis points. Westpac announced a 14-basis-points cut, and ANZ said it would lower its rates by just 12 basis points.

Like clockwork, the near-identical rate cuts left the big four oligopoly all sitting with near-identical standard rates. The decision not to pass on the entire RBA rate cut would reap the banks about $2 billion in extra revenue over a year. It was the same old song from the banks, but they didn't realise the government was starting to sing a remarkably different tune.

A furious Turnbull called a press conference and announced he would be dragging the chief executives of the major banks before parliament to face a twice-yearly public grilling. 'The banks should have passed on the full rate cut,' the prime minister said. 'There is no basis for them, no commercial basis for them other than to improve their profitability … they must provide a full account of why they have not done so.'

Publicly, the banks could do nothing but agree, lest they be subjected to a more rigorous and time-consuming royal commission.

While detractors labelled the parliamentary hearings a show trial, Liberal MP David Coleman worked methodically within the constraints of the inquiry and took care to diagnose the problems with the sector. He found that since 2000 NAB had made no interest rate changes to the benefit of consumers. ANZ and Westpac had both made only two changes that benefited consumers, and CBA had made just one.

'The major banks also tend to follow each other's price increases rather than compete to gain market share,' Coleman said. Since 2000, in the majority of cases where a bank made an out-of-cycle interest rate change, all the major banks followed their rival within a month.

Many of Coleman's proposed remedies, such as a public register for badly behaved bankers, were to be taken up by the government in its next federal budget, but at the time the banks had no inkling of the severity of the crackdown.

Hours before handing down the 2017 federal budget, Treasurer Scott Morrison was confidently cruising around the budget lock-up. He was there to give the banks a valuable lesson in politics. The centrepiece of the night was an onslaught of policies targeting the biggest banks, including a $6.2 billion levy focused solely at the largest lenders. It was known as the major bank levy.

Morrison's response when it was suggested the banks might be a bit unhappy about this? 'Cry me a river.'

The government had laid down the law, pledging to give financial regulators more teeth and tasking the competition watchdog with an investigation to prevent lock-step movement in mortgage-rate pricing. Fines for the big banks would be raised significantly to $200 million per offence.

Speaking at the National Press Club the next day, Morrison told the banks to suck it up. The public 'already don't like you very much', he said. Radio 3AW host Neil Mitchell was more blunt, saying to NAB chief Andrew Thorburn, 'You know people think you're a bunch of bastards. There won't be a lot of sympathy for you.'

The banks, it seemed, had used up all their goodwill with Canberra's politicians.

Fast-forward to mid-2018, during a break between bruising public hearing rounds of the royal commission. Westpac boss Brian Hartzer was hosting a lunch in Sydney. There, he would announce some cultural changes the bank was making in light of the inquiry's early findings.

Seeing and being seen with various businesspeople before he gave his address, Hartzer settled briefly at a table of journalists to shake hands and do the rounds. During the small talk, he mentioned a recent meeting of company representatives at the ABA. When bank executives gather at such roundtables they must bring lawyers with them to ensure no one breaches 'price signalling' laws—the ones introduced by the Rudd and Gillard governments—or engages in cartel behaviour.

I expressed surprise at the fact that the bankers needed to have lawyers with them at all times, but the US-bred Hartzer was never good at seeing the humour in anything. 'It's not funny,' he told the journalists. 'It's very serious. We could go to jail.'

The price-signalling laws, introduced by then Labor Treasurer Wayne Swan, had made it unlawful for banks to disclose price-related information in a number of situations and had evolved from a string of legal defeats suffered by the competition watchdog in high-profile petrol price fixing cases. However, they were crafted by Swan to target just the big four banks. If two or more competitors privately disclosed pricing information, even if there was no proof that competition had been harmed in any way, executives could face hefty penalties. Swan's laws were designed to crack down on 'nod and a wink' pricing manoeuvres that allowed banks to hike interest rates and leave the door open for other banks to follow, but despite the best intentions, they failed to prevent price-following behaviour in the market and the oligopoly remained as it ever was.

Speaking to me about the proposals years after they were introduced, Swan said the behind-closed-doors campaign against the laws, led by the big four banks' chief executives, was vitriolic. 'We tried bloody hard with that package and they were just a culture of arseholes,' Swan said. 'The reason they went apeshit about it was that we targeted them for personal responsibility. The only place you can ever really affect results from the high and mighty—who are basically overpaid and overpowered corporate elite—is when you actually target them. They're really good at hiding behind their corporate veil, but whenever anyone tries to actually hold them to be responsible for one of their actions is when the shit hits the fan.'

Swan said the laws were introduced because the banks were never transparent in their reasoning for changing their variable rates. They could 'just make up a whole lot of stuff about their margins' that was at odds with the financial information published by the RBA. 'If you went back through it all, it was all just bullshit,' Swan said. 'They were taking every figure and bending it all the time. It's just a gigantic spin machine to camouflage the fact that they were gouging drastically.'

Despite spending tens of millions each year on marketing to convince punters of the inherent differences between bank brands, the major banks have shown themselves to be terrible at going it alone. ANZ under chief executive Mike Smith, who was the bank's boss from 2007 to 2015, attempted to delink—in the minds of customers at least—the association of changes in the lender's standard variable rate from changes in the RBA cash rate. By nominating a day each month on which rates would be reviewed, separate from the first Tuesday of every month when the RBA board meets, ANZ tried to make its rate changes appear less reactive to RBA decisions and more related to the lender's overall cost of funds.

But it was spoiled after the other three big banks exploited the plan, waiting until after ANZ announced rate changes to follow with rate hikes or cuts of their own. As the leading bank, ANZ ended up copping most of the flak for moving rates between 2011 and 2014, when the experiment ran.

Starting around the same time in 2011, NAB spent millions telling Australians it was 'breaking up' with the other major banks and pledging to do things differently. Realising that people already hated the bank, NAB decided it would scrap the fees it charged to customers coming on board and would pay rival bank exit fees charged to customers who were jumping ship. True to its word, it also followed through with a promise to charge borrowers the lowest interest rate of the major banks—but, rather pathetically, its rates were the lowest by just 0.02 percentage points.

So it was little surprise that politicians had had enough of the behaviour.

After slapping the $6.2 billion major bank levy on the lenders, the government tasked the ACCC to investigate the interest rate decisions of the big four banks to make sure they didn't just hike rates and pass on the cost of the tax to borrowers. In its report following the investigation, the ACCC remarked that 'one bank considered whether the costs could be passed on to customers and suppliers at a range of different time periods, including after the end of the ACCC inquiry', which finished at the end of June 2018. Hartzer, whose bank was first off the mark with the August 2018 rate hike, was forced to admit before parliament later that the unnamed bank was indeed Westpac.

Time and again, the banks used any excuse to increase the cost of clipping the ticket throughout the financial system. While claiming to be dynamos of innovation at the forefront of technological adaptation, they are in reality in a bread-and-butter business of charging hefty fees for otherwise basic services. With a collective profit before tax of around $30 billion a year, the cost is borne by everyday Australians.

The 'Australian Banks Belong to You' campaign, launched by the ABA during the royal commission, was an odd attempt to soothe public anger at a testing time. Telling Australians that 80 per cent of these profits were paid out to shareholders only served to remind people of the immense windfalls banks were making off the backs of ordinary borrowers every time interest rates were changed. After perhaps considering the fact that about 25 per cent of bank shareholders were overseas institutions and that the average superannuation member held very few bank shares anyway, the ABA pulled the campaign after a few months.

The banks were never interested in changing their ways. Lowering profits would result in lower share prices, which would then feed into lower levels of executive remuneration. It would be better for customers if the banks were barely there, charging minimal fees for basic financial products. But the incentives to make larger profits at the expense of customers proved too great.

The heat applied during the royal commission was the only thing that could make the banks reconsider the way they treated their customers.

4

JUSTICE MUST BE SEEN TO BE DONE

In July 2016, just two weeks after Malcolm Turnbull was re-elected prime minister of Australia, the nation's biggest fund managers, wealth companies, superannuation giants and life insurers gathered in Melbourne for the annual Financial Services Council summit.

Having just survived a Labor election campaign driven by a pledge to establish a royal commission into the financial sector, the wealth industry wanted to tell politicians they had had enough. They were sick of the constant reviews.

You could forgive them for thinking so. Since the end of the GFC, almost every aspect of financial sector regulation had been looked at. A 2009 parliamentary joint committee review of the financial sector led by Labor MP Bernie Ripoll changed the face of financial advice in Australia. There was a wide-ranging 2010 review of the super sector, led by former ASIC deputy chairman Jeremy Cooper. Former Commonwealth Bank boss David Murray was commissioned for the 2014 root-and-branch Financial System Inquiry. Former APRA member John Trowbridge in 2015 pulled apart the commissions and kickbacks strewn through the life insurance sector in a major review.

All in all, the various arms of the financial sector had been subjected to more than a dozen major reviews, the industry complained. There was an obvious sickness at the heart of the financial sector, but the chief lobbyist for the wealth management industry believed that all symptoms had been diagnosed and were quickly being treated.

'The financial services industry has been under intense scrutiny for the better part of a decade—with fourteen different reviews and inquiries examining financial advice, superannuation and life insurance,' FSC chief executive Sally Loane told the powwow. 'Many of these reviews have been subject to further follow-up inquiries. The current and ongoing PC review into superannuation is a review into the recommendation of an inquiry that stemmed from a previous PC review. A time-consuming and costly royal commission into the financial system would undoubtedly delay important consumer-focused reforms. It should not be considered. It is a last-resort measure.'

Just on the numbers, Loane had it wrong. There had actually been fifty-one substantial reviews, investigations and inquiries since the financial crisis, of which twelve were ongoing at the time the royal commission was later announced. But just the fact that there had already been an avalanche of inquiries was an oft-repeated argument, mainly sprouting from the financial sector itself, that a royal commission was unnecessary. What more could there possibly be to inquire into, they begged. They were already snowed in.

In some ways, they were right. Countless hours had been spent trying to plug the holes in the battered financial-sector ship.

The Murray inquiry report had been a landmark document, forcing regulators to ensure that the banking system was 'unquestionably strong' with financial buffers large enough ostensibly to withstand the worst economic crises. It had also made the financial sector pick up the tab for ASIC's funding, reviewed the capabilities of financial watchdogs, and looked at the state of the current regulatory architecture to ensure rent-seeking firms weren't gouging customers.

The Cooper review had reformed the nation's retirement nest-egg system and chopped down to size rampantly high fees that were being charged to customers who had no idea they were paying them.

The Ripoll review had sparked the Future of Financial Advice (FOFA) reforms, from then on making advisers act in customers' best interests, while clamping down on lucrative kickbacks across the sector.

But for all the work, the broader public hadn't been placated. There was review after review, committee on top of committee, penalty upon penalty, enforceable undertaking on enforceable undertaking, slapped wrist after slapped wrist, but the banking sector was still Australia's biggest producer of scandals by a country mile. Whatever the reviews had done, they hadn't gone to the heart of the misconduct.

The average Australian didn't care what David Murray had recommended as the adequate level of regulatory capital banks needed to have to weather downturns. Moreover, most of the reviews had been carried out in back rooms without the interest or scrutiny of the mainstream media to amplify the process and explain it to the broader public. Once recommendations were handed to the government, a Treasury consultation process would begin in which the industry could simply lobby to water down any prospective reforms. Then, as implementation was handed back to governments, recommendations were quietly shelved indefinitely or weakened. Strong proposals were victims of ideological governments.

Following the Cooper review, the Gillard Labor government was privately incensed when Treasury modelling revealed how much superannuation tax breaks were costing the federal budget. Superannuation is the jewel in the crown of the Labor Party's reform legacy, but Treasury's modelling showed how the world-leading retirement system was failing in its basic task of taking pressure off the federal budget. The government was still spending much more on tax breaks for superannuants than it was saving on the age pension bill, and it would be doing so until about 2070.

The party's close relationship to the super industry meant Labor was rarely able to gather the steam to properly reform the super sector. What the Australian public needed was an inquiry with teeth.

Just over a year after the FSC leadership summit, when the chairmen and the chief executives of the big four banks made their collective decision to write to the treasurer and ask that a 'properly constituted inquiry into the financial services sector' be established, they did so with the purpose that it would 'put an end to the uncertainty and restore trust, respect and confidence' in the industry.

To restore the public's trust, the public had to be able to trust the review itself. A royal commission was the only way to ensure this. For justice to be done, justice also had to be seen to be done.

Such had been the determination of Lord Chief Justice Gordon Hewart in 1924 when he created the influential legal precedent that even the mere appearance of bias would be sufficient to overturn a judicial decision. It came after a motorcyclist known as McCarthy was prosecuted for dangerous driving after he was involved in a crash. As it turned out, a clerk working for the justices deciding on McCarthy's case was also a member of the prosecutor's firm that was chasing McCarthy over a separate civil claim stemming from the same accident.

When McCarthy appealed his case, even though the justices had sworn affidavits that they had made their decision to convict him without consulting the clerk, Justice Hewart overruled the decision because of the paramount interest of maintaining faith in the courts. 'A long line of cases shows that it is not merely of some importance, but is of fundamental importance that justice should not only be done, but should manifestly and undoubtedly be seen to be done,' Hewart said.

It was an acknowledgement that there were two conversations going on: one inside the courtroom to persuade the judge, and the other outside the courtroom to persuade the public. As the Turnbull Government drew up the terms of reference for the banking royal commission, it would have two conversations in mind: one, that it would need to properly inquire into misconduct in the financial system, and two, that it would need to be seen to be doing this.

And so began the best corporate blood sport in Australian history.

Looks can be deceiving.

While royal commissions look like, sound like and are even referred to as judicial inquiries, they are not at all proper courtroom proceedings. Although witnesses are asked to take oaths or affirmations, and the proceedings take place in courtrooms across the nation, royal commissions are arms of the executive government. As such, they are used to serve government purposes.

In some cases, those purposes are political.

Before it launched the banking royal commission, the Coalition government had set up inquiries into former prime minister Kevin Rudd's home insulation scheme, known as the 'pink batts' scheme, and into misconduct in the trade union movement. The latter attempted to skewer Labor leaders Gillard and Shorten over historical conduct.

In other cases, royal commissions are used to allow the public to release pent-up angst. The government is able to be seen to be pursuing something, which lets the public know that things are being taken care of. A few heads on spikes, so to say. After the first royal commission into the banking sector was established in the 1930s, one of the commissioners, Professor R.C. Mills, told a Sydney bank manager that 'the commission was superfluous except for giving some people a chance to blow off steam'.

While governments can give off the impression that they are tackling important issues with a royal commission, recommendations that come from the commission's final report can also be ignored.

The Royal Commission into Aboriginal Deaths in Custody, which ran for four years from 1987 to 1991 and took the work of five commissioners, ended up making 339 recommendations. Some thirty years later, only two-thirds of its recommendations had been fully implemented, over which period the rate of Indigenous incarceration had doubled.

Pointing to the successes achieved by any royal commission can be a mug's game, but most of the inquiries do attract public confidence as impartial, non-political and independent. The appointment of judges, ex-judges and senior lawyers to run the show helps with the veneer of credibility, even though the lawyers are not essential to the process. They are chosen because they are experienced in assessing evidence and understand the impact investigations can have on people and organisations.

High-ranking judges are also aware of the unique and unbridled power royal commissions have at their disposal. In all states and territories, royal commissions have powers greater than those given to police and prosecutors, especially the power to force witnesses to give evidence and to subpoena documents. The power of royal commissions to demand answers from witnesses exceeds that given to regular police.

However, where royal commissions fall short is in the ability to make formal findings of guilt or innocence. What they are allowed to do is recommend findings against individuals and companies, which can then be passed to prosecutors to properly stack up in a court of law if there is enough pressure to do so.

While royal commissions are given a wide degree of freedom, the temptation is still there for governments to attempt to constrain the process should they think an inquiry will backfire on them, their supporters or their electoral chances. The government controls the selection of the commissioners and their staff, the scope of the terms of reference, and the level of funding attached to the inquiry.

When Turnbull and Morrison announced the banking royal commission on the morning of 30 November 2017, they were instantly hit with criticism from opponents who believed the terms of reference would leave the inquiry hamstrung. Labor accused the government of failing to consult with victims of rogue financial outfits before designing the terms, and said the inquiry had been constructed on the banks' own terms. Greens leader Richard Di Natale and Greens treasury spokesman Peter Whish-Wilson wrote to Morrison lobbying for broader terms out of concern the commission would miss some of the main systemic problems within the sector.

Morrison had earmarked $75 million to spend on the commission, which would have twelve months to investigate the banks, wealth managers and superannuation funds before reporting back to the governor-general. It would be led by one commissioner, who would also not be given the power to recommend any compensation be paid to victims.

Concerns about the commission soon fell away after the government announced the inquiry's commissioner: former High Court justice Kenneth Hayne.

In some suburbs at least, Hayne became a household name. Hyped as a black-letter lawyer who would do things by the book, the generally media-shy judge was thrust into the spotlight. 'He is renowned for his brilliant mind, his forensic skill and his deep sense of justice,' Turnbull said when making the announcement.

Along with his talent, Hayne was also well known for his tireless work ethic. After leaving the High Court in 2015 at the age of seventy—the mandatory retirement age for the nation's most powerful justices—he had continued practising law. He served on the High Court for seventeen years, and when he left the bench his wife, Michelle Gordon, took his place. He kept a low profile on the High Court, often siding with the majority vote of the seven-member bench. He participated in more than 400 judgements during his time, including a contentious ruling against the government in 2014 when 157 Tamil asylum seekers were held at sea by the Australian Navy; Hayne had recommended that the refugees be able to sue for damages. It was one of his more controversial decisions.

Banking executives attempting to read the tea-leaves for what Hayne would be like as a royal commissioner could look to prior decisions he had made. Some of these suggested the financial sector needed to hold itself to higher standards. For instance, Hayne had been one of three High Court judges who refused to allow Westpac off the hook over a blunder involving the dishonouring of thirty rent cheques sent by a western Sydney–based real estate agent. In that case, Westpac had to stump up $50,000 for libel in a 2010 judgement that overruled lower-court decisions that had said the bank was covered by the defence of qualified privilege.

'To hold banks responsible to their customers not only in contract, but also for damage to reputation, is conducive to maintaining a high degree of accuracy in the decisions that banks must make about paying cheques,' said Hayne along with his colleagues Chief Justice Robert French and former judge Bill Gummow. An accurate and efficient banking system was part of 'the common convenience and welfare of society', the judges said.

In a prescient decision, Hayne had also contributed to a landmark ruling allowing third parties to fund class actions in Australia. By the time he handed his royal commission report to the government, a dozen class actions would have been launched against Australia's biggest banks and wealth managers. In one instance he sided with Andrew 'Twiggy' Forrest's Fortescue Metals against the corporate regulator in 2012, while in another he forced a new vote after the bungled 2013 West Australian Senate election.

Hayne was born in Gympie in Queensland and schooled at the prestigious Scotch College in Melbourne. The bleak city became his home after he had a stint as a Rhodes Scholar at Oxford.

The justice soon developed a reputation for embarrassing barristers with his sharp intellect and his obvious impatience with long and protracted waffling. He was known to shame counsels by asking them to 'help me to understand better than I do now the submission you have just put'. Other times, he would warn dithering lawyers that it would be 'unwise to go back into the lion's den to recover one's hat'. In a 2013 case, he told a lawyer: 'If you sit on the fence too long, Mr Solicitor, it becomes deeply uncomfortable.'

Appointed to the High Court by Prime Minister John Howard in 1997, Hayne was often pigeonholed as a conservative for his rather strict interpretation of the law. Indeed, he had been appointed by Howard in a bid to settle what was increasingly seen to be an activist court, following a string of high-profile controversial decisions. But while he played with a straight bat, Hayne was not afraid to go against the establishment.

His relationship with his wife was also out of the ordinary for an establishment judge. Hayne met Gordon, his second wife, when he was acting for the Bank of Melbourne during a 1990 case about the botched sale of a life insurance business. Three years after the case Hayne divorced his first wife, with whom he had four children, married Gordon and had another son.

Hayne was seventy-two years of age when he was appointed to the banking royal commission, and his formidable work ethic would be put to use in his new role. With the government giving him just twelve months to trawl through a decade's worth of misconduct in the country's largest industry, he would not be able to dawdle.

Hayne once attempted to schedule proceedings, unknowingly, on a Saturday. When this was brought to his attention, he quipped: 'I am all in favour of the legal profession running a seven-day week, but others may have a different view.'

Multi-tasking was a necessity. Witnesses dragged onto the stand would sometimes wonder if Hayne was paying attention to the proceedings. He would be viewing various screens and scrolling on his iPad, or sitting back in his chair and looking at the roof, only to interject about an apparent inconsistency in testimony that had been missed by all the other lawyers in the room. 'I am not using this to play Angry Birds,' he told them.

However, the former High Court judge had made some mistakes. In 1995, after he had just been appointed to the newly created Victorian Court of Appeal, he decided to give reprieve to a young offender who had been sentenced for trafficking the drug ice, seeing good prospects of rehabilitation for the young offender. That man, Carl Williams, eventually became one of the kingpins of the gangster underworld in Melbourne and would have spent thirty-five years in jail for three murders if a fellow inmate had not beaten him to death three years into Williams' sentence. 'I am not altogether certain that these events completely fulfilled the excellent prospects for rehabilitation which we had so confidently predicted twelve years earlier,' Hayne told a gathering of lawyers in 2014. 'The lesson? None of us is infallible.'

No one was infallible. Especially not the treasurer who had long opposed the royal commission.

Despite voting against a banking royal commission twenty-six times by Labor's count, Scott Morrison was soon shocked by what the inquiry turned up. Just days into the commission's second round of public hearings, Morrison was forced to call a press conference to regain control of the narrative, which had been quickly escaping the government. To be fair to Morrison, few others had seen it coming either.

AMP, the Sydney-based wealth manager, had never been lumped in with the scandal-prone four major banks. The so-called fifth pillar of Australia's major financial conglomerates, AMP had been a perennial underperformer for shareholders but was otherwise known to the public as a reliable financial advice provider with a respectable brand. A demutualised mutual friendly society with a history stretching back 169 years and a headquarters fronting onto Sydney's harbour gateway at Circular Quay, it had long been paraded as a bastion of sound financial management.

But by the end of the second round of hearings in April 2018, that reputation was in tatters. AMP was revealed to have charged millions of dollars in fees to customers without providing any service in return. Then the company's board, which was dotted with darling veterans of the Australian corporate scene, had gone on to mislead ASIC at least twenty times over the heist when the regulator started asking questions.

The scandal triggered a wholesale clean-out of the upper ranks of the company and cost it close to $1 billion in refunds for wrongly charged fees. The AMP share price was smashed to smithereens, falling more than 50 per cent and in the process wiping out $7 billion in market capitalisation.

In a series of rolling crises, the AMP disease spread to nearly every facet of the organisation. Its financial advice arm was sordid, its superannuation business a disaster, and its life insurance unit rotten. Chief executive Craig Meller was quickly pushed out of the company and chairman Catherine Brenner, a high-profile member of the Sydney corporate establishment, soon followed. Half the board vanished, and a raft of other executives and managers had to leave the group.

The extent of the scandal took pretty much everyone by surprise—including the treasurer. 'What has occurred here and what has been admitted to in the royal commission by AMP is deeply disturbing,' Morrison told reporters outside his Bligh Street office in a hastily organised press conference. 'This type of behaviour can attract penalties which include jail time—that's how serious these things are.'

The threat of jail time for executives, until that point, had not been seriously considered. For years Australians had been told there was no point in even holding a royal commission, and yet after just a few weeks of public hearings, prison sentences were being discussed.

After the treasurer's comments, other members of the government that had blocked the royal commission were flushed out with admissions they had been wrong to oppose it. 'In the past I argued against a royal commission into banking,' said former deputy prime minister Barnaby Joyce. 'I was wrong. What I have heard so far is beyond disturbing.' A few days later, Turnbull reluctantly conceded that the government shouldn't have resisted the commission: 'All of the commentators are right when they say we would have been right to establish one earlier.'

Turnbull's admission was a few days late for the rest of his Cabinet members, who had not been given the go-ahead to offer messages of regret to victims of financial malfeasance. They were still under the impression that a government could not be seen to be fallible. In a bizarre exchange with the ABC's Barrie Cassidy, Financial Services Minister Kelly O'Dwyer had refused to make the concession just days earlier on national television. Cassidy had wanted to know whether the Coalition thought it had made an error in resisting the inquiry, but O'Dwyer wouldn't engage with the idea.

> O'Dwyer: I've answered your question.
> Cassidy: No you haven't.
> O'Dwyer: I have answered your question.

Cassidy: You haven't said whether you were wrong or right to delay it.

O'Dwyer: I've said we've established it. We have in fact established it.

Cassidy: You have established it, but it took a long time coming. Were you wrong?

O'Dwyer: Well let me put it to you this way. We would not have done all those other things that we would otherwise have done to address these actions.

Humiliated for a week after the exchange, O'Dwyer had to clear the air. 'With the benefit of hindsight we should have called it earlier. I am sorry we didn't, and I regret not saying this when asked earlier this week,' she said.

For Morrison it would take a few more months, a few more rounds of hearings and one more leadership spill until he made the same concession as Turnbull had. It would also take one of the most galling examples of misconduct to extract the apology, like a sore tooth, from Morrison's mouth.

This was as the commission revealed how the boiler-room insurer Freedom Insurance had repeatedly refused to cancel a funeral insurance policy sold through a cold call to a man with Down syndrome. The man was audibly disabled and had been pressured into buying something he did not understand. Despite his father, Baptist pastor Grant Stewart, repeatedly requesting the company to stop deducting money from his son's bank account, the call centre workers had refused to end the policy, and Stewart had then been mocked by Freedom Insurance employees as a 'bloody whinger' for attempting to cancel the useless and expensive insurance policy.

Morrison, who had for so long resisted the commission and then resisted admitting it had been wrong in hindsight to block the inquiry, could no longer resist. 'Of all the problems I was seeking to address in the banking and financial industry, the real hurt being felt by Australians also needed to be addressed,' he said under assault during parliament's question time. 'I regret we didn't do it earlier.'

The inquiry was so powerful that under the glare of the spotlight, the big four banks were also forced to acknowledge their regret. After years of pushing back against such an inquiry, the landslide of wrong-doing was proving too great a weight to hold back. 'I was wrong,' said ANZ chief executive Shayne Elliott. NAB boss Andrew Thorburn said, 'It is now clear to me that the royal commission is necessary and justified.' Westpac chief Brian Hartzer and Commonwealth Bank boss Matt Comyn agreed.

They were forced to admit their contrition not just because of the clarity and weight of the evidence of misconduct: they were also help-less in the face of a deeply talented team of counsels chosen to assist the royal commission, who drove the show. Along with the support of twenty solicitors on secondment from the Australian Government Solicitor, Hayne had handpicked a handful of key counsel to spear-head the inquiry. With the top ranks of the Australian corporate world glued to the royal commission, the solicitors would go on to become lauded figures in their own right.

Rowena Orr, QC, was one of these solicitors. Her time at the royal commission and her careful cross-examination of befuddled banking executives would earn her fans across the nation, and the *Financial Review* would later name her 'Australia's favourite barrister'.

Described as a reluctant rock star, the closest Orr came to having a catchphrase was 'Can I show you a document?' This was delivered multiple times to witnesses when, unbeknown to them, they were about to be shown proof they had been lying for the past hour. The tactic quickly earned her the nickname 'Shock and Orr'.

Before being catapulted to fame at the royal commission, Orr had already had a stellar career. A previous commission was even under her belt: she had acted as a senior counsel assisting in the Victorian inquiry into family violence.

Born in Sydney in 1973, Orr trained in Queensland in law and economics before working for High Court judge Michael McHugh, where she popped onto Hayne's radar. She then worked as a solicitor for the Commonwealth Director of Public Prosecutions and went on to study criminology at Cambridge University.

While she has more recently made her name tackling well-heeled executives, her case history prior to the royal commission was markedly different. It included an inquiry into the death of one-year-old Jaidyn Leskie, who was abducted and murdered in 1997. The toddler's babysitter, Greg Domaszewicz, was charged with murder but subsequently found not guilty in 1998. The murder goes unpunished to this day.

Another case, the most recent before her stint at the Hayne inquiry, was representing an Iranian-born woman who was resisting extradition to the US on charges of skirting around sanctions. She lost.

Other cases she won. One was the defence of Paul Yore, a young artist who was fighting child pornography charges over an exhibition of collages where children's faces were pasted onto adult bodies. Another was for the ACCC over a dodgy vacuum cleaner company that was preying on elderly women with high-pressure door-to-door sales.

Orr was already known in the legal community for her ability to be across a brief and show intimate knowledge of the evidence at her disposal. Executives were powerless to obfuscate and bloviate under her calm and methodical examination, not for want of their lacklustre attempts to outsmart her. Before the royal commission wrapped up, legal eagles around Melbourne were whispering that she would go on to become a judge.

Whereas Orr was a powerful examiner, her colleague Michael Hodge, QC, showed a profound grasp of how the spider-web of financial system laws and regulations drove banking misconduct. Hodge earned the nickname 'Babyface' due to pundits' inability to place his age—he had been a silk for barely a year before he was called up to the royal commission.

The young silk had a penchant for drama. A barrister by day, he was also the co-author of an off-Broadway hit, Clinton: The Musical, with his brother Paul. The play, which won plaudits from the *New*

York Times, followed the colourful administration of the former US president.

When not penning stage plays, Hodge had worked on major cases such as the Grantham floods inquiry and the Queensland Rail Strachan inquiry.

Whereas Orr earned her stripes in the first round of hearings, taking apart the banks over loose lending standards, Hodge made headlines after demolishing AMP's head of financial advice, Jack Regan, in the second round of hearings on wealth management. In a wry exchange between Regan and Hodge, the executive had to be walked through just how many times AMP had misled ASIC over its fees-for-no-service debacle. The bumbling Regan lost count of the number of transgressions as he was plied with more and more evidence. It made for excellent nightly news grabs for the commercial TV stations.

'By my count this was the fourteenth false or misleading statement by AMP to ASIC?' Hodge asked Regan, who was by this point unable to give a response. 'You're losing count?' Hodge said, to laughter in the Melbourne Federal Court hearing room.

'I'm in your hands in that regard' was the best Regan could muster.

From there, the count of documents showing AMP misleading ASIC kept rising. 'I think that takes us to seventeen false or misleading statements by my count,' Hodge said at one point.

'Were you counting that as one or two?' asked Regan.

'I only counted that as one—do you think I should count it as two?'

'I think in fairness, Mr Hodge, you should.'

'OK. The eighteenth false or misleading statement by AMP to ASIC.'

While show business was a certifiable skill for the QC, Hodge also grappled with some of the more complex aspects of financial services laws during the commission. These included the notoriously abstruse arrangements between superannuation funds, their trustees and the related parties owned by the corporations. The complexity was used as a tool to siphon as much cash out of unsuspecting customers as possible. Behind the scenes, Hodge would spend hours working with the PC to get his head around the current regulations that allowed this discreet heist to occur, and to understand what changes were needed to prevent it from happening again.

Then there was Mark Costello, a barrister with the Victorian Bar. He played a smaller role in the public hearings than his colleagues Orr and Hodge, but hit the headlines after putting a witness in hospital with his examination.

Costello had previously acted for the Commonwealth in the high-profile dual-citizen fiasco cases considering the eligibility of MPs to hold office, including Barnaby Joyce, Malcolm Roberts and Nick Xenophon. But it is the examination of Dover Financial boss Terry McMaster that may come to be Costello's most fondly recalled career highlight.

McMaster was the sole owner of Dover Financial, an advice shop maligned within the corporate regulator as the 'licensee of last resort' for its habit of hiring dodgy planners who had been booted out of slightly less maligned institutions. During a gruelling interrogation that stretched for hours, Costello told the commission that McMaster was the head of the only company that had refused to respond to the inquiry's initial request for information on misconduct.

'The word "decline" is strong,' McMaster said. 'A better word is "didn't respond".' It was clear to Costello that McMaster wouldn't go down easily.

However, when it came to discussing Dover's cutely named 'Client Protection Policy', McMaster was left speechless, and then uncon-scious. Under the policy, clients were made to agree that Dover would not be held responsible if a financial adviser failed to do a long list of things that customers of any other organisation would expect to be routine. These included considering a customer's circumstances before giving them advice, and undertaking adequate research about a product before selling it to them.

Customers also agreed to hold any investment for at least a decade without complaining, no matter how bad the product was. Dover told its customers: 'You are responsible for ensuring our advice to you is implemented on a timely basis notwithstanding you may have engaged us to implement it for you.'

Costello put it to McMaster that it was 'Orwellian' to describe the policy document, which sought to insulate the company from any liability, as providing protection to a client.

Here, Hayne interrupted to ensure the witness knew the seriousness of providing a misleading document to his customers. 'I should perhaps say that if it were misleading or deceptive, that might draw attention to relevant provisions of the ASIC Act about making misleading or deceptive statements,' he said.

McMaster, who had fixed one eye firmly on the wall-mounted clock as the day's hearing entered its twilight hours, began to fret. He soon turned sickly pale and began breathing heavily, and then, without so much as a whimper, he collapsed in the stand.

Hayne stood up out of his chair and demanded that triple-0 be called before ordering the public out of the courtroom. Then, for the full glory of the evening's news bulletins, McMaster was stretchered out of the Federal Court and wheeled into the back of an ambulance. An absent look, tinged with relief, was all that was sketched on his face as he was trundled off to hospital.

Thus, the moniker Mark 'Heart Attack' Costello was born. It was showbusiness. It caught the attention of the public. And Canberra wanted a piece of it.

While some of Australia's best reporters were given the job of following the royal commission's every move, a few politicians decided to go and experience the show for themselves.

Labor MP Tim Watts, whose electorate was just a stone's throw away from the Federal Court in Melbourne, was the first to sit in on the proceedings. He relayed the action by live-tweeting the event and it was such a hit that Labor leader Bill Shorten shared the tweets with his own followers.

About a month later, One Nation's Pauline Hanson called a press conference outside the courtroom to proclaim her involvement in setting up the inquiry. She applauded the work of the commission but, sniffing opportunity in the political winds, tried to extract maximum capital from the show. 'I hope that at the end of this there is justice,' she said. 'For the people here, and I've spoken to these people here today, there is a fear that there has not been justice, and there is a feeling that justice will not prevail at this royal commission. There have been over 5500 submissions and a lot of them will not get their chance on the floor of the Federal Court to have their case heard. And that will be a shame.'

Despite the commission eventually handling more than 10,000 submissions from the public detailing all sorts of misconduct and tales of woe, the commission chose to publicly examine only twenty-seven 'case studies'. These came from a carefully curated set of witnesses who were called up to give evidence on the stand before the commission questioned the executives responsible for the misdeeds.

The solicitors knew how to choose them. From the cast of thousands, the royal commission found the witnesses who could convey the most impact, could relay the most harrowing tales of misfortune, and had circumstances that were the most able to illustrate where the problems lay and, from there, the avenues of possible resolution. To allow all 10,000 complainants to give evidence on the stand would have proved too unwieldy, even if each of them had genuine input, but the curation provided enough of a gap for some politicians to claim the royal commission hadn't gone far enough.

Like flies to the carcasses of Australia's corporate heroes, Opposition and crossbench MPs buzzed in from across the country to the royal commission. Renegade MP Bob Katter flew into Brisbane to attend the hearings there, but whereas other MPs complied with the dignity of the proceedings, the member for Kennedy first fell asleep, snoring in the corner, and then, cap-in-hand, made demands to the bench as the hearing was in motion.

Just before the commissioners took a break for lunch, Katter interrupted proceedings to demand why Hayne had not yet delivered proposals to clean up the finance sector. 'Could I just ask—are we going to address why these things happen and what we can do to improve it in the future?' he said. The inquiry had only been going for three months at this point.

It was the second interjection from the independent MP, after he had earlier yelled out 'Can't hear ya', as Orr began to interrogate ANZ executive Benjamin Steinberg.

Hayne shot down the unruly MP, saying, 'All I will say to you is that we are looking at these things at the moment through the lens of particular case studies and there is a deal of work that goes on behind the scenes before, during and after. Ultimately the fruits of that work are going to have to appear in my report and that's the way that I will have to deal with that. You're not the only one who is concerned, Mr Katter—a lot of people are concerned.'

Hayne's message fell on deaf ears with members of other political parties. Not long after the Katter episode, Greens leader Di Natale and his treasury spokesman, Whish-Wilson, assembled out the front of the Melbourne Federal Court as it returned for its investigation into bank-owned superannuation funds. Di Natale used the setting to launch the party's banking policy, designed to fix the 'cancer at the heart' of the banking and financial services sector.

Launching the policy to break up the banks just moments after Hayne had raised the prospect that NAB may have committed a crime by taking money from superannuation customers to which it was not entitled, Whish-Wilson said current regulations had failed: 'At what point is too much profit too much? That's what's at the heart of the royal commission. Malcolm Turnbull said this is not capitalism on trial. Well, in a sense it actually is.'

Labor's financial services spokesman, Clare O'Neil, also joined the show. In late September, she sat quietly in the public gallery as the commission examined the nation's biggest insurance companies. She must have liked what she saw, because two weeks later she would announce, with the backing of Shorten, that Labor would be holding its own version of the royal commission. The so-called community banking roundtables would take place in cities and towns not visited by the royal commission, ostensibly to hear stories from victims who had not been given the opportunity to share their complaints in public on the stand at the real banking inquiry.

'Australians across the country deserve their chance to be heard. Unlike the Liberals, Labor will listen to victims,' Shorten said.

It was a chance for Labor to show voters it was the only party that genuinely cared about banking victims. Local MPs from Geelong to Adelaide were told to head along to the roundtables held in their electorates. More than a dozen were held across the country. It was brazen politics. At the same time as Labor was campaigning for the royal commission to be extended, it was running its own second-rate concurrent inquiry into banking misconduct.

It looked exactly like the political stunt it was designed to be. Each time Labor called for the royal commission to be extended, the government responded that it would indeed grant Hayne extra time if he asked for it. But still Labor continued to demand the extension, despite Hayne making a note of his disinterest in an extended timetable in his interim report. 'The banking system is a central artery in the body of the economy,' he wrote. 'Defects and obstructions in the artery can have very large effects. Likewise, prolonged injections of doubt and uncertainty can affect performance. Therefore, I must execute my tasks promptly.'

Shorten, O'Neil and Labor had either not read his report or did not care for what the commissioner had to say. For a party that had campaigned for the royal commission for so long, Labor seemed uninterested in working with the commission on Hayne's terms. In its submission in response to the interim report, the party chose not to answer the more than 100 policy questions put forward. Instead, it sent the royal commission a glossy booklet outlining the lessons it had taken from its own community roundtables.

The eighteen-page Labor report was not designed to be read by the commissioner or his counsel assisting. Rather, it was a public document for potential voters, mostly useless to the solicitors who had painstakingly trawled through the 10,000 submissions made to the commission. In it, Labor retold stories from people who had attended the fifteen roundtables held across Australia. It seemed to fly in the face of the instructions outlined by Hayne, who called for responses 'on policy issues identified in the interim report' and specifically said he was 'not seeking information relating to individual disputes or instances of misconduct'.

On both counts, Labor had ignored the requests.

But what could one expect? Royal commissions are political beasts, set up by the government for political purposes. It is only natural then for the Opposition to want to use them for its own political purposes. The banking royal commission and its counsels and solicitors, and the witnesses who had built up the courage to tell their stories, were just collateral damage in the carnage of the Corporate Colosseum.

5

IRRATIONAL EXUBERANCE

It was just eight days into the royal commission when Australia was first warned it should brace for bad weather. After twenty-seven years of unbroken economic growth fuelled by the world's longest housing boom, the country found itself sitting on a $7 trillion powder keg that was threatening to explode.

For some time Jonathan Mott, one of the country's most respected analysts at investment bank UBS, had been extremely concerned about tumbling lending standards in the banking sector. Just like a patient who misleads their doctor about how many times a week they drink and exercise, borrowers had routinely been over-egging their levels of income while underselling their living expenses when applying for a loan.

The banks and mortgage brokers had been happy to join in on the fantasy. The less scrutiny applied to the borrower, the more likely it was that the bank could approve the loan. And the larger the loan, the bigger the kickback for brokers, bankers and executives.

There was seen to be little problem with the deal. First-time home buyers and investors alike were assured that house prices only went up—and who could forgive them for thinking otherwise? Since 1986, house prices across Australia had jumped by 700 per cent. In Sydney, prices had risen tenfold over the period to 2018. It was one of the world's biggest-ever debt binges. By early 2018, Australia's household debt-to-income ratio had hit 200 per cent, the highest in the English-speaking world and beaten only by a handful of other heavily indebted nations.

Luckily for Australia, it had emerged unscathed from the GFC. However, it soon became apparent the financial system had suffered several hairline fractures in the GFC turbulence, and those fractures were now threatening to crack open under the weight of the debt.

After just one week of public hearings for the royal commission—which was examining its first topic, residential mortgage lending—the doctors who guard the health of the financial system had given enough evidence to conclude that Australia had poisoned itself, drunk on debt.

For Mott, the hangover was both inevitable and imminent as he sat down to relay the bad news to his clients. 'Only eight days into the banking royal commission, evidence has been presented of fraud, bribery, false documentation, failure to verify customer income, not assessing expenses, failure of internal controls, and failure to report misconduct to ASIC,' he wrote. 'The banking royal commission has shone a spotlight on systemic misconduct. As banks address irresponsible lending, could this result in a credit crunch?'

Those two words—credit crunch—at the end of Mott's short note reverberated around the financial system. A credit crunch is a sharp and sudden reduction in the amount of bank lending in the financial system that, as happened in the GFC, can threaten to sink the entire economy. The Reserve Bank, Treasury and APRA were all put on notice to watch potential developments in the housing market.

Having been shamed into actually complying with responsible lending laws after decades of loose behaviour, the major banks pulled back sharply from the mortgage market. Whereas once brokers could hand in a few paper scraps with guesstimations of a borrower's income and expenses, they were now required to list, in painful detail, every dollar going in and out of a bank account. Gym memberships, pet insurance and subscriptions to Netflix were all accounted for.

The guilty habits of each home loan applicant were supplied to the banks. If you wanted a loan, you had to fess up.

Under the Credit Act, should it have been properly applied, banks were allowed to lend to someone only if the prospective borrower could prove and verify that they could afford to pay back the loan. As soon as scrutiny was applied to the sector, it was more than obvious this wasn't the case. The big four banks, which sell up to 80 per cent of mortgages in the system every year, had been operating in the margins of the law.

CBA-owned mortgage broker Aussie Home Loans came under fire after executives revealed it lacked a system to detect loan fraud, which, of course, was rampant. ANZ was found to have lacked a system to check information provided by brokers about customers' living expenses. How could it even pretend to believe it was properly selling loans? NAB had been repeatedly targeted by scammers, with white envelopes stuffed with money passed across tellers' counters to bribe bankers into giving out fraudulent home loans as part of a scam involving six branches in western Sydney.

Westpac was labelled by ASIC in 2015 as the 'most resistant' of the big four banks to obeying the law during a dispute about an apparent breach of responsible lending obligations. Indeed, APRA chairman Wayne Byres also labelled Westpac a 'significant outlier' in responsible lending standards after a review found that a third of loans at the nation's second-largest bank failed minimum income verification checks, such as sighting a pay slip.

Meanwhile, all the banks were using a heavily discredited formula to automatically approve loans. The Housing Expenditure Measure, which had been used to approve as much as 80 per cent of all loans, continually underestimated the level of expenses households had to comply with.

In terms of scandals, it was colossal. Millions of borrowers were in over their heads.

For the country's biggest institutions, whose bread and butter is the sale of home loans, to wantonly disregard laws that ensure borrowers can repay loans was, to say the least, concerning. The banks panicked into compliance, but when they did so, the regulators grew concerned they were overreaching. After being accused of being too loose with their standards, the banks were now copping flak for being too tight.

And no one would be specific about what the Goldilocks standard looked like. With $1.6 trillion in home loan debt still to be repaid atop a housing market worth $7 trillion, analysts were concerned the financial system was about to run off a cliff.

Just six months after the credit crunch warning, the financial system began to groan as the lenders raced to shore up their loose lending. By late 2018, official statistics revealed the total value of housing finance sold by the financial sector had slumped 14 per cent compared to the same point a year earlier. It was the worst result in eight years, mirroring the credit crunch that had followed the GFC.

As lending became constrained, borrowers were cut off from accessing larger loans—if they were lucky to gain approval for a loan at all.

It quickly filtered through to property prices. Sydney house prices had by this point in late 2018 tumbled 10 per cent from their peak, with Melbourne prices not too far behind. After years of strong growth, house prices began to slide down the other side of the peak, and economists began to warn that the housing market could fall 30 per cent over the next few years, in what would amount to the steepest fall in decades.

The government was put on the back foot and was unprepared to deal with a turning housing market. The prime minister had changed since the start of the royal commission and Scott Morrison was now in charge. His junior treasurer, Josh Frydenberg, was having to deal with the fallout.

Auction rates across the country plummeted, including to a thirty-year low in Sydney. Upset borrowers were miffed they couldn't now access finance when just months earlier their less creditworthy peers had been sold into huge debts.

Frydenberg was attempting to catch a falling knife. In a desperate attempt to keep the housing market from falling in, he took to the front page of the bankers' bible, the *Financial Review*, to urge the lenders to 'keep the books open and don't lose sight of the broader public good'. 'We all know the royal commission has brought into focus the issues of responsible lending and examples of misconduct. While both issues are important, I do see them to some extent as separate, with different responses required,' Frydenberg pleaded. 'Great care needs to be taken around any further changes to responsible lending in order to prevent an unnecessarily restrictive approach to credit.'

The minister appeared to be encouraging the banks to ditch a long-overdue reassessment of their compliance with the law, and the pointy heads in Treasury were concerned. Just days earlier, they had made a forceful submission to the royal commission's interim report that warned against derailing any regulatory crackdown on loose lending. Rather than being concerned about a downturn in property prices or angry borrowers voting out the government, Treasury saw a bigger threat in the continuation of loose lending, which could threaten the stability of the financial system.

'Given the relationship between credit availability and macro-economic performance, the value of a sound and trusted system of credit provision cannot be overstated,' said the government's key economic department. 'Lax lending standards and poor credit allocation that boost economic activity in the short term can come at the cost of longer-term performance when a segment of borrowers fails to perform.'

Luckily for the staff inside Treasury, they could put forward sensible advice without needing to face the wrath of voters. In contrast, Frydenberg was all too aware of what falling house prices would do to the government's hopes of re-election. When it was pointed out to the treasurer that the advice from his own department directly contradicted his public coercions for the banks to continue to lend with gusto, he was exasperated. 'Look, you've got to understand what

I'm dealing with here,' Frydenberg said as I told him I was preparing the story for the next day's paper.

Seasons change, and there were signs a cold snap was set to hit the housing market after twenty-seven years of economic summer. As house prices drove higher and higher and as debts grew and grew, the government had failed to take note of the autumnal leaves. Persistent warnings about the country's love affair with ever-rising household debt were ignored again and again.

The economy was over-reliant on the housing market, and the situation was worsened by a perverse tax system that rewarded unbridled property speculation. It was all managed by a banking sector that was blind to its own risk-taking.

What can seem insignificant at first can seem very important later on.

For example, what started with just five ATMs at Commonwealth Bank ended in the largest penalty in Australian corporate history. Those first five yellow-and-black-painted cash machines deployed by CBA in 2012 would end up teaching the Australian financial industry more about their failings than a steady stream of high-profile scandals strung out over the course of a decade.

The rollout of the bank's so-called 'intelligent deposit machines'—a fancy new breed of ATM that allowed business owners to deposit tens of thousands of dollars at a time into their accounts—would expose CBA to the biggest money-laundering scandal in Australian history.

Hungry for more revenue, the bank rushed out the ever-expanding network of the machines, all the while ignoring warnings from its own staff and regulators. The oversights left CBA open to being used as an instant international transfer service for drug cartels, criminal syndicates and suspected terrorist financiers. Tens of millions of dollars washed through the network of flawed ATMs, and from a Vietnamese restaurant in Sydney's Bankstown to a bank branch in Beirut, Lebanon, CBA was being used by the top tier of organised crime in Australia and by globetrotting suspected terrorists overseas.

By early 2018, the bank was forced to submit to a $700 million penalty, the largest ever slapped on an Australian corporation. But while the lawsuit only became public late in the process, the contraventions of the law at the bank had stretched back for years. At the core of the scandal was a folly of risk management and leadership at the nation's biggest bank, and what could be seen as an isolated event at the bank was indicative of a broader sickness that had infected the country's largest financial groups.

The anti-money-laundering regulator, the Australian Transaction Reports and Analysis Centre (AUSTRAC), first filed the explosive legal suit against the bank in late 2017, alleging more than 50,000 breaches of the law over half a decade. Corporate Australia was shaken from its slumber, and over the course of the following year, the chairmen and chief executives of Australia's largest banks came to learn just how much of an education the country had missed out on following the GFC. The rest of the world had been forced to return to basics and diagnose where it all went wrong as the financial system crumbled around them during the GFC, but Australia was blissfully unaware of the ensuing wave of management reforms that swept over the biggest financial institutions across the globe, who looked to diagnose the causes of the downturn and head off another significant credit crisis.

At the centre of the movement on both sides of the Atlantic was a focus on 'risk culture', a hard-to-explain concept that meant nothing to those who were unfamiliar with it but everything to those attempting to train the banks in how to avert financial disaster. Risk culture was important because what may seem relatively small events in one financial institution can end up causing major problems in other companies, or indeed the system at large.

For example, when US giant Bear Stearns sneezed during 2008, the global economy caught a severe cold. With every aspect of the financial system becoming more interconnected and interdependent, what goes on in one firm is of increasing importance to every other organisation. Small decisions taken by staff inside a company can snowball dramatically internally and spill out onto other groups and the broader system, like financial butterflies on one side of the world causing economic typhoons on the other.

Risk culture, and the promotion of it, is aimed at preventing these storms. A successful risk culture is one where discussion of risks in the organisation is thorough, transparent and acted on. It can be as simple as a lowly worker raising their hand and asking 'Should we be doing this?' and as complex as ensuring the person whose job it is to monitor a bank's balance sheet is properly skilled and listened to.

Australia's heightened engagement with the concept came from unremarkable beginnings when CBA rolled out its project aimed at bringing its ATM network into the twenty-first century. The first five machines in 2012 soon ballooned into a network of more than 800, but each machine was sent out into the world and installed without a daily transaction limit. Customers could deposit as much as they wanted, whenever they wanted, and CBA would collect the fees on the way through.

Unlike CBA, the other major banks had listened carefully to a confidential briefing from AUSTRAC in 2015 about the risks posed by these machines. When the other banks rolled out their own versions of the intelligent ATMs, they instituted modest deposit limits of between $4000 and $5000—half of the $10,000 threshold that triggers a legally required transaction report to the regulator.

CBA never sought to restrict its depositors, and in the end customers—some of whom were criminals—enthusiastically took up the machines. In the first month of their operation, just under $1 million was deposited through them. By mid-2017, this had grown to a monthly $1.7 billion in deposits made through the smart ATM network. It was a boon for business and CBA was reaping the rewards.

So it came as something of a shock when, in August 2017, AUSTRAC sued CBA for breaching the Anti-Money Laundering Act more than 50,000 times. Within days, CBA chairman Catherine Livingstone would announce the early retirement of chief executive Ian Narev, slice executive bonuses to zero, and put in motion a wholesale clean-out of the bank's tarnished board of directors. CBA briefed journalists that it had been 'ambushed' by AUSTRAC, and Livingstone publicly contended that there was much in the legal suit that the bank had learned for the first time when it read the statement of claim.

Behind the scenes, CBA had known for some time of the issues with its compliance with the law. In early August 2015, AUSTRAC had written to the bank asking why it had not handed over two transaction reports relating to deposits made through its smart ATMs that were connected to a suspicious-matter report CBA had filed a few days earlier.

At first the bank was confused, but it went back to its compliance team and found the two transaction records—they were nestled among 53,504 other transaction reports that had never been sent off. A coding error was blamed for the mistake, but later investigation confirmed that the bank had never carried out a proper risk assessment of the ATM network to check the machines were compliant with the law, and the problems were never communicated to the bank's top brass. Managers at the bank were tight-lipped. They never told their seniors of the massive problems they were uncovering as they went about their business. If there was bad news, those at the top didn't want to know about it. And even after the legal action became public, the bank resisted making any changes lest it be cut off from the lucrative deposit fees it was earning through its cash machines.

It was a failure that left the bank continuing to fall foul of the law it was accused of breaching for more than six months after the legal action was first filed in the Federal Court. In the end, CBA submitted to reality and sought to implement AUSTRAC's advice to limit the amount of money that could be pushed through its machines by mid-2018—more than six months after it was first sued.

Reams of documents obtained under freedom of information laws revealed the bank was busy pleading its compliance bona fides with AUSTRAC in the months leading up to the filing of the Federal Court allegations. At the same time, chief financial officer David Craig was sceptical of AUSTRAC's pleading that the bank needed to commit more money to its obviously faulty compliance systems. It was later forced to spend more than \$400 million bringing its systems up to scratch.

Was CBA ambushed by AUSTRAC looking to claim a big scalp? 'It wasn't a surprise,' AUSTRAC chief executive Nicole Rose told me when I asked about the lodging of the lawsuit. Rather, the scandal once again pointed to what is now abundantly clear: a longstanding lack of leadership and prudent thinking about risks at the bank. According to the statement of agreed facts in court documents, the breaches 'were caused by a lack of risk management, assurance and oversight that endured for close to three years'. It's an oversight that jeopardised the safety of the community and the ability of authorities to tackle organised crime and the financing of terrorism.

It showed just how from little things, big things can grow.

The money-laundering scandal threw the spotlight for the first time in Australia onto the concept of risk culture—the idea that small events could have systemic implications.

Several branch managers and staff at CBA had raised alarm bells about the smart ATM networks being used by shady customers, but senior executives ignored the warnings and failed to ensure the machines were sending transaction reports to authorities.

Although the AUSTRAC scandal didn't threaten the stability of the bank or other financial institutions, APRA saw large gaps in CBA's risk management procedures that could leave the lender—and the broader financial system—vulnerable to a far more devastating scenario. If CBA was this bad at dealing with obvious risks relating to shady customers, how bad was it at making sure its balance sheet wasn't going to implode during an economic downturn?

The failings would push APRA to launch a prudential investigation into CBA's 'governance, culture and accountability' that ran for six months. After the findings were handed down, APRA asked all other major institutions to mimic the exercise and report back to the regulator. Until then, Australia's banks had largely been left out of the global discussion on risk culture and the effect internal culture has on the way companies operate.

Although there are countless examples of executive hubris ending in disaster, risk management and culture is a relatively new focus for the centuries-old global banking industry.

In 1987, the US bank Merrill Lynch suffered what was then a $250 million trading loss when a banker took a highly questionable billion-dollar position in mortgage-backed securities. Memos written to senior managers warning of the risk attached to the trade if interest rates rose were ignored. As luck would have it, six weeks later interest rates surged and the Wall Street bank recorded what was then the biggest trading loss in history, prompting a shareholder lawsuit against it. When the dust settled, Merrill Lynch created the world's first market risk management group, looking to ensure such a thing never happened again.

One of Australia's first experiences of careless risk management was during the Russian financial crisis of 1998, when the former Soviet nation devalued its currency and defaulted on its debts. Many banks around the world lost billions on Russian bonds. At the time, ANZ was the sixth-largest investment bank in the world and held about $160 million worth of Russian bonds through its London-based investment arm. However, the incredibly large stake in the Russian bond market was basically unknown to ANZ chief executive John McFarlane. Back at the bank's Melbourne headquarters, executives had no idea of the massive emerging market-bond trading program that was being run out of London, and ANZ suffered massive losses on the operation during the 1998 crisis. Executives at the bank simply didn't have a good grip on what their employees were up to.

Then we can fast-forward to 2004, when NAB was blindsided by a $360 million loss sparked by the actions of just four rogue traders in the lender's foreign exchange trading division. The bank itself was completely destabilised by the affair, which led to the departure of its chief executive, Frank Cicutto, and a clean-out of its senior management and boardroom. When NAB's new boss John Stewart arrived in Australia from Scotland, he said the bank's executives had been warned by ANZ of the rogue traders in their bank, but instead of acting, NAB had responded by cutting off the loans it held with ANZ.

APRA launched an investigation into NAB after the scandal in what was the world's first investigation of bank culture. The regulator found certain failures in risk controls, audits that were ignored, and issues with reporting lines among staff, but it concluded that culture was at the heart of the bank's problems. 'That this could occur is symptomatic of an organisational culture that did not have sufficient regard to the risks attendant with these products,' APRA said.

The NAB investigation is a case study that is still used around the world because it points to the influence of culture on banking problems. But the lessons were not taken on board at the other major Australian institutions.

A good risk culture is one that cultivates an environment where bankers can tell their bosses when they're doing something stupid. Any executive wise enough would want that to be the case, but Australia's approach to risk culture was extremely laid-back for a long time. The long period of unbroken economic growth that underpinned both a strong housing market and ever-increasing bank profits left the sector complacent.

The so-called 'reputational' scandals that caused so much brand damage to the local banking sector—such as the financial planning disaster, dodgy claims-handling in life insurance divisions, and the money-laundering debacle—were all lucky not to threaten financial stability. But the housing market is a different issue.

Surging house prices and extreme levels of household debt have left financial regulators anxious. If banks have shown themselves to be so underwhelming at raising issues internally about obvious misconduct, how vulnerable was the financial system to a widespread downturn if lending standards weren't being adhered to, they wondered. While one bad loan here or there may not seem significant to a mortgage broker, hundreds of thousands of dodgy loans pose a serious threat to the health of the entire economy. Meanwhile, all the evidence was pointing to a financial sector that had let standards slide as profits were put ahead of prudence.

In the years leading up to the royal commission, the Reserve Bank took to conducting new stress tests of the entire financial system, ASIC began investigating banks for compliance with responsible lending laws, and APRA launched new restrictions on excessive lending.

For APRA chairman Wayne Byres, risk culture was a topic close to his heart. Byres had seen the 1998 Russian bond market implosion up close from London when he was on secondment with the Bank of England after more than a decade with the RBA. In 2014 he returned to Australia after working with the Switzerland-based global-standard-setting body for banks, the Bank for International Settlements. Then, as incoming chairman of APRA, Byres began to seriously discuss risk culture with the Australian banking sector. One of his first major programs was to shore up standards in the mortgage sector. In 2014 he announced the first of a number of new measures to clamp down on loose lending in the sector, dramatically limiting the amount of loans that could be sold to property investors and speculators.

Then, in 2016, APRA moved on to defining the term 'risk culture' for the local banks. In doing so, Byres drew on a definition that had been adopted by European and American banks a decade earlier. 'One of the more widely accepted definitions of risk culture', APRA told the banks, 'is the norms and traditions of behaviour of individuals and of groups within an organisation that determine the way in which they identify, understand, discuss, and act on the risks the organisation confronts and the risks it takes.'

That definition came directly from a 2009 report written by the Washington-based International Institute of Finance, titled 'Strengthening Practices for a More Stable System'. It was written at the peak of the GFC, when there was a growing consensus that culture was paramount to the risks faced by the world's biggest banks.

By comparing notes between banks that had fared well during the financial crisis and others that had received a shellacking, the review found numerous ways in which bad culture inside a firm coincided with a bank's weak risk management. Weak risk management was found in banks where workers didn't speak up, bad news didn't travel upwards through the organisation, managers were overconfident and staff were lazy.

Importantly, the review also found that culture could be shifted. It was malleable. Whenever a chief executive changed, the culture of the entire bank changed. Organisations could proactively shape and evolve their culture.

A decade after the financial crisis, Australia found itself still behind the curve, stubborn in its ways. Numerous scandals that should have prompted a review of risk culture were batted away by the banks, which claimed the issues were caused by a few misguided workers. The financial planning disaster revolved around a number of 'bad apple' advisers. The rigging of interest rates by all four major banks was put down to a few rogue traders. Instances of mortgage fraud were solved by sacking a few greedy mortgage brokers.

However, after just eight days at the royal commission, the latter had been shown to be false. The mainstay of the banking sector, selling millions of mortgages, had been predicated on ignoring responsible lending laws for decades. The more mortgages that were sold, the bigger the profits. The bigger the profits, the more executives got paid. It didn't matter who was getting sold into a loan, just as long as they were with your bank and not a rival lender.

Once again, warnings were ignored. The banks didn't want to hear the bad news.

In 2011, then–ANZ boss Phil Chronican gave an unusual speech. It was unusual because the banker used it to take aim at one of the sector's sacred cows: investment property loans and housing speculation.

'Governments might want to look at whether the current extent of negative gearing tax breaks are fostering an unhealthy focus on housing as an investment vehicle, thereby compounding affordability issues,' he told a business lunch in Sydney. Real estate, Chronican said, was being used as a speculative investment vehicle to get rich, rather than as 'a place to live in, sleep, eat and raise your family'. It was a call to arms that subsequent governments failed to take up, leaving the country's economic managers with few options to safely unwind soaring levels of household debt.

Australia's tax breaks for property investing, such as negative gearing and capital gains discounts, helped create the precarious situation the financial system found itself in as soon as the royal commission began. Tasked with countering surging house prices and the erosion of lending standards, APRA and the RBA were forced to put limits on the number of investor loans being sold. The government was too scared to end the negative gearing tax rort that was pumping up house prices to dizzying heights, and the financial regulators had few options at their disposal. In late 2014, APRA put a 'speed limit' on growth in investor loans. Individual banks would be restricted to a maximum 10 per cent increase each year in the amount of investor loans they sold. When this failed to cool the market, the regulator said it would be putting a limit on interest-only loans, restricting the sale of these mortgages to 30 per cent of all new lending.

Australia, it turned out, was an outlier in terms of property speculation. Property investing was a national sport, and we were the international champions.

In the UK in 2016, when the proportion of interest-only loans going to investors reached a heady 17 per cent, the Bank of England was given unprecedented new powers to tighten lending to investors. In 2017, by the time APRA got around to enforcing its own limits on interest-only loans, almost 50 per cent of all loans in the system were being written on an interest-only basis—three times the rate that had led the UK to launch much stricter conditions.

Interest-only loans are an odd financial product for a bank to be selling. Unlike normal home loans, interest-only loans don't require the borrower to chip away at the loan's principal amount and pay down their mortgage. Monthly payments of the interest accrued on the loan are all that is required to be paid, usually for a period of five years, when the loan can then move to a principal-and-interest basis. But because borrowers are able to refinance their loans with another interest-only loan, this means a mortgage could be held for thirty years and the borrower would be no closer to paying it off than when they started.

Interest-only loans, which overwhelmingly are sold to investors, are considered more risky to the financial system as speculators are more likely to dump properties onto the market if house prices head south. In Ireland during the GFC, investors rushed for the exit when the property bubble burst, and house prices in Dublin fell by more than 50 per cent.

Australia's enormous concentration of both investors and interest-only borrowers in the market owes much to negative gearing and capital gains tax breaks. Under negative gearing laws, losses on investment properties, and the interest repayments, are tax deductible. A generous capital gains discount of 50 per cent also means investors have a greater incentive to speculatively buy and sell properties. It's hard to lose money, and when you do, the government picks up the tab.

'For investors, it's unambiguously obvious that one of the attractions of an interest-only loan is maximising the tax deductibility,' said Saul Eslake, a former chief economist at Bank of America Merrill Lynch and long-time critic of negative gearing. 'Given that an interest-only loan typically is for five years, for many investors the intention would be to sell the property before, or at the time, the interest-only period expires. The fact that the interest is tax deductible is the whole attraction.'

To make matters worse, interest-only borrowers are also able to borrow larger sums compared to first-home buyers shopping for an owner-occupier mortgage. This is because investors are sold loans often based on the rental income they can expect to earn on the property, whereas owner-occupiers are measured against their personal income and expenses. This gives property speculators the ability to outbid borrowers who aren't able to supersize their loans from the bank, and in the process artificially inflates house prices.

It's a vicious circle that encourages property buyers to seek out larger and larger interest-only loans to be able to keep up with runaway house prices and compete with property investors who have more financial firepower.

In one of his first speeches after taking over as head of the central bank in 2016, RBA governor Philip Lowe said the popularity of interest-only loans was explained largely by 'the taxation arrangements that apply to investment in residential property in Australia'. 'Over the past year, close to 40 per cent of the housing loans made in Australia have not required the scheduled repayment of even one dollar of principal, at least in the first years of the life of the loan,' Lowe said.

The incentives built into the tax system, while aiding property investors to bid up house prices to foolish levels, pushed owner-occupiers and first-home buyers to the fringes of the market. Just twenty-five years ago, first-home buyers and investors each received around 18 per cent of new home loans. Refinancers got the rest. By 2018, the share of first-home buyers was less than 10 per cent, while investors received around 45 per cent.

'I'm genuinely surprised that there isn't more anger among young people,' Eslake told me. 'When people say that negatively geared investors are just mums and dads trying to get ahead, the question nobody seems to ask is: of whom are they seeking to get ahead? The reality is it's their own kids.'

Worryingly, a large percentage of investors are geared several times over. In other words, they've used equity from one property to put into another property, and again to put into another property. By 2017, the fastest-growing part of the property market was investors who owned six or more properties.

If the market is going up, that's all fine. As long as rental returns are increasing, the maths works out. But in 2018, Australia found itself in a situation where property prices were not going up and where rental returns were going down.

Inspecting the home loan market in closer detail, the situation was even more worrying. A survey of mortgage holders by UBS analyst Jonathan Mott concluded that one-third of borrowers with an interest-only loan didn't realise they weren't paying back any of the loan's principal. They had essentially been sold into loans they didn't understand by brokers chasing large trailing bonuses (ongoing bonuses that are paid out at regular intervals to advisers for years after the sale of a product).

By late 2018, lawsuits were beginning to roll in from borrowers who had been sold interest-only loans they didn't realise were interest-only loans, and that they couldn't afford when the interest-only period expired. Monthly repayments on interest-only loans jump by about 50 per cent at the end of the interest-only period.

The problem was that whereas a borrower used to be able to simply refinance their loan with the bank and extend the interest-only period, the royal commission had led to a situation where no lender wanted to get pinged for irresponsible lending. Although a borrower may have previously qualified for a loan with perhaps a wink and nod, lenders were no longer prepared to skirt the law. On top of this, APRA's new restrictions on investor and interest-only lending meant that many banks were simply not in a position to be able to lend, even if they wanted to.

By 2018, a total of $360 billion worth of interest-only loans were due to roll over to principal-plus-interest over a three-year period. For the average borrower, that meant about $7000 a year in extra repayments.

For ASIC boss Greg Medcraft, the situation had been clear for some time. As the head of securitisation at French bank Société Générale, he had been working in the US in 2008 when the subprime mortgage crash unfolded. So he had firsthand experience of a housing market going pear shaped. While the situations in Australia and the US were not identical, the rise in interest-only loans was as sure an indication as any that many people were buying properties they could not really afford, just as had happened in the US a decade ago.

When Medcraft spoke to overseas regulators, they could not fathom how the Australian financial system allowed one in every two home loans to be sold on an interest-only basis. 'I've been saying for a while I thought it was a bubble. Other people are catching up now,' he told a lunch in 2017—but it was of no apparent concern to the local banking fraternity. Indeed, interest-only loans were so lucrative that the banks would have been shooting themselves in the foot if they'd willingly stopped the mortgage frenzy. Because the principal on an interest-only loan takes longer to pay down, a bank could collect more fees for many more years than it could with the sale of a regular loan. These were highly profitable products.

In the case of Westpac, the worst offender of the major banks, more than half of the loans outstanding on its $400 billion mortgage portfolio were held on an interest-only basis. As the banks' chief executives rolled up to parliament for a committee hearing in mid-2017, the responses by Westpac and ANZ to concerns about interest-only loans couldn't have been more different.

Westpac boss Brian Hartzer was flippant about his company's addiction to the interest-only drip, revealing it had only moved to curb its lending after the regulator forced it to do so. On the other hand, ANZ chief Shayne Elliott said his bank had targeted its interest-only book in April 2016 and had at that point begun to pull back from the market, nearly a year before APRA's crackdown. 'We saw that the risks in our portfolio were changing,' Elliott told the parliamentarians. 'It's not in our interest to lend money to people who can't afford to repay.'

For nearly three decades, Australia's banks had counted themselves lucky. They had been spared the worst from a run of global financial crises that had sunk bigger institutions across the world. But as the royal commission took a peek beneath the tent, it was clear that the structure of the housing market was held up by nothing but hot air. When they were subsequently forced to sell loans only to borrowers who could afford to pay them back, the housing bubble began to slowly deflate. Whether it will burst completely depends on which way the winds blow.

6

LIARS AND THIEVES

Ian McKenzie had been waiting patiently for his turn to speak. It was 10 May 2018, and the Savoy Ballroom at Melbourne's Grand Hyatt was packed out with hundreds of grey-haired AMP shareholders. McKenzie had been a shareholder in AMP since it had demutualised and listed on the stock market back in 1998, and had travelled more than an hour to attend the meeting.

The company's annual general meetings usually drew a good crowd of seniors, some of them lured by free sandwiches and tea at the end of the proceedings, but this year was different. This year, everyone wanted to come. Commercial TV vans full of reporters with their snappers in tow battled to find parking out the front of the Hyatt. The Finance Sector Union national deputy secretary, Nathan Rees, had flown down from Sydney to attend, and activist shareholder from the Australian Shareholders' Association Stephen Mayne had traipsed into the ballroom with a notebook full of prepared questions under his arm.

Less than a month earlier, the reputation of AMP, which had been painstakingly built up over 169 years, had been destroyed in a matter of hours by the royal commission. The value of shares in the company was shattered, along with the brand of the once-venerated institution.

It wasn't that the scale of the heist was particularly egregious. Of the damage wrought by the industry-wide fees-for-no-service scandal, AMP was just a minor player. Although its refund bill for wrongly charged fees would later explode to close to $1 billion, the first estimation of its take in the fees-for-no-service scandal—$4.5 million—was minor compared to the other major wealth companies. For instance, Commonwealth Bank was, at this point, estimated to have siphoned $105 million in fees-for-no-service from its customers, and ANZ had racked up a $50 million bill.

AMP had a trusted brand and loyal shareholder base. Until the royal commission, it had dodged much of the scandalous sludge covering the rest of the financial services industry. Indeed, with such a small bill for its fees-for-no-service rort, it looked almost saintly compared to its peers. However, it wasn't the crime that damaged the company: it was the cover-up. As the commission trawled through a ream of correspondence between AMP and ASIC, it discovered an ill-fated attempt to shield the company's most senior executives from the scandal.

It all started after ASIC stumbled upon the wealth management industry's dirtiest little secret: the unusual habit of charging a fee where no service was exchanged for that fee. This was not isolated to just one major Australian institution. ASIC asked the biggest wealth managers to launch independent reviews to find out how the practice had bubbled away in their divisions for years without action to clamp down on what was essentially the theft of customer savings.

Law firm Clayton Utz, which was tapped to investigate AMP, would have its 'independent' report into the scandal redrafted twenty-five times by senior AMP executives. AMP's head of financial planning, Jack Regan, was forced to admit at the royal commission that the company had then fed ASIC a 'fiction' about why it was charging fees to financial advice customers where no service was given. This was a company with a $17 billion market capitalisation misleading the regulator over a tiny $4.5 million slip-up.

Executives had told ASIC the snafu was initially an administrative error, but when they were presented with the stream of emails, their claim turned out to be false. The practice was in fact a deliberate decision made by AMP management, and for at least seven years tens of thousands of customers had been paying fees they shouldn't have been paying.

AMP had under its control the largest number of financial advisers of any company in Australia—almost 3000—but many of them operated largely as independent contractors. Under a scheme known as 'buyer of last resort', AMP agreed to buy back the portfolios of financial advice customers from these contractors when the contractors left the industry. AMP would then hold onto the portfolios until it sold the customers on to another adviser. If a customer wasn't immediately taken up by another planner, the client was left as an 'orphan', without an adviser, for as long as it took to find them a willing buyer. Meanwhile, under the law, financial advisers must provide ongoing services to clients, such as checking how their investments are performing and doing regular analyses of those investments. For this service, clients pay a fee. Without a financial adviser in charge of the customer, AMP couldn't actually deliver these services. But rather than stopping the regular service fee or conducting the services themselves, AMP continued to collect the fees without telling customers it was doing so.

Clayton Utz's investigation into the issue was supposed to be independent, but the commission heard that AMP's top legal officer, chief counsel Brian Salter, looking to spare the company's former head of financial advice, Rob Caprioli, had repeatedly asked for changes that watered down references to involvement by the former executive. AMP's chief executive, Craig Meller, also had his name deleted, exonerating his boss in what was supposedly the final version of the Clayton Utz report.

The scandal dragged in AMP chairman Catherine Brenner, a darling of the Australian corporate scene. Brenner, a former trainee of ANZ chairman David Gonski, held several of the highest corporate seats in Australia, including on the board of construction giant Boral and the local arm of Coca-Cola.

On 11 October 2017 Salter sent an email to Clayton Utz partner Nicholas Mavrakis after Brenner asked for the inclusion of a statement that Meller was 'unaware of the practices or their illegality'. The interjection by Salter and Brenner was unusual, as Regan, the head of the financial planning division, was one of only two executives dealing regularly with Clayton Utz during its review of the financial planning arm. Meanwhile, AMP board members were responsible for maintaining governance standards across the company, so it was extremely unusual for members of the board, let alone its chairman, to be intervening in the construction of an 'independent' report.

As the royal commission began to pick apart Regan's and AMP's dealings with the regulator on the witness stand in mid-April, the company's share price entered a freefall. Soon after Regan stood down from the stand, AMP forced Meller out the door, and less than two weeks later, a crisis board meeting convened to see that Brenner would exit the company too. Salter was unceremoniously sacked via a public statement; it was the first he knew of it. In just two weeks, AMP shares sank 16 per cent, wiping off $2 billion in shareholder value.

The royal commission's run of hearings was bookended by a recommendation from counsel assisting Rowena Orr that AMP had committed a criminal offence by misleading ASIC. It was an explosive suggestion, and the first potential criminal finding of the year-long commission. What was more, it shot directly to the company's top brass.

'AMP adopted an attitude towards the regulator that was not forthright or honest and demonstrated an attempt to mislead,' Orr said. The behaviour was 'attributable to the governance and cultural practices at AMP', she said, pointing a finger squarely at Brenner, Meller and 'particularly' Salter, who had 'either marked up or suggested amendments to the Clayton Utz report'.

The scandal, along with revelations of a wild culture of fee gouging in its financial advice business and the company's failure to prevent dodgy planners from shunting customers into unsuitable products just to earn kickbacks, marked the beginning of a torrid year for AMP. Soon, the royal commission would carve open other arms of the

AMP conglomerate to find that each division was as rotten as the last. Its superannuation business, one of the largest in the country, turned out to be worthy only of contempt, with member savings apparently kept by the company just so it could slowly whittle away balances for its own profits. Its life insurance business turned out to be charging dead customers for cover they obviously no longer required, and failing to refund the difference. Meanwhile, advisers were 'churning' customers by cancelling cover and then signing them up to the same policy, just to draw down bigger commissions.

Despite the further revelations of poor behaviour, AMP's fate had been sealed by the time of the second round of hearings into the fees-for-no-service scandal. With its annual general meeting following just weeks after these hearings, the company was already falling apart. Following the untimely departures of its chairman, chief executive and legal chief, AMP board directors Holly Kramer, Vanessa Wallace and Patty Akopiantz also bowed out of the organisation. Two class actions had been announced against the company before the 10 May general meeting, and another three would follow.

Shareholders were rightly pissed off, and they wanted to make it known to the company.

As interim chairman Mike Wilkins took to the stage at the Grand Hyatt, he was pummelled by shareholder after shareholder lamenting the mess the once-great AMP had become. One was the former meat trader McKenzie, who had travelled a long way to let the company directors—or what was left of them—know what he thought.

Wilkins had been profusely apologising for the situation shareholders found themselves in. Many had a fair chunk of their life savings wrapped up in AMP shares. But while mea culpa was welcome, shareholders were still in the dark as to why the board was being cleaned out at the same time Wilkins was arguing that Brenner, Meller and the other directors had done nothing wrong. AMP was still claiming innocence.

'Why don't you disclose these things?' McKenzie demanded as he stepped up to the microphone. 'I think it's just absolutely imperative that you become a bit more transparent because the minute you want to become transparent, the word "apology" comes out—"We're very sorry for what we did". There are a lot of mums and dads here that are more than sorry. They would like to see you on a spit.'

No explanation was forthcoming. 'I don't think I would be very tasty,' Wilkins responded weakly.

The industry could offer no narrative countering what the royal commission had revealed during its wealth management hearings. The public could be sure of only one thing about the industry: liars and thieves wanted to get their hands on your money. It was the only explanation following the devastating picture of the financial planning industry that had been painted by evidence at the inquiry.

Even after years of scandals in the sector, the revelations at the royal commission came as a shock. One planner had tipped his clients into buying property through a business he secretly owned, another had pretended to have qualifications he did not have, and another had straight up stolen hundreds of thousands of dollars from customers. What was more, a Labor-led crackdown on bad financial advice in 2013, with reforms known as the Future of Financial Advice (FOFA), had failed to prevent the grift.

As the supply of easy money from trailing commissions started to dwindle after the reforms banned the kickbacks, dodgy planners had turned to the growing honey pot of fees provided by the ballooning self-managed super fund (SMSF) sector. This sector had grown 65 per cent over five years to become the largest in the $2.7 trillion super system by 2018. With about 600,000 funds and more than $700 billion in assets, SMSFs now housed a third of all the money in the super system.

That growth, coupled with the greed of financial planners, put the sector on the radar of the corporate watchdog—so much so that during the royal commission hearings, ASIC deputy chairman Peter Kell revealed that a survey of planners had found that 90 per cent of the times an adviser told a client to set up an SMSF, the advice was not in the client's best interest. But the fees available for the planners to set up these funds were irresistible.

If it did nothing else, FOFA had crystallised a requirement that planners had to act in the 'best interests' of clients. The SMSF sector showed they were ignoring these provisions. As one source of fees was closed off to financial advisers, another was opened. A cottage industry of 'one-stop shops' popped up where you could get financial advice, pay to set up an SMSF, and be charged for the service of having a property investment loan signed into your name along with an investment property thrown into your portfolio. The adviser would collect fees at every point of the transaction.

It was a move beloved by financial planners, Kell said, 'where clients, irrespective of their circumstances, get placed into a very, very similar strategy ... particularly in the SMSF context where people are being encouraged to undertake borrowing to invest in real property'.

It was a system that escaped the control of the regulator, too, which simply didn't have the resources to investigate every financial advice business. Many were backyard operations run by two men and a dog.

While the sector was littered with bad apples, the royal commission revealed that the cart itself was well and truly rotten. The financial advice sector was so big, with tentacles touching nearly every part of a customer's financial life, that it was impossible to escape—even if you were dead.

In early October 2018, as the royal commission continued to demolish the nation's financial companies, the ABA put the media on alert: the next morning, the lobby group would be making an important policy announcement.

If they had made such an announcement just six months earlier, it would have been thought of as a joke. No one could have guessed that the country's most powerful industry, which had campaigned so strongly against a royal commission, would be forced to make a commitment to banning the charging of fees to dead people. It was a graveyard smash. 'This issue of charging fees without service, particularly when customers have recently died, was raised during the royal commission and identified as unacceptable,' ABA chief executive Anna Bligh told reporters. 'When someone loses a loved one, they need support and compassion as they finalise their loved one's financial affairs. Charging ongoing advice fees to dead people is clearly unacceptable.' Because of the adverse publicity, the sector now wanted to put the nail in the coffin of one of the most high-profile scandals of the commission by making sure the public knew the graveyard sting was going to end.

While many of the commission's revelations were too technical or dense to penetrate mainstream consciousness, stealing money from the dead was the sort of banking scandal taxi drivers liked to talk about. It was dubbed the 'I Fee Dead People' scandal, a graveyard robbery carried out by executives with pinstriped shovels.

It started early in the year-long inquiry, in April 2018, when Commonwealth Bank's former head of wealth management, Marianne Perkovic, was called back to the witness stand for a second day of questioning. She had spent the first day largely attempting to avoid straight answers.

The commission learned that CBA's financial planning subsidiary, Count Financial, had been charging fees to customers for almost a decade after they had died. On top of this, management barely cared about the practice. One planner's client had been dead for seven years before the adviser contacted his widow, but then he had taken 'no action' to fix the continuing charges. When management found out about the planner's behaviour, which included such misdemeanours as failing to conduct reviews for his legally required ongoing service obligations, they punished him with only a warning.

Another Count Financial adviser had sold a plan to a customer in 2003 who died the following year. 'Adviser is aware the client is dead but the ongoing service fee continues to be charged,' said a management document. Again, the company's solution? 'Depending on outcome, possible warning to adviser.'

If that wasn't enough, a third planner had failed three quality assurance reviews that found he was not giving any advice to customers but was continuing to charge fees to them, including in instances after the customers had died.

Charging fees for no service—including to the dead—was so rife that it appeared to be part of CBA's business model. As was the case with AMP, Count Financial had an 'orphan client book'. CBA's version brought in $1.5 million a year in revenue.

Under examination by counsel assisting Michael Hodge, QC, Perkovic admitted Count had known as far back as 2012 that its clients were being charged for services they never received, but the company did not report the breach of the law to ASIC until late 2014.

What was at first a tragicomedy soon became a farce. It turned out that emptying the pockets of the dead wasn't just routine for CBA— the rest of the industry were as thick as thieves. After it was revealed that CBA had been opening up caskets for cash, the other major banks began to investigate whether they too had left their fingerprints on corpses. By the time NAB's superannuation chairman, Nicole Smith, was put in the dock in August, the company had discovered it had taken fees from more than 4000 savers who had died. The bank had made $3 million from these ex-customers, and the rip-off had only begun to come to an end in May after NAB decided it should bother to check if it was at risk of the same issue as CBA.

For CBA, the rigor mortis spread beyond the fence of the bank's financial planning arm and into its superannuation business. Its superannuation trustee, Avanteos Investments, found it had charged fees to dead customers as early as 2015, but rather than ending the fees it thought an appropriate course of action was to update the product disclosure documents with the fact that dead customers would be charged fees.

CBA's superannuation boss, Linda Elkins, had, like NAB, only begun to examine her own backyard following the first admission of the scandal at the commission. 'You're saying in 2015 and 2016 the view wasn't that it shouldn't be done—the view was that it needed to be notified to the members,' Hodge asked her. 'But in 2018, the view is it shouldn't be done?'

'That's right, yes,' Elkins said

While Elkins professed that CBA believed it now to be wrong to charge the dead, the bank was not exactly living up to its claim. An internal 2016 presentation tabled by Hodge on the topic of 'fees post death of the member' showed that CBA was continuing to charge the fees but was 'looking to put controls in place after, say, three months'.

'Was a control ever put in place for the fees to stop after three months?' Hodge asked.

'No,' said Elkins.

The nation's fifth-biggest financial services group, AMP, also launched an investigation into itself after CBA admitted its sins to the commission, and found it was charging dead people for life insurance even after being told the customer had died. AMP had ignored concerns from staff members about the practice of charging dead people fees, shrugging them off in favour of aiming to refund life insurance premiums once the policy paid out.

AMP had dirt under its fingernails. It had known since 2016 that it had been charging life insurance fees to dead customers. Upon reopening the casket, it found it had to now refund more than $1.3 million in wrongly charged life insurance premiums to more than 4600 dead customers.

How could Australia's biggest firms have such a disregard for the dead and their loved ones?

Kenneth Hayne cut right to the point in his interim report. 'Why did it happen?' he asked. 'Too often, the answer seems to be greed—the pursuit of short-term profit at the expense of basic standards of honesty. How else is charging continuing advice fees to the dead to be explained?'

Days after Hayne's interim report landed, the ABA wanted to put the issue behind it as fast as possible and announced the 'ban' on charging fees to the dead. However, it wasn't easy to drag the industry along with it. A short time later, AMP would look to maintain its innocence. The company, which by this point barely had a legitimate business to defend, said it was within its legal right to charge dead people fees. 'It has always been AMP's policy to refund premiums incurred after a member's death. It is inevitable and appropriate that premiums will continue to be deducted after a person's death and before AMP is notified of that death,' the company argued in a submission to the inquiry.

While it may have been policy to refund the premiums, it wasn't the company's practice in reality. In the real world, financial advisers and wealth managers never let go of a dollar that easily. And as the royal commission ground onwards, it appeared that more often than not the money obtained by the sector was wrongly sucked out of customers' pockets in any fashion possible.

Just before the commission was scheduled to start tearing up the practices of Australia's wealth management industry, I received an unusual phone call. Annabel Spring wanted to meet me.

Spring was the former chief executive of Commonwealth Bank's wealth management division. Before rising to the head of the division in 2011, she'd had a fairly illustrious career as a managing director of US investment-bank giant Morgan Stanley, and had worked across North America and Asia in high finance. Now, seven years after she'd joined CBA, she was out on her own.

CBA had a few months earlier announced it was letting her go after the bank decided to get rid of its scandal-ridden life insurance business and look at possible options to carve off its wealth management business. With no more work to do, Spring was essentially redundant, on gardening leave.

Both major scandals that had helped build pressure for a royal commission, CBA's financial planning disaster and its dodgy life insurance operations were in the division that had been overseen by Spring. Now, they were about to be given their most thorough examination at the royal commission.

Spring, who by this point was handing her résumé around town in a bid to get hired again, was nervous about what might come out during the round of hearings. A bit of expectation management was in order, she figured. Although I had written regularly about the problems in her business, she had been well insulated from the media. Now she was ready to defend her legacy.

Inevitably, we discussed just how CBA had come to be accused by ASIC of charging more than $100 million in fees-for-no-service.

Before the introduction of the FOFA reforms, the wealth industry had been addicted to the easy revenue garnered from shunting customers into any old product. Advisers were able to claim big kickbacks and trailing commissions or small, bite-sized ongoing service fees. The sector had a mentality of 'set and forget', with customers unknowingly charged huge sums over the years for advisers who did little else than send out an annual letter alerting clients to the fact that their investments were still being looked after. When ASIC began to look at whether companies were actually complying with their ongoing service obligations, it soon became clear they weren't.

The fees-for-no-service issue was the hallmark of ASIC's Wealth Management Project, which began in 2014. Spring claimed that CBA's first estimation of a $100 million fees-for-no-service bill had been so large because the bank had surrendered in the early stages of the investigation. It had bought the financial advice licensee Count Financial in 2011 and had inherited its other planning business, Financial Wisdom, when it took over Colonial First State in 2000. Whereas CBA had processes for document management and digital storage, its acquired businesses did not. Apparently, they housed boxes upon boxes full of document scraps that were meant to show where and when a financial adviser had complied with laws, but the paper trail was such a mess that CBA threw in the towel early. Unable to quantify the extent of its non-compliance, or indeed its compliance, the company instituted a broad-based refund for fees that had perhaps been charged where there was the possibility that no service had been provided.

Spring would be watching the royal commission from the comfort of her own home when counsel assisting the inquiry Mark Costello grilled Elkins, the executive general manager of CBA division Colonial

First State. Elkins had to help Costello pull the thread of CBA's fees-for-no-service practices, and they unravelled from there.

Between 2007 and 2015, CBA and its financial planning subsidiaries had failed to provide annual reviews to more than 30,000 customers but charged the customers money for the reviews anyway. The bank had already put aside $118 million in refunds for the customers.

'You'd be the gold medallist if ASIC was handing out medals for fee for no service,' Costello said.

'Yes,' Elkins responded.

But CBA shouldn't have been given the gold—it was merely first across the finish line in the first heat. The other competitors in the fees-for-no-service marathon were just gearing up. ASIC's first estimate of the extent of the theft across the entire industry was a lowly $180 million. By the end of the public hearings at the royal commission, the figure was racing towards $2 billion.

ASIC's fees-for-no-service investigation started with a small admission from ANZ in a letter it handed the regulator in late 2013, about a low-key 'non-provision of financial advice' issue discovered within its own business. At the time it seemed small and contained, but ASIC asked the other major banks and AMP if they had similar issues. Together, CBA, Westpac, NAB, ANZ and AMP had responsibility for about half of all financial advisers in Australia. What ASIC unearthed was a systemic issue. The industry was taking fees to which it was not entitled and keeping them. The ever-increasing profits provided a nice little windfall for executive remuneration. It was exactly the type of fee gouging that the FOFA reforms had been designed to prevent, but the industry, which had fought so hard against the reforms, revealed itself unable to properly submit to them when they became law.

The FOFA reforms were introduced in 2013 by then Financial Services Minister Bill Shorten to provide consumer protections in wealth management and to clamp down on commissions and fees for advice that had been rolling into banks and superannuation firms. The reforms finally became law under the Abbott Government, but not before a huge lobbying campaign by the wealth management industry that pushed

Finance Minister Mathias Cormann to wind back some of the key protections. Luckily, the Senate crossbench forced Cormann to back down.

Despite the new law, the spirit of the reform was, in the end, ignored. To the industry, the savings of their financial advice customers were just a biscuit tin, and the government had allowed them easy access to the shelf on which it was perched. While the reforms killed off all new trailing commissions, the sector was able to keep the trails that were already in place. These became known as grandfathered commissions, and it was thought that in time they would wither on the vine.

But the industry wasn't going to let go of the money so easily, and the grandfathered payments flourished.

For the executives at CBA, trailing commissions were known as the Hotel California. They wanted a situation where they could count on the continued flow of the commissions after their superannuation members pulled up stumps on their working lives and switched from contributing wages into their nest eggs to drawing down a pension; and they were determined to make sure members who'd checked out of the financial products in the accumulation stage could never leave the Hotel California in the drawdown stage.

Documents presented at the royal commission laid out the true extent of CBA's furious lobbying of key government figures during the FOFA reforms, including two assistant treasurers, Arthur Sinodinos and Josh Frydenberg, and key figures in the Treasury bureaucracy.

The lobbying effort by CBA began at a key moment of opportunity for the financial services sector, shortly after the September 2013 election that turfed out Kevin Rudd's Labor government and installed the Liberals, headed at the time by Tony Abbott. CBA and the other banks were keen to water down consumer protections that had been introduced by Labor, and wanted to make this known to the new government.

So a month after the election, a CBA delegation led by Harvey Russell, who was head of advocacy for the bank's wealth management arm, Colonial First State (CFS), descended on Canberra. The team included the executive general manager of Commonwealth Private, Marianne Perkovic, Colonial boss Linda Elkins, and CBA executive Nicolette Rubinsztein. They met with key Sinodinos adviser Paul Giles as part of the government's 'confidential' consultation with the finance industry on FOFA issues.

'Hotel California' was raised during the chat, according to a CBA file note of the conversation tendered at the royal commission. The government had questioned whether CBA's proposals would result in a situation where grandfathered payments continued indefinitely, and asked whether CBA would settle for a fixed date in the future to end the flow of commissions. 'We argued this would raise constitutional issues. We argued the decline in grandfathered payments would occur naturally and as a result of regulator scrutiny/pressure,' CBA staff members reported back to their seniors.

It was a bald-faced lie, and evidence before the commission revealed it did not happen. Instead, financial adviser portfolios stuffed with clients who were subjected to grandfathered commissions continued to be traded around the industry more than five years after new trailing payments were banned—effectively keeping customers in a situation where they would be heavily fleeced by their adviser in perpetuity.

However, CBA came away from the meeting happy after Treasury explained that the rules would not impact members who moved from the superannuation accumulation phase to the pension phase in the same fund. 'Treasury would consult with CFS to resolve,' the CBA file note recorded. 'A win.'

This was the nation's largest bank, with hundreds of billions of dollars in customer superannuation, arguing for its members to be trapped in a situation where they would be slugged thousands each year in return for no service, just to keep the rivers of gold flowing for the bank's financial advice employees. It seemed completely at odds with the legal requirement that superannuation managers act in their customers' best interests.

Five years after lobbying to keep the fees, Elkins was forced to account for the sins on the witness stand at the royal commission. 'It was more than that, wasn't it,' said Hodge. 'You were lobbying to be able to grandfather commissions when it went from superannuation to pension. How was it in the interests of the members of the fund to grandfather commissions when going from superannuation to pension?'

Elkins responded: 'In hindsight, I would agree that it's not, and we ... shouldn't have been lobbying for that.'

The bank lobbied the government again in February 2015, by which time Sinodinos had been replaced by Frydenberg. In a post-Canberra group email, Rubinsztein told Annabel Spring that Perkovic and others 'had some very productive meetings' in Canberra with Frydenberg's chief of staff, Martin Codina, and Treasury officials. 'Controversial changes are dead,' Rubinsztein recorded.

The Hotel California lived on. Regulators could not kill the beast.

By 2018, $400 million in grandfathered trailing commissions was being siphoned out of the retirement savings of hundreds of thousands of members every year, with many likely unaware they were being slugged the fees. The grandfathered trailing commissions being charged to customers included about $50 million to superannuation members of AMP, $30 million by CBA's Colonial First State, and about $20 million by Westpac's BT Financial. NAB's MLC division sucked out about $40 million in commissions, while IOOF took in about $15 million.

The kickbacks, worth an average of $2000 per customer per year, are loved by dodgy financial planners, but there are no realistic reasons to charge the fees other than to encourage advisers to shunt their customers into products based on who is offering the biggest kickback. The extent of the fee gouging was galling enough in and of itself, but taken from superannuation members, it was stopping savers from being able to amass a decent nest egg for retirement. Thanks to the power of compound interest, the larger a super balance already is, the faster it will grow. Trailing commissions were costing untold thousands in lost opportunity for better superannuation balances. As the royal commission turned the heat onto trailing commissions, it appeared that finally the Hotel California would be closed down.

When Bligh announced the industry would ban taking fees from the dead, she made a concurrent announcement: grandfathered trailing commissions would now be banned from the industry, and the ABA would be looking to lobby Canberra to pass legislation outlawing the practice.

After fighting for so long to keep the kickbacks, the industry's move to dump the fees once the royal commission started scrutinising the practice came as somewhat of a surprise. It was incredible how quickly the banking sector was able to come together to lobby for a legislative change—one that would actually benefit customers—when it turned out that the banks would be the ones paying conflicted kickbacks.

It was some turnaround, and it was because the banks were now tasting their own medicine. CBA, Westpac, ANZ and Macquarie had raced to announce that they would be ending the trailing commissions as the royal commission rolled on. The problem was that they could only ban trailing commissions received by their own salaried advisers. For customers who were paying grandfathered commissions to independent or aligned financial advisers not on the bank's own payroll, ending the kickbacks would cause the banks to break contracts with their advisers. This could end up with angry advisers taking the bank to court, and was the 'constitutional' issue CBA was concerned about.

With only about 30 per cent of financial advisers employed by a major bank, the overwhelming majority were independent or with an aligned financial advice dealership, potentially lining up the banks for thousands of lawsuits. If the banks wanted to now stop customers from paying the commission, someone had to pay the financial adviser their kickback. It left the banks in a situation where they were forced not to ban the trailing commissions but were in a money-go-round situation where they would rebate customers the commissions they had been charged.

The conflicted remuneration was still being passed around the system—it was just that now the companies themselves were paying for it. You still couldn't check out of the Hotel California, but at least now the banks were picking up the room service bill.

The royal commission always kept its cards close to its chest. Companies that were called up to face the fire of public hearings were only ever announced in the week leading up to the proceedings. Witnesses who took to the stand to provide the case studies, along with executives questioned over their conduct, were named just the night before they were due to appear.

So when Fair Work Commission member Donna McKenna was named as a witness for the 27 April hearing, it appeared things would be getting interesting.

McKenna, a workplace lawyer appointed to a statutory body by former prime minister Julia Gillard, was chosen to tell her story of being made a victim of bad financial advice. The press pack at the Melbourne Federal Court was intrigued—usually witnesses were your average customer who had been unknowingly preyed upon by badly behaved banks. To have a serious lawyer make a claim of financial victimhood was unusual, to say the least.

Then came the publication of who McKenna would be accusing of misconduct: celebrity financial adviser Sam Henderson. We could hardly contain our excitement.

Henderson, with his orange complexion and perfectly coiffed blond hair, was a minor TV star and a columnist with the *Australian Financial Review*. His show, broadcast late in the evening on Sky News Business, featured Henderson, who owned his own financial advice business, answering questions emailed in by viewers. The set-up worked a treat, and he had managed to rake in about $170 million in funds under advice at his shop.

The royal commission was Henderson's last show, but it would garner the highest ratings of his career. Not even twenty-four hours after his appearance at the commission, he was dumped by both Sky and the *Financial Review*.

In calm and cold language, McKenna told the tale of how, after seeing Henderson on TV and reading some of his columns, she had sought out his shop, Henderson Maxwell, for advice on how she should prepare for retirement. It was late 2016, and as a single mother she wanted to help her adult children by sorting out her finances at the same time as changes to super tax laws were looming.

Had she taken Henderson's advice, she would immediately have lost half a million dollars.

At her first meeting with him, in November 2016, the conversation was dominated by talk of setting up an SMSF to be managed by Henderson Maxwell. 'It was to be one of the largest slabs of conversation we had at the meeting,' McKenna recalled. 'Mr Henderson persisted in promoting a self-managed super fund with Henderson Maxwell's involvement.' McKenna resisted Henderson's continued spruiking of the idea but eventually agreed to consider it if he would write her out a formal statement of advice.

Henderson also wanted McKenna to invest in funds managed by Henderson Maxwell, pointing out that the firm had recently won an international financial planning award and the 2016 Association of Financial Advisers award for practice of the year. McKenna was wary. A month later, Henderson provided her with a formal statement of advice, ready to be signed. It recommended she shut her State Authorities Superannuation Scheme fund and transfer the balance into an SMSF managed by Henderson Maxwell. This would have cost her $500,000—the difference between an early withdrawal from her state scheme and waiting until retirement to move the money.

'After Mr Henderson had got the overhead projector working, he said to me words to the effect: "We've had a good look at this and we recommend you should set up a self-managed super fund and buy property using a limited recourse loan and that you should have Henderson Maxwell Investments … looking after it for you",' McKenna told the commission. She pushed back against the idea as she was already in a low-cost super fund that seemed to be performing better than what Henderson was suggesting. At this point, Henderson cut the meeting short. 'Mr Henderson said: "I don't have much time, I've got a Christmas cocktail function I've got to go to",' McKenna recalled. The entire meeting was over in fifteen minutes, and she was charged $4950 for the advice.

McKenna eventually got a refund, but the price for getting Henderson on the stand was worth every cent. The bumbling adviser had earlier barged into the courtroom with his legal team in tow, announcing his presence with a bang as McKenna told her story in exacting terms.

By the time Henderson took the stand, the courtroom had already heard audio recordings of phone calls that Henderson Maxwell staff had made where they impersonated McKenna in an attempt to find out about her superannuation scheme. They did this six times. When asked about the conduct, Henderson blamed intransigent junior staff, but it was clear in the background of the phone calls that Henderson was instructing his staff what to do. He denied this.

It only got more embarrassing from there. As Rowena Orr, QC, took Henderson through how he operated his business, every facet of Henderson Maxwell was revealed as a joke. Even the name was ridiculous: Maxwell was Henderson's own middle name, so he had named his company after himself—twice.

When taken to his product disclosure documents and asked to point out where he informed customers that he held a stake in the company that managed the in-house funds, into which he tipped about 84 per cent of his clients, Henderson was unable to find any such reference. It wasn't for lack of trying, though: he spent a good silent minute or two on the stand looking for the reference before giving up and admitting the information wasn't there.

Another piece of vital information was also lacking. Did he actually have the master's degree in commerce that he told his clients he had? 'I apologise for that,' he said, having never actually attained the degree. He hadn't been so apologetic behind closed doors. After McKenna complained to the Financial Planning Association (FPA) about him, Henderson requested the issue be kept under wraps and claimed McKenna was 'aggressive and nitpicking'. In an email to FPA investigating officer Mark Murphy, Henderson said he wished the matter to remain confidential 'given my media presence and potential financial loss as a consequence of FPA publicising the investigation in any way'. Not one to accept responsibility for his deeds, he went on to blame his sloppy advice partly on the trouble of being a single dad and having been forced to fire his children's nanny at short notice when he 'discovered she smelled of alcohol on two occasions at a school pick-up'.

Orr ultimately recommended Henderson Maxwell face a criminal charge for making misleading statements in an official document. As the examination of Henderson dragged on into the late afternoon, she asked Commissioner Hayne if he wanted to sit on for another half an hour so she could finish off Henderson rather than drag the adviser back onto the stand the following morning. Hayne asked Henderson what he would prefer. 'I'd prefer to get it over with,' he said.

And so, with the FPA later concluding that Henderson had breached the group's code of practice a total of nine times, the financial adviser, who is now in the online hamper business, was out of the financial advice profession for life.

At one point when a relative of mine was down on his luck, he could be found selling cherries on the side of the road. He'd sit next to his car on the side of the highway with the boot open to show a trunk full of open boxes with gorgeous cherries on sale for $10 a pack.

He would buy the boxes of cherries cheap from other sellers when the fruit was already on its way out, bruised and starting to decay and would otherwise have been thrown out. Then he'd buy a smaller amount of newer, more expensive cherries and cover the overripe fruit with an appetising top layer. Customers would drive away with a pack and start eating the cherries only to find that beneath the first few they had been sold a box of rotting fruit.

The scam was called 'salting' because the deception was sprinkled on top and covered up the true rotten state of the product to the customer. It was the same scam the banks used to cover up the reality of their financial advice businesses.

No matter how they came, the royal commission revealed the true state of the financial advisers in the industry. Whether they were in expensive suits, dressed up and heavily tanned for television, or faceless guardians of superannuation savings, or among the country's most respected corporate titans, the commission showed that the wealth management sector was not to be trusted.

Just days after he appeared at the royal commission, Sam Henderson was due to give a keynote speech to the SMSF Expo in Melbourne alongside Financial Services Minister Kelly O'Dwyer and SMSF Association chief John Maroney. With no explanation, all references to Henderson were dropped from the program. How could an entire industry association have been unaware of the behaviour of one of its members who had been booked to give the keynote speech at its annual gala? Or was Henderson's behaviour not only indicative of the culture of financial advisers but completely representative?

A month after Henderson's appearance at the commission, ASIC released a study that found a stunning 90 per cent of financial advice given when investors opened SMSFs was not compliant with the law. The Productivity Commission later found that for members with less than $500,000 in their SMSF, the costs of managing the fund were too high and were eroding investment returns. Only 16 per cent of SMSF owners had a balance higher than $1 million. If their financial adviser was actually acting in their best interests, they would have been told to join a standard industry fund that would cost them next to nothing to join. Instead, advisers were leeching off unsuspecting retirees and winning huge kickbacks for shunting them into SMSFs.

In his 2014 financial system inquiry, David Murray recommended banning SMSFs from borrowing to invest in property. It was the only one of forty-four recommendations that the Turnbull Government ignored, and borrowing through SMSFs for property has since become a national sport. The most recent figures from the Australian Taxation Office reveal that the number of DIY super funds that borrowed from banks to invest in property doubled over the past five years to more than 50,000 accounts in 2018. Almost one in ten SMSF owners has accessed limited-recourse borrowing arrangements, which are used to fund the property investments. SMSF borrowing for property has ballooned from $2.5 billion in 2012 to close to $40 billion in 2018.

It was a rort on an enormous scale, and when property prices began to fall at the end of 2018 financial regulators began to worry. SMSF owners had been so wrapped up in the scam that a large proportion of their retirement savings was now dependent on the fortunes of the housing market. The financial advice sector was responsible for the losses but had already come out on top, having won billions in fees.

When interim AMP chairman Mike Wilkins was forced to explain how it came to be that his lauded company had been so tarnished by the behaviour of its employees, he said it was the fault of just a few bad apples. 'I've been asked how could this happen. And I've been honest and explained that no organisation should consider itself immune from such failings,' Wilkins told the AGM. 'At AMP, a small number of individuals in our advice business made the decision not to follow policy and inappropriately charged fees to customers where no service was provided.'

When he was later dragged before the royal commission, Wilkins was asked by Commissioner Hayne whether he still believed what he had said. By this time, AMP's estimate of how much it would have to refund its customers was racing towards $1 billion.

'Mr Wilkins, you said at the annual general meeting of the company in May this year that—and I think I quote you accurately—a small number of individuals in your advice business made the decision not to follow policy and inappropriately charged fees to customers where no service was provided. Do you regard that as a proper characterisation of what happened?'

Wilkins replied: 'Yes I do, Commissioner.'

'A few bad apples?' said Hayne.

Wilkins agreed, but he needn't have said anything. Anyone else could see the financial advice industry was troubled by more than just a few bad apples. Given the opportunity, it seemed large swathes of the industry would take as much as possible, whether you were living or dead, until there was nothing left.

7

BOOM AND BUST

Standing on the ridge overlooking the dusty plains, the ANZ boss looked out of place next to the brewing billy tea.

Mike Smith was indeed a long way from home. The chief executive of the Melbourne-based banking giant had previously had little reason to visit Carisbrooke State at Winton, halfway between Mount Isa and Longreach in central west Queensland. The akubra on his head was pristine. There was no salt starched onto the brim. It appeared to have been plucked off a mannequin just hours earlier.

Smith had flown more than 2000 kilometres to outback Queensland as part of a public relations stunt. He was there to apologise to 81-year-old farmer Charlie Phillott, who had been forced off farmland that had been in his family for fifty years until ANZ seized the property during a drought in 2014.

The story of the Phillotts was symptomatic of tales being told by thousands of other farmers across Australia following the GFC, but the publicity attached to Phillott's own personal turmoil provided one of the key turning points in driving the National Party to push for the banking royal commission.

On his land, Phillott had run a successful cattle and tourism business until struck by a prolonged drought in 2011. The family took out a $1.5 million loan with the agribusiness lender Landmark in 2008 to consolidate their debts. Then, in 2009, ANZ rushed into a takeover of the Landmark business, paying $2.4 billion to acquire the rural financier and in doing so becoming the second-biggest agribusiness player in the Australian market.

But the takeover—at the peak of the GFC—coincided with a sharp increase in deteriorating loans on Landmark's mortgage books. When the drought hit, it served only to exacerbate the number of borrowers falling behind on payments, and many of those borrowers soon slid into technical default. In a bid to shore up its own standing, ANZ went about revising down the valuations of the farmland on its books. This resulted in ANZ slashing valuations at the worst time for the market.

The bank halved the value of Phillott's plot, erasing the family's equity entirely and putting them in technical default despite the farmer never having missed a payment on his loan. The bank then doubled its interest rates, and Phillott continued to pay until he couldn't anymore. He was given just fifteen days to leave his property by ANZ when the family farm fell into distress.

It was a situation being repeated countless times across drought-stricken Australia. By 2013, $722 million worth of Landmark loans—a total of 1050 loans—were impaired or considered high risk, and the bank ended up forcing 162 farmers off their land.

When the scandal became public, Mike Smith decided to intervene. He had grown up at an English boarding school and was better known for collecting Aston Martins and Jaguars, and yet here he was, uncomfortably grasping an enamel camping mug, apologising to Phillott in front of *60 Minutes* cameramen.

Weeks earlier, the news crew had flown Phillott down to the bank's Melbourne HQ for a surprise visit to Smith. In front of the cameras, the company's chief spinner, Stephen Ries, had to inform the farmer that Smith was not there that day.

'I really apologise for what we put you through,' Smith told Phillott. 'It's not been our finest hour, I don't think. And sorry I wasn't there when you came down to Melbourne. I felt we had not covered ourselves in glory, to be perfectly honest. I think there was quite a bit of fault on our part.'

While the Phillotts eventually got their land back with the apology from Smith, thousands of other farmers were not as lucky. And for the banking sector, the damage had been done. Farmers already viewed the banks with a jaundiced eye, but as the stories of roughshod bankers tipping farmers off their land spread throughout regional Australia and over tea and scones at Country Women's Association meetings, opposition to the sector only soldified.

Soon, politicians began to take up the cause. Independent MP Bob Katter attached himself to rural bank customers who had been foreclosed upon. One Nation senators also jumped on board, and by early 2017 the minor party had set up a small parliamentary inquiry into farm lending; short-tenured One Nation senator Rod Culleton had personally been foreclosed on by a bank. The Nationals also took up the fight, wanting to flush out the truth of what had been an industry-wide practice to push farmers into default and sell off their land at miserable prices when times were tough.

The big four banks dominated the rural lending sector, but it was not their speciality. Agribusiness customers were a different beast to the suburban mortgage holders the lenders were used to dealing with. Rural debt, covering 130,000 farm businesses, amounted to about $60 billion in 2018—equal to the value of Australia's gross annual rural production—and the big four banks hold 96 per cent of this debt.

While the big four controlled the market, the royal commission revealed that they did not understand it.

For many farmers, their property is not only a business but an inter-generational home, one that is subjected to years of drought, moments of devastating flash flooding, and a fickle, unpredictable environment of volatile farmgate prices in which each move can threaten to make or break the whole operation. It's also a world of isolation. When intergenerational farming land is taken out of the hands of a family, what follows are divorces, suicides, drugs and violence. Many farmers never get over being forced off their land.

They also don't trust bankers from the big smoke who come onto their country and make out as if they understand the struggles of the land. 'These people have no idea,' said Queensland senator Barry O'Sullivan, a former grazier and a proponent of the banking royal commission. 'They undo their tie, take their crisp white shirt and fluff the collar, and then go out west to manage a complex circumstance of properties that are in drought,' he told parliament as the commission geared up to examine rural finance. 'They honestly would not know the difference between a mulga bush and a Christmas tree, and yet they're sent in to try and keep thousands of stock alive.'

It wasn't always so antagonistic between farmers and bankers, but over the past few decades, the relationship had undergone a dramatic shift. The changes had come in slow waves, but each one was a new plague forcing farmers to change the way they worked and lived.

In the 1980s Australia opened itself up to the world, making its agricultural markets accessible to the rest of the globe. With that opening, farmers were suddenly vulnerable to sharp changes in global commodity prices. Deregulation, such as scrapping the centralised Australian Wheat Board, meant farmers could no longer control volatile prices. Instead, they were expected to buy financial products that could help them hedge against such price movements, which meant more trips into town to meet with branch managers who were selling increasingly complex products.

As international markets developed, the banks then needed to find funding to buy new technology or to expand their landholdings to compete with the advent of factory farming. American farmers were told by Richard Nixon's secretary of agriculture in the 1970s to 'get big or get out'. Australian farmers were now in competition with these US farmers, and found themselves needing to get bigger, and to fund that expansion through the banks.

This situation was mostly uncontroversial when Australia's banking sector was less concentrated. Smaller, regionally focused lenders were staffed with bankers who came from farming families and understood the vagaries of agribusiness finance, the unpredictable economic and environmental cycles, and the risks that were present when lending against them. Years of healthy crops can be followed by seemingly endless drought, only for the climate to bounce right back again.

While farmers were adapting to their new way of life with their lenders, the big four banks were increasingly salivating over the prospect of the growing farming market. Looking to increase market share and search out new sources of profit, the city-based banks turned to the bush. But while they made the trip out, they brought with them a lack of knowledge about how to lend to farmers. They were used to doling out generic home loans for suburban families, or signing up tradespeople with small businesses to relatively minor loans. With their borrowers having steady incomes from urban jobs, the banks could expect smooth rates of mortgage repayments.

When they came out to rural and regional towns, they figured they could run the show how they saw fit. Specialist rural lenders would no longer be staffed by bankers who could properly value land and who understood seasons. The city lenders would send junior bankers with no farming experience out to the bush to work their way up the corporate ladder.

The banking executives had looked out from their top-floor offices and seen a big expanse of land laid out in front of them. They thought it would be theirs for the taking, and started counting their chickens.

It was dubbed Project Conserve.

When ANZ initiated its takeover of Landmark Financial Services in a bid to become a 'super regional agribusiness bank', it made sure to do the due diligence on its target. It worked out it could acquire almost 10,000 customers and more than 100 agribusiness finance specialists across Australia, and gain more than $5.5 billion in annual turnover. This would cement the bank as the nation's second-largest rural lender.

However, while ANZ put numerous executives to work to crunch the numbers for the potential acquisition, it was spectacularly underprepared for the aggressive expansion into the sector—it just didn't know it at first.

At the time of the takeover bid, Landmark reassured its customers nothing would change under its new owner, and ANZ said it would soon be in touch to ease the transition. But the bank had no structures in place to ensure it could deliver on this commitment. The process was bungled from the start, and the slow drip of bad news soon started gushing into ANZ.

An independent consultant's report from McGrathNicol told the bank it had probably paid too much for Landmark, and as it looked closer at the acquisition, the consultant told the new parent bank it needed to ensure almost all Landmark's experienced bankers came along during the transition—otherwise, a great deal of expertise would be lost.

Farmers trusted their specialist bankers, who knew intimately how a family business was run. ANZ would need their expertise to ensure the loans complied with the bank's new risk procedures when it took a scalpel to examine the quality of the loan book it had just purchased. However, only two-thirds of Landmark's relationship managers stayed with the business during the takeover, and a further 10 per cent left during the first six months. They could spot an out-of-towner from a mile away, and they weren't interested in helping ANZ get the lay of the land.

Soon, the bank found nearly half of all the loans it had just bought were not backed up with the right kind of collateral. It became increasingly disappointed with its new purchase as the sheen wore off, and it started to game-plan a way out of the mess it found itself in. Documents later revealed that ANZ executives David Hisco and Joyce Phillips suggested hiking rates on the farmers so the bank could draw in an immediate $6 million extra in revenue. They also recommended that the bank should start trying to foist wealth management products on the farmers in order to make sure it could turn a profit.

No matter how ANZ tried, it couldn't kick Landmark into gear. The division was beset by technical issues, accounts were unable to be opened, and minor problems such as incorrect interest-rate charges plagued customers. McGrathNicol soon warned ANZ that in order to cover the expected cost of defaulting loans, it would need to set aside four times more capital than it had first prepared for. Almost half of the loans in the Landmark portfolio were given a poor credit-rating grade of D, E or F.

The timing for ANZ was already bad, as it had bought Landmark just as the GFC hit, but it worsened when, in late 2010, floods swamped Queensland. To top it off, the Gillard Government banned live cattle exports in 2011, which sparked an immediate and unresolvable oversupply of beef in the Australian market. The farmers had no one to sell their cows to, and prices for livestock plummeted.

Stupidly for ANZ, it hadn't even bothered conducting stress tests of the loans on the books of the Landmark acquisition before it bought it in 2009. And soon after the takeover, about a third of the loans became impaired or were considered to be at high risk of imminent default.

To save its own hide, ANZ cracked down on the farmers with a ruthless vigilance.

Steve and Janine Harley in Western Australia, whose family had owned their sheep farm for more than a century, were given just one day by ANZ to vacate their property after their debt fell due. The letter from the bank telling them to leave came just a few weeks after Steve had suffered a heart attack.

The Harleys attempted to pay down $1.6 million worth of their $2.5 million debt before the deadline, and asked for an extension so they could take advantage of spring sales, when the prices they'd get for selling their land would be better. ANZ wouldn't allow it, and engaged administrators who forced the family to sell all of their nine properties, including their home and their sheep. The receivers then hocked the properties for 30 per cent less than they were worth, almost $600,000 below a recent valuation. When those sales left the Harleys with debts of more than $300,000 to ANZ, the bank threatened them with bankruptcy proceedings.

Then there was Queensland cattle farmer Elizabeth Handley, whose properties had suffered through fire, flood and drought. When she and her husband, Roderick, asked the bank for a brief reprieve as she had just had been diagnosed with breast cancer, ANZ refused.

ANZ's hands were not clean in this case: the Handleys had been duped by the bank. Their loan files revealed ANZ managers had falsely witnessed signatures for the loans, overcharged fees and default interest, failed to extend a promised overdraft, and incorrectly bounced Elizabeth's cheques because of the bank's own system failures.

Victorian farmers Arthur and Rhonda Cheesman were among the other thirty-plus farmers to complain to the royal commission about their treatment by ANZ after the Landmark takeover—the most submissions received on any single scandal examined by the inquiry. The Cheesmans, third- and fourth-generation farmers, had been forced to sell three farms, including one of their homes, along with tractors, cropping machinery and cattle, all to get ANZ off their case as it threatened foreclosure. The bank refused to grant them extra time to sell their property, and the family lost hundreds of thousands due to the quick sales of land that had been in their possession for decades.

The Landmark acquisition was a bona fide disaster.

The bank initially resisted fessing up to the dire state of its rushed and bungled acquisition. It took Charlie Phillott visiting ANZ headquarters in Melbourne to make chairman David Gonski realise that the brand damage could spiral out of control on the bush telegraph. He ordered a thorough review of the Landmark acquisition, which would ultimately provide a valuable education for the bank. Minutes of an ANZ board meeting from August 2015, presented to the commission by counsel assisting Rowena Orr, showed that the board directors discussed a paper titled 'Farming Segments Support Strategy'. In that meeting, which was attended by the man who took over from Smith as chief executive, Shayne Elliott, the bank considered there was 'a lesson to be learned from the Landmark acquisition'.

ANZ had never bothered to properly do its homework before rushing into a market it never truly understood. It had gone into agriculture with great hope, and created only scorched earth.

This wasn't unique to ANZ. The scandal was repeated across the banking sector.

The farmers who lined up to castigate ANZ at the royal commission were just a handful of the thousands who had been done over by their lender and wanted retribution. The other major banks had made the same mistakes as ANZ.

Commonwealth Bank gained a substantial agribusiness lender when it took over Bankwest for $2.1 billion during the GFC. When it inherited the business, the Perth-based Bankwest saw a big opportunity to make an expansion into farms along the east coast. But then, following the devastating Queensland floods at the end of 2010, ensuing droughts and the impact of the live cattle export ban, the bank was forced to withdraw from the market with its tail between its legs.

Bankwest was already in distress when CBA was asked to take over the business during the crisis. Bankwest had a business loan portfolio that was packed full of commercial property loans and bad debts. Under the notorious 'Project Magellan', CBA reviewed more than half of the loans on the new acquisition and tipped many Western Australian businesses into default. While the foreclosures angered many business borrowers who to this day complain of a wild conspiracy by CBA to take over assets it wasn't entitled to, the royal commission could find no fault with the WA management program. CBA's east coast agribusiness expansion, however, was rife with mismanagement.

Bankwest was established as a rural lender in 1895 by the state government as the Agricultural Bank of Western Australia. More than a century later, its new British owner, HBOS, wanted to expand into the other side of the country, where the big four banks dominated the landscape. It was this expansion that would ultimately contribute to HBOS's unwinding as its empire grew too large and too unwieldy.

All the while, Bankwest was treating its farming customers as if they were regular city-based home borrowers, plying its bank employees with incentives to sell as many loans as possible.

Mel Ruddy, a cattle farmer from Toowoomba, was one of the victims. In the space of a few years he lost one of his two farms, was reduced to driving bulldozers at age sixty-eight to pay bills, and had to watch 100 of his cattle die because he could no longer afford to feed them.

It was a Bankwest regional manager who convinced Ruddy to take a larger loan over his two cattle properties when he had originally planned to sell one of them, after the banker valued the properties at a generous $2.3 million. Ruddy signed with Bankwest in late 2011, but his farm was soon hit by a savage drought and cattle prices plunged after the live export ban. Bankwest re-evaluated his properties in 2014 at $1.65 million and deemed them outside its loan-to-valuation ratio rules. Ruddy was now in over his head, according to the bank, which forced him to sell one of the landholdings.

Ruddy fought the bank over a four-year period but eventually lost his farm, known as Sunrise. As the bank crippled him, he had to cut the number of cattle on his other property, an outback station known as Arranfield in far western Queensland, because no other lender would deal with him when he needed to borrow money for licks.

The scales were tipped against Ruddy from the start, for he was dealing with a Bankwest manager who was a 'rural champion'. The title was not because he championed his customers or because he had an unbeatable understanding of life on the land—it was because he sold the highest number of Bankwest loans to his customers as was possible. For his efforts, the banker was sent on a trip to Hayman Island after he hit 134 per cent of his sales target of $25 million. In a single year, he sold $33.5 million in loans and processed more than sixty applications, most of which were for new clients of the bank. The banker, who couldn't be named for legal reasons, also scored a bonus of $15,000 in 2010, and $35,000 the next year.

CBA had foisted the same sort of sales target on its branch tellers and wealth management employees in the city, where staff were pushed to sell as many products as possible in return for endless bonuses and prizes. But farming finance was a different game, and there were severe consequences when bankers tried to double their annual salary by hitting the sales targets. Indeed, there was no recognition of other KPIs: Bankwest was only rewarding sales targets. Internal documents showed that its incentive scheme from 2012 urged the company to 'dangle the carrot and reward top performers' for selling loans, regardless of the economic environment.

In order to garner the bonuses, the champion banker inflated farm valuations and fudged numbers to meet targets. He gave two unconditional letters of finance approval to customers when their loans had not even been approved. A number of times he gave verbal commitments that the bank would definitely stump up finance, before any formal decision was made. He also arranged and advised an elderly customer to withdraw a $350,000 term deposit ahead of schedule, and then transferred the funds to another of his customers. By inflating property valuations, he was able to steer farmers into bigger and bigger loans—but if the bank revalued the land lower, the farmers would find themselves breaking their debt covenants. It was a sure-fire way to get farmers kicked off their paddocks.

Bankwest became aware of the issues around the time the champion manager resigned in March 2012 under a cloud of misconduct. Other customers were found to have problems with him after CBA contacted his clients when his phone was handed in. The employee had even gamed the company's bad-behaviour register, entering into CBA's 'Genesis' system to reset to zero the number of 'dishonours' marked against him.

After the banker was 'assisted' out of the company, the board of CBA was briefed on the rogue employee as part of a broader investigation into its Bankwest arm. When it discovered widespread misconduct by the banker after digging deeper into his files, CBA kept mum and decided against telling other farmers who had dealt with the man about his bad behaviour.

Ruddy had never sought out this man's services. He would not have entered the deal if the banker hadn't personally approached him. 'Bankwest offered such a good deal. Being an optimist, I thought I would give it a go,' Ruddy told the royal commission.

Bankers were moving from farm to farm like locusts, stripping them of all they could, just to earn bonuses.

It wasn't just the city banks that tried to harvest everything they could out of the farmers: specialist agribusiness lenders were also in on the act. Australia's biggest rural financier, Rabobank, owned by the Dutch multinational bank of that name, is the world leader in food and agricultural finance. In Australia, its pay model for its bankers was beset by aggressive lending targets that wrongfooted farmers.

Grazier Wendy Brauer of Theodore, Queensland, was nearly ruined by Rabobank. She had chosen to bank with the lender for her farm, based south-west of Rockhampton, despite its higher interest rates, because it had a solid reputation for agribusiness. The Brauers ran nearly a million cattle on their farm, Kia-Ora, which had been in the family since 1974.

One day, after they had temporarily moved to the US in 2009, the family received an unsolicited email from a Rabobank employee. Although they were not looking to purchase any more land, the banker was offering them the property next to their Queensland farm. He even offered to split the land two ways, looping a neighbour into the deal. This way, the Brauers could buy the lion's share of the property and the neighbour would take a smaller slice.

The deal was too good to resist, and they signed up to a new $3 million loan to purchase the property and buy new cattle to run on it. But it soon turned sour. In late 2010 and 2011, severe flooding devastated the region. A tenant who had been on the Brauers' land decided to throw in the towel and did not renew their lease.

The family came back to Queensland from the US and, confronted with the dire situation, asked the bank if they could access some of their loan facility. Rabobank agreed to let them access their money, but only if they paid back the $3 million debt in just two years. This would be impossible to do after the damage wrought by the floods, and the live cattle export ban was just about to hit too.

It was not the deal they had agreed to, and the Brauers had to sell one of the properties and refinance with another bank. By the end of the ordeal, they were out by about $1 million.

'They put us backwards. They came hunting for us, they came looking for us to buy this block, and twelve months later they wanted us to pay them back more than we'd borrowed,' Brauer told the royal commission. 'And to think I'd recommended these jerks to other people because they had said they were a specialist rural bank that understood the ebbs and flows and cycles of farming.'

As they sifted through the wreckage, the Brauers discovered that not everything with Rabobank was hunky-dory. It had been working on all sides of the fence during the deal. The original valuations of the farm it was offering were conducted by Rabobank, not an independent party, and the same employee was also acting for the family selling the land, not just the two neighbours buying the property.

All the while, Rabobank was threatening the banker with no bonus if he didn't make a target of writing $15 million worth of new loans each year. By inflating farm valuations he edged closer to meeting his targets, and as the bankers enjoyed their bonuses, the farmers would be tipped into bankruptcy come the first dry spell.

The banks, it turned out, didn't care about the farmers—they only wanted to recover their money as fast as possible. As the downturn hit, quick sales of farmland erupted across the country. Properties that had been passed down through families for generations were taken over by liquidators and sold within weeks or days for far below what they were worth.

Despite finally being able to hold the banks to account, farmers were still angry. While the banks were in the dock, the receivers were still at large. The role of the liquidators—guns for hire by the banking industry—was the missing examination from the royal commission. Hayne had been precluded from looking into why bankers took such little care in overseeing what receivers and liquidators did with the distressed farmland in their possession. The commission's terms of reference did not include the scope to examine the industry.

It was a major oversight.

As was the case with so much before the GFC hit, Australian farming was enjoying a period of excess. Big prices were being paid for agricultural land as farmers placed bets on the prospect of significant capital gains while ignoring the fundamental ability of the land to produce decent yields for their labour and investment.

When the GFC hit, interest repayments on debt spiked and banks were no longer as comfortable to lend for long periods at such low rates. Farmers struggled through, earning just enough to get by, pay their bills and keep their land.

The final straw was the 2011 live cattle export ban the Gillard Government established after an investigation discovered that Indonesian abattoirs were mistreating cows that had been shipped to that country for slaughter. With one of Australia's biggest export markets for live cattle closed off, farmers had nowhere to sell their livestock, and as the price of beef crashed, the value of the land they were holding plummeted. How could you sell a farm when the produce generated on the land was worthless?

As rural electorate offices were flooded with tales from angry farmers on the brink of disaster, Treasurer Wayne Swan called an urgent meeting with regional MP Bob Katter. The topic of rural debt was thrust into focus on the national stage, and banks were put on notice that Canberra would be taking a closer look at their dealings.

As farmers struggled, the receivership industry blossomed. Billions of dollars in non-performing loans were now trapped on the books of the major banks, and the lenders were drafting in liquidators for a series of rapid land sales across the country.

Liquidation couldn't have come at a worse time. Not only was the value of the produce crashing, but there was a severe drought that was dragging the price of farmland even lower. When the situation blew up in their face, the banks panicked, appointing as many receivers as they could across the country to hock the distressed land as quickly as possible. The banks needed their money back.

Under-stress loans in ANZ's Landmark division were expected to be 'resolved' within eighteen months. This meant the farmers would either have to get back to an acceptable debt position or sell their land.

As was the case with WA farmers Steve and Janine Harley, who sold their land for almost $600,000 below a recent valuation—30 per cent below what the land was worth—under pressure from their receivers, the authority given to the liquidators seemed out of kilter. Counsel assisting the commission Rowena Orr went straight to the heart of the matter. 'Was there any reason for ANZ to think that agents for a mortgagee in possession could achieve a better price for the sale of the remaining parcels of land than the Harleys could?' she asked ANZ head of commercial lending services Ben Steinberg.

Steinberg, who was facing his third day of examination in the witness stand at the Brisbane Magistrates Court, could respond only with the bank's official line: 'What we were looking for, Ms Orr, at this point in time was to bring this matter to a conclusion and certainty. They were the drivers behind this particular decision.'

As more tales of destruction at the hands of liquidators were heard, the royal commission came under pressure to examine the role of receivers in agricultural lending, even though the inquiry's terms of reference excluded any investigation of administrators. There was a seemingly endless number of farmers complaining of repossessed farms that had been sold below market value, pushing them further into debt. It didn't make sense for the banks to be so brash with the farmland. 'If you appoint a receiver, a receiver will move to sale promptly?' Hayne asked Steinberg.

'If the receiver believes the best outcome would be to hold back a sale, I would expect a receiver to come back to us with a strategy around what the best method of realisation for that property is,' Steinberg said.

In reality, this rarely happened. ANZ had an interest in getting the assets off its books as quickly as possible. Steinberg said holding a loan that was under financial distress attracted an additional capital charge for the bank, as was required by the regulator: 'That capital comes to the bank at a cost.' However, the commission could not subpoena any receivers to come to the inquiry to explain their behaviour.

The rural politicians who had fought hard to establish a royal commission were disheartened by the failure of the inquiry to really take a knife to the receivers. It was unfinished business for the senators who had helped push the government to set up the commission in the first place. During the hearings, they made a plea to expand the inquiry from Canberra. The formal motion, although passed on the voices, was ignored by the government, but it does set the stage for a further examination after a change of government. The Greens-led motion was sponsored by a variety of crossbench senators, including Fraser Anning, Derryn Hinch, David Leyonhjelm, Brian Burston, Rex Patrick and Peter Georgiou.

Labor senator Chris Ketter even said the role of external administrators when dealing with distressed rural borrowers was 'an issue that warrants further scrutiny into the future'. 'There are stories about rural properties being sold for half their original worth in times of drought,' Ketter said. 'I know that I expressed some concerns about the behaviour of valuers, and I am concerned about the inherent conflict of interest that exists with the profession of valuers.'

When the government did not alter the terms of reference to include receivers, more than 100 dispossessed farmers travelled to Canberra from every state in Australia a month later for a hearing arranged by Anning, who was then a senator for Katter's Australian Party. Amid the political pressure, the regulators were finally forced to act. APRA said it intended to formalise in its prudential standard the requirement that land valuations be done at arm's length from the bank, in line with international practice. ASIC said there was a 'tension' between an independent valuation and its usefulness to both the bank and the customer. 'Evidence before the commission establishes that independent valuations of the farms are a significant cost, which are often charged to the customer,' the corporate regulator said. It added that if valuations were conducted internally, it should be by a qualified person separate from the areas of the bank interested in recovering the loan.

Still, the banks bit back at this in their submissions to the royal commission. They believed they were well within their rights to value the land as they saw fit. It didn't help that the bankers facing questioning on the stand were hopeless at giving simple answers. For example, Steinberg frustrated the process significantly, demanding to see evidence to back up each of the assertions made by Orr. James Thompson from the *Financial Review* joked that Steinberg was the sort of person who would ask to see a copy of his passport before he confirmed his date of birth.

By extending the time period for public hearings into rural lending, Hayne was acknowledging the intense political scrutiny on the farming finance round of hearings. Under the weight of the stories told by the farmers, he was also forced to delay an examination into natural disaster insurance. He said the commission had continued to receive information about its case studies for its examination of the farming finance sector as the week of hearings wore on.

'That's why as a result some of those studies are going to take longer to produce than first anticipated,' Hayne said. 'It's important that they're done and that they're done properly. That will give us enough time for the farm finance case studies to be dealt with properly. As I say, it is very important that they are.'

With the focus on the hearings, it seemed that at least some banks were about to start paying attention to their farming customers.

A month after the farm finance hearings, NAB chief executive Andrew Thorburn took a trip out to the regional NSW town of Wagga Wagga. It was time, he thought, to try to mend some fences.

Just weeks earlier, the royal commission had been told the story of Ken and Debbie Smith, who had financed two farms in Queensland through NAB to the tune of $3.1 million. Like many others, they had been hit by droughts, plunging cattle prices and floods. When it looked like they would have trouble paying back the loans, NAB did the worst thing possible: it jacked up their interest rate to 19 per cent.

It was a procedure known as 'default interest'. Banks across the sector were known to punish their borrowers with it in an attempt to claw back as much of a loan as possible before a farm went under, all in the knowledge that no other lender would take the risk to refinance the loan.

When the Smiths tried to enter talks with the bank, NAB told them they would leave the branch with nothing but the clothes on their back if they didn't sign its mediation plan. All the while, it refrained from pulling the trigger on a forced sale of the land, which would have put the farmers out of their misery quickly. Internal documents showed bankers thought a fire sale 'might not be politically acceptable'. So the bank left the Smiths paying extreme amounts of interest for years. By the end, their debts more than doubled to $8 million. It was another tale of a bank doing everything to a customer they shouldn't have.

So there was Thorburn, making the five-and-a-half-hour drive from Melbourne to Wagga to announce that the bank would no longer be applying default interest to struggling farmers. He also announced that the bank would introduce new policies to allow farmers to use much-needed offset accounts against agribusiness loans. Farmers had been fiercely lobbying for the offset accounts for years.

The bank would also find ways to keep banking services in regional communities, Thorburn promised. NAB in particular had been hit by strong criticism for shutting down its regional branch network over the preceding decade. The bank of choice for one in three farmers, in the previous year it had closed several branches around the Riverina region surrounding Wagga. Branches were shuttered in Ardlethan,

Lockhart, Grenfell, Culcairn and Barham in NSW, and Boort and Euroa in Victoria.

Even Deputy Prime Minister Michael McCormack, whose federal electorate centred on Wagga, got in on the bank bashing. He warned that there could be a rise in ransacked businesses if owners—concerned by the rising methamphetamine addiction in regional Australia—were forced to keep more cash on premises because of the banks leaving town.

Now, deeply bruised after several rounds of the royal commission, NAB was attempting to usher in a new era for relations with farmers and other customers in the bush. For Thorburn, the bank's ties with regional Australia became personal. One of NAB's recently closed branches in the western Victorian town of Casterton had been managed by his great-grandfather. 'I sometimes wonder what he would think of how the banks have treated regional Australia in recent times,' Thorburn told a community roundtable.

Until the royal commission, bankers rarely paused to think about how they treated regional Australia. And why would they? Three-quarters of the Australian population live in urban centres. For all the myth-making about the bush, Australians are terrified of the country's big red centre, with most people clinging to the coastal fringe for fear of falling into the harsh desert interior. The banks had dominated the country just fine by targeting their products to city dwellers. In their hubris, they had believed themselves insulated from any backlash when they were pushing farmers into destitution with their ramshackle attempts at entering the agricultural market.

Angry farmers were isolated, disconnected. They were spread too thinly across the great expanse of the continent to cause too much of a fuss, the banks thought. But they underestimated the bush telegraph that connected farmers across the country and turned the collective opinion of the regions against the nation's most powerful industry.

When Nationals politicians and regional MPs cottoned on to the discontent bubbling through their towns, they vowed to take swift action. They forced the banks to reap what they had sown.

8

A SORRY BUSINESS

In 2017, a gathering of Indigenous elders, academics, delegates and activists from across the country asked Australians to listen to them.

In time, it is hoped that the Uluru Statement from the Heart will be seen as the most important political document produced in Australia for decades. At its core the statement is a demand to be heard. It holds out an invitation to non-Indigenous Australians to walk with their Indigenous brothers and sisters into a shared future.

The statement is also an invitation to speak together. The overwhelming conclusion from decades of policymaking targeting Aboriginal Australia is that long-term failure has been caused by a lack of Indigenous voices in the legislative process. Put simply, white Australia has not listened to Indigenous Australia.

The Uluru Statement was dismissed by the Turnbull Government with no consultation. The way its central proposal—the establishment of an Aboriginal advisory body to parliament—was shunned without so much as a batted eyelid from the government was not so much a break with tradition as a continuation of the status quo. Since settlement, mainstream Australia has made decisions that are then foisted on Indigenous people, barely listening along the way.

The treatment of Aboriginal people at the hands of the financial sector has been much the same.

Without a doubt, most of Australia has been generally well served by its financial industry. It has enriched large swathes of society with the ability to finance home ownership, fund business loans and drive decent levels of retirement savings. But the system is purpose-built with the overwhelming majority in mind. The 3 per cent of Australians who identify as Aboriginal or Torres Strait Islander can find themselves underserved by the sector or, at worst, discriminated against.

For hundreds of thousands of First Australians that live in regional and remote communities, the situation is often the latter. In the Northern Territory, for instance, 80 per cent of Indigenous Australians live outside the Darwin capital city area. Just as they are likely to face difficulty in getting the services that are enjoyed by the rest of the country, dealing with the financial system can be just as, or more, difficult. Often, Indigenous people don't start on an equal footing with mainstream Australians when they go to deal with a bank.

Being sidelined from the economy through many generations has left little in terms of wealth being passed down in many Indigenous families. Although many historical policies are now no longer in place, Aboriginal people were for generations excluded from accumulating wealth, home ownership or running a business, and this history continues to burden the current generation.

Currently, Indigenous Australians are twice as likely to be unable to access products that are right for them, or that are affordable. Because of this financial exclusion, more and more Aboriginal people are forced to turn to predatory payday lenders and dodgy credit salespeople who charge crippling interest rates for tiny loans. Aboriginal and Torres Strait Islanders locked out of the mainstream lending system have 'become a captive market' for these black economy credit providers, which include hotels, stores, hawkers and taxi drivers, according to Australian National University academic Siobhan McDonnell.

The absence of wealth and financial engagement can be traced back over many decades. Aboriginal people were forced from their land more than 200 years ago, dispossessed and marginalised. Then, missionaries took to replacing traditional customs with skills for a 'new economy', such as forcing women to cook, clean and mend clothes for white homes.

The depressing irony is that the early white Australian economy relied on Aboriginal labour. Men were put to work on livestock stations but were never paid like their white brethren. Instead, they received payment in food scraps, alcohol and basic housing such as corrugated-iron humpies. Into the early 1900s in Queensland, the government withheld wages or systemically underpaid Aboriginal workers, who could work all their lives and see very little of their own money. Others were subjected to 'income management policies', barred from making decisions about their own finances and thus never learning how financial products worked.

All of this makes attempting to deal with the current complexity of the superannuation system worse for Indigenous Australians than for non-Indigenous people. Even for non-Indigenous Australians, the system is often an opaque mystery.

For many Indigenous people who were subjected to debentured labour policies under previous governments, large chunks of their salaries were sequestered off into trust accounts and referred to as 'stolen wages' by Indigenous workers. In some communities today, superannuation is still contextualised as stolen wages. For a worker who had their wages taken away from them all their life to one day learn that they have a large savings account they can only access once they're old is bemusing, to say the least.

As Indigenous people were excluded from the mainstream financial system, their traditional kinship arrangements not only survived but were relied upon. The accumulation of wealth among Aboriginal people in remote communities is found primarily in forms of social capital, such as connections to traditional country, rituals and inter-generational knowledge. Material forms of wealth, such as cash and consumer goods, are shared through cultural obligation among a community that is tied together by land and kinship. It has been this way for up to 60,000 years. 'Money has only really been in Aboriginal and Torres Strait Islander society … [for] just on three generations,' says Lynda Edwards, a Wangkumara woman and financial capability coordinator with Financial Counselling Australia.

Although the superannuation system affects almost everyone earning a wage in Australia, for an Aboriginal person, negotiating the system can be like trying to struggle against a heavy river. 'You're just tired from swimming upstream and so you give up. And by giving up, you're losing out on things that could actually benefit you,' Edwards says.

Financial counsellors report spending 90 per cent of their time with Indigenous Australians in trying to access their superannuation. On average, their superannuation balances are just under half of those enjoyed by other Australians.

One woman who approached Edwards for help gaining access to her super account needed the funds to help pay for dental work that was expected to cost $20,000. It took six months for the super fund to finally approve the early release. 'Although getting the dental work done would cure the pain she was suffering, the most important reason for it was so she could smile in photos with her family,' Edwards says. 'Her daughter was murdered and there aren't any good photos of them together smiling. The main purpose of getting the money for the dental work was so she could create positive memories through photographs of her and her family for her grandchildren.'

Centuries of deliberate destruction have left deep scars throughout Aboriginal communities, but calculated discrimination has given way to a situation of indifference and neglect. What often starts with the best of intentions languishes as lip service. Australian financial corporations parade around Reconciliation Action Plans and preside over policies that, at best, fail to properly serve Indigenous people in remote areas, and at worst, actively discriminate.

It's often cheaper to fly to Los Angeles on short notice than to book an unexpected flight to Darwin from one of Australia's southern capitals.

Despite this, the royal commission decided to take its travelling tour of public hearings to the top end of the Northern Territory.

It was more of a symbolic decision than a practical measure. The commissioners wanted their visit to such a remote part of the country to be instructive—to show there was a need to travel to see the people affected by the bank's policies.

Unfortunately, the royal commission would be fighting to gain the attention of the public. The round of hearings coincided with a particularly special Territory Day—the fortieth anniversary of the moment the NT had been granted self-governance. About 370 tonnes of fireworks were ignited on the NT's infamous cracker night the Sunday before the week of hearings, leading to twenty-seven injuries, 770 calls to emergency services and nearly 700 grass fires across the territory.

Sky News had flown its presenter Paul Murray to Darwin specifically for the occasion to revel in the festival and its lack of nanny-statism. He was recording live when Territorians fired roman candles at him, forcing him to run away from the camera and dodge small explosions. That week, the front page of the local *NT News* tabloid newspaper read: 'Why I Stuck a Bunger in My Bunghole'— a not-so-subtle nod to its 2012 Walkley Award–winning effort, 'Why I Stuck a Cracker Up My Clacker'.

Territorians reading the same paper in search of an account of the royal commission's hearings at the Supreme Court of the Northern Territory that week would have been forgiven if they couldn't find an article. The commission was given far less carriage than the wreckage and fires sparked by cracker night. For some news organisations, Darwin was a four-hour flight too far to send their reporters for a week to cover the royal commission. Still, the ABC, Sky News, the *Australian Financial Review* and *The Australian* sent people from Sydney and Melbourne to cover the events.

However, there was much less public interest in the commission's inquiry into Indigenous financial issues than in the Territory's cracker night, and as such, the coverage lacked the same penetration as previous rounds.

It wasn't because of a lack of galling tales.

The royal commission heard about Cairns-based used-car salesman Colin Hulbert, who sold old cars on the verge of breakdown to Aboriginal customers who had recently come into money from relief payments made to victims of Cyclone Yasi. Hulbert sold car loans at interest rates of 48 per cent, the highest legal rate, preying on his customers' misunderstanding of how interest rates worked: a number of them believed that the higher the interest rate, the better the deal.

Then there was Sydney-based life insurer Select AFSL, which sold thousands of funeral insurance policies through high-pressure cold calls to Indigenous Australians. Kathy Marika, a sixty-year-old Arnhem Land woman, was wrongly signed up to the policies along with her seven children and grandchildren. Select AFSL had plied its army of British backpacker telemarketers with rewards such as shopping vouchers, Vespa scooters and a cruise to the Sunshine Coast as incentives to sell as many policies as possible. Chief executive Russell Howden attempted to hide this behaviour from the royal commission when it began asking for documents.

While there were many examples of Indigenous customers being ripped off, the Darwin chapter of the royal commission's hearings lacked the financial power of other rounds of hearings, during which billions and millions in wrongly gained windfalls were revealed. Rather, it was probing individually tiny amounts of money that had been sucked out of the hands of Australians who needed to make every dollar count.

The recently installed ASIC boss James Shipton made a surprise visit to the commission's first day of hearings in Darwin. He was there under the guise of being in town to meet with the watchdog's regional NT commissioner, Duncan Poulson. But Shipton was leading by example and wanted it to be known. He wanted more executives from southern capital cities to go out to remote and regional Australia and see how their policies were affecting a certain slice of their customer base.

'I do not want any sector of our society, including our First Australians, not having access to the full benefit of our financial system; nor do I want them to fall victim to unscrupulous behaviour,' Shipton told me at the end of the week of hearings. 'I want to encourage financial firms, especially their senior leaders, to actively engage in closing the financial inclusion gap in remote and Indigenous communities. And by that I mean coming to remote areas, meeting local people, listening to the issues they face and understanding the barriers they encounter.'

When it launched its 2016 Reconciliation Action Plan, ANZ decorated the pages of the document with the artwork of Emily Anyupa Napangardi Butcher. 'The symbolism depicts a future where people and communities thrive by coming together, with ANZ's core values at the centre,' the bank said. However, the goodwill it had in its reconciliation plan was of little consolation for Thy Do, a family support worker at Save the Children.

Do was based in Katherine in the NT when she attempted what she thought would be a simple task to open a bank account for a client, a Dalabon woman who was a single mother of three and lived an hour and a half outside the town. The banks around Katherine were already known as having a curious resistance to serving people who came in from the surrounding communities, but Do did not expect it would take ANZ four months to open a basic fee-free bank account for her client.

The arduous attempt to open the account began after the Aboriginal woman, who struggled with English and relied on Centrelink benefits for income, discovered she was being charged regular direct debits by a photography-package scam that was known to other Aboriginal and Torres Strait Islander people. It routinely preyed on isolated communities, where photographers would offer to take pictures of Indigenous Australians for a small fee. After they signed over their bank account details, the fee would be debited from their account over and over again.

This particular woman, who couldn't be named for legal reasons, was being stung with $200 a month in fees, including dishonour and overdrawn fees, and fees for checking her balance. For many in remote communities, fees for checking a bank balance at an ATM can escalate quickly when they are waiting for their welfare payments to arrive.

Travelling to Katherine to set up the new bank account was no small feat for this woman. Her community of about 400 Aboriginal people had no bank and just a single communal computer at the local council office, and it was often cut off from Katherine during the wet season.

When the woman went with Do to the ANZ branch in town, she was told by a staff member that the bank no longer offered the fee-free account. This seemed strange. Afterwards Do phoned the ANZ call centre, which informed her that the account did, in fact, still exist. So she and the woman scheduled another meeting with the ANZ branch. After organising the account, the woman discovered that ANZ had opened a savings account attached to another account that attracted monthly fees and overdraft fees—not what the woman, who was trying to escape overdraft fees, wanted.

After Do complained again, ANZ opened a pensioner's account for the woman, which still attracted fees. It added insult to injury when she was then told she couldn't change the account to a fee-free account without a password verification. To do this she would have to return to Katherine again.

It took four months and a formal complaint to ANZ before the woman was eventually set up with a basic account, and another two months for the bank to send her the debit card so she could actually access the account.

'It's been a long, confusing, frustrating process. It never crossed my mind that it would be this difficult to open a bank account,' Do told the royal commission. 'The last time I opened a bank account for myself it took me two minutes, and I did it on my laptop. There are particular cultural, language, geographical barriers that are experienced by Indigenous consumers in and around Katherine that, perhaps, weren't taken into consideration by ANZ staff members.'

This case is instructive regarding the way in which many Indigenous Australians are treated by financial institutions. While many Indigenous Australians receive the same unremarkable treatment as the rest of the country when they enter a branch, those in remote communities can be severely underserved. There is as much diversity among Aboriginal and Torres Strait Islanders, in terms of financial knowledge, as there is in the broader population. However, a small but significant chunk of the Indigenous population lack the English skills needed to feel their way around an increasingly complex financial system. Many of them have suffered, too, from generations of poor policy developed by government and businesses. Australia's biggest banks can be armed with all the goodwill in the world and still fail to devote proper resources to understanding the needs of hundreds of thousands of Aboriginal people who live in traditional communities.

The government is also responsible for designing financial laws that are out of step with the reality of remote life. These can affect the simplest things, such as the need for a banking customer to provide identification documents with a name and address. For many Indigenous people, a driver's licence is unheard of and births, deaths and marriages are unregistered. Then, when birth certificates are issued, many don't display the names Aboriginal people understand to be theirs. Many have standard birthdates such as the first of January or July in the year that is a best guess of the year of birth.

Some Aboriginal and Torres Strait Islanders have traditional skin names, different birth names and an adoptive name. If they do hold formal identification, all three versions of their name can be seen printed on different documents. Where this leads to difficulty with the Australian banking sector is with anti-money-laundering laws, which require lenders to fully identify their customers using a range of documents that corroborate the same information. For many Indigenous Australians in remote communities this is impossible, and it means they are locked out of the financial system.

Financial regulators have only recently put in exceptions to these rules, which are known as Know-Your-Customer (KYC) laws. Banks can now accept a letter from a community elder as ID. However, these exceptions to the laws aren't widely promoted or known about within many financial companies. ASIC is often forced to step in and remind firms that there are exceptions for documentation rules when Aboriginal Australians are locked out. Top executives might be aware of the exceptions but front-line staff might have no idea, and customers are turned away when they simply want to engage in the economy like the rest of the country.

'While the guidance is there, and we see commitment to implementing it by the financial services industry, we're still not seeing a real reduction in the difficulties that people are having identifying themselves on the ground,' said Nathan Boyle, ASIC's Indigenous policy analyst. Boyle, a Wiradjuri man who grew up on Biripi country, has been working on financial services issues for Indigenous Australians for the past decade and helps companies to improve their understanding of Aboriginal and Torres Strait Islander customers.

Not only is documentation an issue for Aboriginal customers, but questions that might seem simple to the majority of Australians have no relevance to customers in the bush. What is your street address? In remote communities, there are no street names. 'They will be asked three or four times what the street address is, whereas if they were asked, "What number is on the front of your house?" then they can answer that question,' Boyle said.

For Boyle, some problems could be easily solved. Something as simple as a map of the local area in a bank branch could help staff members work out whether a customer is coming from a remote community and might benefit from a fee-free bank account. It's a simple solution, but not something that has been taken up by the industry.

'I think the biggest change that would really benefit things for Indigenous consumers is if there was a concerted effort to make sure all of the members of that service, right down to the coalface, to the people who are on the telephone or who are dealing face-to-face with Aboriginal and Torres Strait Islander people, are aware of the policies that have been agreed to by the industry,' Boyle said. 'What I would really love to see is more executives from banks, and more policymakers from banks and from financial services institutions who are making these policies, going out to Aboriginal communities to see how the policies are actually working on the ground.'

Lynette Melcer believed her company treated all its members equally. Melcer, the head of technical advice at the $95 billion superannuation fund giant QSuper, had little reason to think otherwise. Established by the government in 2013, the fund operated on a not-for-profit basis and was delivering in spades for its savers.

Melcer's beliefs changed when she travelled to Lockhart River in Far North Queensland in 2014. It's a community of 600 people about 2500 kilometres from Brisbane. To get there, you need to take a flight from Brisbane to Cairns, then another regional plane. 'Lockhart River is a beautiful place. Life is quiet, I suppose. I wouldn't say harsh, but it's not city life at all,' Melcer said. 'Driver's licences didn't exist, passports didn't exist. People who did have driver's licences or birth certificates, often they were wrong.'

Even getting a justice of the peace to certify a photocopied picture was difficult for the locals. One man who brought Melcer a photograph for identification had to have the document lightened because the picture was too dark to show his features. 'He looked at it, he looked at me and he laughed. He said they don't make photocopiers for blackfellas,' she recounted.

When Melcer travelled to Anangu Pitjantjatjara Yankunytjatjara, the problems were compounded. In the APY Lands, nestled in the corner of South Australia that butts up against the state lines of Western Australia and the NT, the 2500 residents who call the area home only recently had mobile phone towers switched on for the first time.

'Most of the people in those communities don't speak English at all, so we had to work through interpreters,' Melcer said. 'I learned that there is no Indigenous word for superannuation.'

According to Melcer, these problems are not understood or dealt with unless executives have on-the-ground experience. 'I thought we did everything for members and I thought we treated all our members equally,' she said. 'Going out to the communities made me see how hard life is there, and how equal isn't the same for everybody.'

Rather than pouring more resources into regional and remote areas, Australia's banks are deserting hard-to-reach parts of the country. Closing bank branches in remote communities has removed one of the last physical connections the city-based corporations have with people on the land. Over the past decade, 2000 bank branches have been closed across the country, and these closures have affected regional areas more than metropolitan centres.

The community of Mutitjulu, at the base of Uluru, is 470 kilometres from its nearest bank branch.

ANZ's retail branch network across the entirety of northern Queensland and the NT is overseen by one executive: Tony Tapsall. His responsibility covers a region three times the size of Texas, and many of his 130,000 customers live in remote communities. ANZ has almost twenty branches in remote communities across Australia, and five are under the watch of Tapsall. It's an enormous expanse of land to manage in a responsible way.

Over the course of Tapsall's evidence to the royal commission, it became clear that despite the best of intentions, ANZ had been treating its Indigenous customers with at best indifference, and at worst neglect. Staff members in its remote branches had not been given any specific training in assisting Aboriginal or Torres Strait Islander people. Instead, ANZ had put a lot of effort into making sure its frontline staff were pushing as many products onto customers as possible, irrespective of the customers' situation.

Staff at the Katherine branch had been coached in making sure they performed the so-called 'A to Z review', which took prospective customers through an arduous process of listing all the financial products the bank has in order to sell them new things they want or have come to the bank to get. The woman who made the three-hour round trip to Katherine with Thy Do was forced to go through such a review.

Rather than simply listening to what a customer requests, Tapsall said the A to Z review was the key to unlocking exactly what a customer wants. 'It's what our bankers will go through with a customer, whether new or existing, to discuss the customer's needs,' he told the royal commission. 'It's a tool to support a conversation between the banker and the customer. It's used, as I said, as part of the conversation to understand a customer's need and goal.'

According to the Finance Sector Union (FSU), bank staff are barely encouraged to offer fee-free accounts. The overwhelming pressure on front-line branch staff is to promote the products that are most profitable for the bank. ANZ has its A to Z review, NAB has a customer 'Mindmap', and Commonwealth Bank leads its customers through a 'Financial Health Check'. 'There is nothing … that would vary by reference to where the employee worked,' the FSU said in a submission to the inquiry. 'The requirement to conduct these reviews is the same for the employee at the Toorak or Point Piper branch as it is for the employee at the Katherine branch.'

In the case of several ANZ account holders on Groote Eylandt, a large island in the Gulf of Carpentaria off the NT coast, customers were given access to informal overdrafts without asking if this was what they wanted. These 'shadow limit' overdraft accounts were causing headaches for the people living on Groote Eylandt, which is home to about 3000 Warnindhilyagwa people. One man who was on Centrelink benefits was charged nine overdraft fees in the space of two weeks by ANZ, costing him $54. He did not know how an overdraft worked and had not asked for one. If customers went more than $50 into the red, they could be hit with interest rates of up to 17 per cent on the overdrawn amount as well as a fee of $6 a day—up to a maximum of $60 a month. While these numbers may seem insignificant to many capital-city customers, they are punishing sums for people who rely on welfare.

ANZ had only recently made changes to exclude people who receive Centrelink benefits from the informal overdrafts, but it was having trouble implementing the change. Tapsall was taken to documents showing the Groote Eylandt man's bank account. Centrelink payments were coming in, and then money was going straight back out to pay the bank its fees. 'Would you give this customer an overdraft?' Commissioner Kenneth Hayne asked.

'No,' Tapsall said. And yet, ANZ had given the customer an overdraft without him asking.

'Isn't there a tension between giving clients informal overdrafts when, if they applied for the overdraft, you would say no?' Hayne said.

For more than 200 years, Indigenous Australians have been grappling with a frontier financial system brought by European settlement.

Former High Court justice Michael Kirby has said a charitable interpretation of the relationship between non-Indigenous and Indigenous people since 1788 is 'a tale of indifference and neglect ... A less charitable interpretation is that it represents a cruel assertion of power: sometimes deliberate, sometimes mindless, resulting in the destruction of Aboriginal culture, unparalleled rates of criminal conviction and imprisonment and massive deprivation of property and land.'

If ANZ's treatment of remote customers was indicative of indifference and neglect, the behaviour of a company called Aboriginal Community Benefit Fund (ACBF) typified the cruel assertion of power.

ACBF was already on the radar of financial watchdogs before the royal commission. The company was in the business of selling funeral insurance, and for nearly three decades it had travelled around the country selling its policies to Aboriginal and Torres Strait Islander people. In the process, it had signed up thousands of children and babies to funeral plans. The policies could cost customers close to $100,000 over a lifetime, depending on how many lives were insured under the policy. If the customer missed a single payment, the entire funeral benefit and any money paid to the company were seized. The customer lost everything.

Before the royal commission, I spoke to a woman who had been sold a funeral plan by ACBF in 1998. Tania Porter was at home when a stranger knocked on her front door. The representative from ACBF convinced her to buy funeral policies for herself, her partner and her family of seven young children. Porter's youngest son, Anthony, was just two years old when he was signed on to the funeral plan.

Porter lived out in Moree, more than 600 kilometres north-west of Sydney. It was a long way from the Gold Coast, where ACBF was based. She couldn't recall every detail of the conversation with the man who signed her up to the policy, but remembered he was a 'real big fella'. When ACBF couldn't find Indigenous Australians to do its door-to-door sales, it often drafted in people who had dark skin or appeared to be Aboriginal.

'They told me if one of my family members died, like my brother or sister, it could help,' Porter said. 'I should have realised then, but I thought I was doing the right thing for my family—that I could wake up every morning and be at peace.'

Porter's cousin-in-law, who was at her house that day, signed up too. They passed over their bank details, and their Centrepay benefit details too. ACBF was kind enough to arrange to deduct the funeral insurance premiums straight from the welfare payments. That way, they wouldn't miss a fortnightly bill.

Twenty years on and $22,000 later, Porter missed two payments. ACBF told her it would be ending her cover and she would get no refund.

ACBF claimed to be looking after Aboriginal communities, but it was doing anything but. The company was run by a Gold Coast family with no ties to Indigenous people or community groups, but from the way it presented itself to customers, you'd be forgiven for thinking otherwise—its advertising material and policy documents were replete with Aboriginal art and symbols such as the rainbow serpent.

The company was also geared towards providing a product for the Aboriginal cultural phenomenon of 'sorry business'—the significant journey surrounding death in Indigenous communities. However, while it promised customers it would take care of the financial costs surrounding sorry business, the company was found to abandon policyholders at the first missed payment.

ACBF saw a morbid opportunity to profit from the cultural attachment to sorry business. The grieving process can extend for months after a death, often involving an entire community. Families will travel from all over the country to the place where a funeral is held and stay with the host family for weeks at a time. Many Torres Strait Islander people wait until a year after burial before laying a traditional headstone for the departed. Because of the weight attached to the mourning process, the price for a funeral can escalate into tens of thousands of dollars. The burden is often shared across kinship lines.

Over its three decades, ACBF sold policies to about 30,000 Aboriginal and Torres Strait Islander people. Over the five years to 2018, it cancelled more than 13,000 of these policies, clawing millions of dollars out of customers in the process.

In a sort of colonial irony, the founder of ACBF, Ron Pattenden, had come to Australia from Britain. The former pub manager set up ACBF in 1992. Not long after the company came into being it began to be targeted by regulators, but several legal actions failed to kill it. After each court case, ACBF would go back to the drawing board and find another loophole to exploit. This had the result of turning it into a complex web of interests that ended with its corporate structure crossing international boundaries.

In 1993, a year after ACBF was established, the NSW Department of Consumer Affairs forced it to split into two funds after Pattenden failed to register it under the proper Funeral Funds Act.

It lost a 1999 court case against ASIC over misleading its customers. ACBF was forced to stop using the Aboriginal flag on its advertisements and ASIC made it declare to any prospective customers that it was a 'private company, not sponsored by or otherwise connected with any governmental or similar body or an Aboriginal organisation'. After the court case, global insurance giant AXA stopped underwriting the funeral insurance policies. When the insurance company became aware of ACBF's behaviour, it said the relationship would no longer 'be in either AXA's or ACBF's, or more importantly in the ACBF members' best interests'.

After AXA pulled the plug on ACBF, no other insurer was willing to step in. In a bid to keep the company alive, Pattenden's accountants, who were then represented by KPMG, told him to set up a holding company in Vanuatu. There, capital of just $200,000 was needed to set up the business—a cut price on the $5 million needed to license the company in Australia. From that point on, premiums paid by ACBF customers were funnelled out of the country and paid into a company called Crown Services in Vanuatu.

Then, in 2004, ACBF was hit by another Federal Court case brought by ASIC. This one forced it to stop selling funeral 'insurance' products. Anti-hawking provisions prevented door-to-door pressure selling of insurance products. Consequently, ACBF set up a 'funeral expense policy' in 2005 whereby the money went towards paying funeral costs to funeral service providers and not to the policyholder. Because it wasn't considered insurance any longer, ACBF was able to skirt the anti-hawking rules.

While Pattenden helped keep the company alive from Vanuatu, the founder's involvement in its day-to-day operation became the subject of uncertainty. According to a 2011 court case relating to a dispute between Pattenden and the Australian Tax Office, different arguments about the nature of his role had been put forward without a clear answer. When ACBF was asked to face up to the royal commission, it wasn't easy to tell who was actually in charge of the company. Pattenden didn't attend. Instead, ACBF's fresh-faced chief executive, Bryn Jones, was sent to Darwin to answer questions.

Jones had only recently been put in charge of ACBF, getting the top job in December 2017 just a month after the government had announced the royal commission. This was despite his having no formal qualifications, no expertise in insurance, and no professional experience working with Indigenous Australians. Indeed, Jones, a muscular, blond young man, had previously been a children's sports coach and an IT worker. He'd got the chief executive job after meeting Pattenden one time in a coffee shop. Pattenden was a banking client of Jones's father, and Jones said Pattenden had suggested at their meeting some ways to 'modernise the company' and 'combat some of the negative publicity' circling it.

At the royal commission, Jones wasn't able to shed much light on who was steering the ship. Michael Wilson, the ACBF chief executive before Jones, had 'ceased all involvement' with the company in November 2017, and Jonathan Law, a non-executive director of ACBF, was apparently not involved at all. Meanwhile, Pattenden's appointment as director of ACBF 'was made simply to comply with legislative provisions' relating to the required number of directors on company boards, Jones explained.

Watching Jones in the dock at the commission could have given the impression that he was just a patsy for Pattenden. Indeed, the ABC's Dan Ziffer put this question to Jones directly as the reporter chased him down the street after his examination.

As Jones was sitting in the witness chair with little knowledge of the company's history or policies, counsel assisting the royal commission Rowena Orr was forced to pick through the inconsistencies in his responses and the information contained in his formal witness statement. 'Did you write this statement, Mr Jones?' she asked.

'Obviously, it was in consultation with counsel and those that I needed to source the information from,' Jones said. He said he was appointed because a 'fresh and transparent' perspective was needed at the company. When he got the job, he 'immediately' contacted one of ACBF's biggest critics: the head of the Indigenous Consumer Assistance Network (ICAN), Aaron Davis, wanting to see what the company could do better.

'Bryn and I met once at my office and I told him in no uncertain terms that until they stopped selling funeral insurance to children, ICAN would have nothing to do with them,' Davis later told me. 'I believe Bryn has a great ability to ease his conscience with Indigenous mortality stats.'

He was right. ACBF used the fact that Aboriginal Australians die on average roughly ten years younger than white Australians to bring a sense of urgency to its funeral policy sales. ACBF deployed these statistics to sell to children and young people in communities where they had little need for the product. The company even had a flat rate it charged babies and children whom it recruited to its funeral plans. It was a boon for business: about 30 per cent of ACBF policyholders were younger than eighteen, while a further 15 per cent were aged between eighteen and twenty-five. Anyone under seventy could be signed up for a policy—which was great news for Indigenous men, who currently have a life expectancy of just sixty-nine years.

In 2015, the federal government banned the ability of ACBF to take premiums straight out of customers' Centrepay benefits. In a bid to survive, the company launched a Federal Court challenge to the decision and won. The ban on the Centrepay deductions was overturned by Justice John Logan, who believed it 'paternalistic'.

When the government later appealed the decision, the ban was reinstated. The court action forced ACBF to abruptly end funeral expenses cover for about 6000 customers because it could no longer access the welfare payments. When the company attempted to call the customers to get new bank account information to continue to deduct money from them, it found it hadn't actually bothered to keep track of where its customers were living.

Another of ACBF's victims was Tracey Walsh, who hailed from Mooroopna, the town across the river from the city of Shepparton in Victoria. In 2005, she signed up to a funeral plan worth $8000 when her friend Leslie passed away. Leslie's family had had to break into their superannuation to pay for his funeral, and Walsh didn't want to leave the same burden on her own family.

An ACBF worker had left posters around her workplace, an Aboriginal cooperative, that were emblazoned with the rainbow serpent. Under the impression it was an Aboriginal company, Walsh signed on when the dark-skinned salesman came back. Despite the previous court case forcing ACBF to stop presenting itself as an

Aboriginal organisation, the company had been advertising its policies on the National Indigenous Times website, in the *Koori Mail* newspaper, on national Indigenous radio services and in television ads without the disclaimer that it had no connection to the community.

After signing up, Walsh paid as much as $10,000 in fortnightly premiums to the company over the next decade for a policy that would cover only $8000 worth of funeral expenses.

When she found out that ACBF would not pay out the balance to her family as she expected, Walsh tried to cancel the policy. She was told in no uncertain terms that if she stopped paying the premiums, she would lose all the money. 'They had me over a barrel,' she told the royal commission.

Walsh complained to the Financial Ombudsman Service but ACBF, through its lawyers, attempted to force her to drop the complaint. Just days before ACBF was forced to face the royal commission, it settled the dispute and increased Walsh's cover to $10,000 with no further premiums to be paid.

'People are in the same position as me, that they think they will get all their money back,' she said. 'All I get at Christmas time is a bloody calendar. I've got elders that have been in these funeral funds for years, and they plan to give the money to their families so that they can survive. Now, these elders will go to their grave not knowing how hard it will be for these families. These people have been used and used and used over the generations and it's just another profit making off our backs.'

The royal commission recommended finding ACBF had breached criminal laws regulating misleading conduct.

Despite the poor publicity at the banking royal commission, just a few months later ACBF was spotted spruiking its products and handing out toys to children at the Koori Rugby League Knockout in Dubbo. Small footballs emblazoned with the ACBF logo were being thrown around by children on the field. Alongside other stalls being operated by education providers such as universities, NSW services such as transport, and community services such as the Financial

Rights Legal Centre and Mob Strong Debt Help, ACBF was handing out show bags with plush kangaroo toys displaying the company's logo. The ACBF stall also featured a football-passing game and the chance to win a large-screen TV. An ACBF representative took down contact details for the company's next victim.

9

WORKERS' CAPITAL

'Bedtime!' calls out the mother to her daughter, who is standing in the backyard next to the chicken coop. 'Goodnight, Doris,' the daughter says to one of the hens, before turning back into the house.

As the mother and daughter retreat inside, a fox watches on from the bushes. Dusk turns to night. 'The big banks want to get their hands on your super,' a voice-over tells us. A trio of foxes encroach on the henhouse: 'And they're putting pressure on our federal politicians,' continues the voice as a disembodied hand unlocks the gate to the coop, 'to let them in.' By the end of the television ad, the viewer knows Doris the hen is dead.

In killing just one chicken, the fox-and-henhouse ad gave birth to a fierce new battle between the Coalition government and the Labor Party over control of the fourth-largest pile of money in the world.

By the end of 2018, Australia's pool of superannuation assets had grown to almost $3 trillion. By the end of 2040, it will have grown to $10 trillion. Due to the sheer amount of money, whoever controls it could wield significant power over corporate Australia, not to mention over the economy and the future shape of the country's financial sector.

The pool of superannuation savings is basically split three ways. A third of the money is held in SMSFs, which are similar to a family trust. Then there are 'retail' funds, which are owned by the banks and wealth management industry and are run on a for-profit basis and open to the public. They include funds such as the Colonial First State funds owned and managed by Commonwealth Bank; the bank profits from managing the savings by charging management and administration fees.

The final third is owned by not-for-profit superannuation providers. Some of these are corporate funds run by a company for their own workers, and some are run by the government for the nest eggs of public servants. However, most not-for-profit funds are 'industry' funds that cater to a specific group of employees, such as those in construction. These industry super funds have longstanding ties to the Labor Party. Their boards are made up of a split number of directors who are either employer group representatives or worker group representatives. The latter are in most cases union delegates. For instance, the construction workers' super fund, Cbus, takes its board directors from employer groups such as Master Builders Australia and from worker groups such as the CFMEU and the Australian Council of Trade Unions (ACTU).

Because of the close relationship between the union movement, industry funds and the Labor Party, the industry fund sector has regularly landed in the crosshairs of the Liberal Party.

The Liberals believe there is good reason to worry. Because of the enormity of the pool of retirement savings, fund managers are now able to take control of entire companies. They are also able to dictate how company boards behave and have an increasing say in company standards relating to environmental, social and governance decisions.

To the Liberal Party, the traditional home of capital management and big business, this is not just a threat to the power and autonomy of the business community, it is also an increasingly viable danger coming from their political enemy. Financial managers of the economy are under threat of control by the party of the worker, and if things continue, business as usual will become a thing of the past.

The industry fund sector knew the government was out to get it, and saw every piece of legislation from the conservative government as another attempt to buckle the sector from asserting itself. It didn't matter if it was an apparently sensible policy, such as a law to improve the qualifications of board directors, or measures to ensure only those members who needed insurance were automatically charged for it—the industry funds saw each bill as the first move towards death by a thousand cuts.

One of those cuts was the bill put forward by Assistant Treasurer Kelly O'Dywer under the Abbott Government in 2015 that sought to require all super fund boards to be composed of one-third independent directors and an independent chairman. The directors, who would be drawn from neither the employer nor the worker nominating groups, would be appointed to keep an eye on governance standards should either side of the table not fulfil its directors' duties.

The lobby group representing the union funds, Industry Super Australia (ISA), waged a campaign against the legislation, accusing the government of an ideological attack on industry funds. It was during this skirmish that ISA created the fox-and-henhouse advertisement.

As the debate over the bill came down to the wire, ISA commissioned two versions of the ad and tested them with a focus group of 200 Australians in October 2015. The focus group research showed that ISA's message resounded with voters. The secret polling showed more than two-thirds of respondents agreeing that 'Industry super funds are right to warn us about what the banks are trying to do' and more than half agreeing that 'Liberal governments tend to give banks what they want even if that's at the expense of ordinary people'.

Despite the positive results in the polling, ISA decided at the last minute not to run the ad. A separate lobbying campaign, behind closed doors in parliament, managed to convince crossbench senators Jacqui Lambie, Glenn Lazarus, John Madigan and Nick Xenophon to join Labor and the Greens to vote down the government's super fund governance bill. In exchange for voting against the legislation, the senators got the industry fund sector to agree to a review of governance among the funds, to be carried out by former Reserve Bank governor Bernie Fraser.

Fraser was a friendly appointment, having previously been a director of the largest and most powerful industry fund, the $140 billion AustralianSuper. He was given a year to work on the review. Six months into it, Malcolm Turnbull cleared parliament for a double dissolution election in mid-2016, and Fraser put the review on the backburner. Why bother finishing it when Labor looked like it had a decent chance to take back government? When Turnbull was returned with the slimmest of majorities, Fraser belatedly got around to finishing the review, handing in the final version nearly a year overdue.

His report was slammed as a whitewash by the Coalition government. It said little other than questioning why independent directors would be necessary when industry funds had delivered far better for their members than the rival retail funds had for theirs.

On the face of it, the point seemed fine. Industry funds, as a collective, had given savers an extra 2 per cent more every year in investment returns than the retail sector. Over a decade, this would give savers an extra 20 per cent and could mean a difference of tens of thousands of dollars.

It was an argument repeated ad nauseam by the industry funds. The 'Compare the Pair' advertising campaign showed that if you were in an industry fund you'd retire with tens—if not hundreds—of thousands more in your nest egg than if you chose a bank-run fund.

However, by the time the Fraser report was handed in, O'Dwyer had already revived the independent directors legislation. The sector also appeared to have lost the support of the Nick Xenophon senators, who were pissed off with the tardiness of the review. They had given the funds the benefit of the doubt, but it had been thrown back in their face.

On top of this, O'Dwyer had tasked the Productivity Commission with the huge undertaking of inquiring into every facet of the so-called 'default' superannuation sector.

The default system of superannuation was the source of industry funds' power. Because of the way the super system had been established by Labor, a large part of the savings of workers was defaulted into industry funds. Employers and unions would strike deals through enterprise bargaining agreements to decide which fund would be the default superannuation manager when job applicants were signing on to work. If new employees failed to nominate their own super fund, which happens overwhelmingly with younger workers at the start of their career or when they are signing on to part-time jobs while they are studying, 10 per cent of their wages will be carved off and managed by the default fund.

Usually, the default funds are union-backed industry funds. Up to 80 per cent of workers accept their employer's preferred fund, and industry funds receive on average 50 per cent more of the new money flowing into the super system each year than retail funds.

The Productivity Commission, under the guidance of the department's deputy chair, Karen Chester, was asked to evaluate whether the current system was delivering for the millions of Australians who were handing over their livelihood to companies they had little knowledge about.

Just the existence of the PC review incensed the industry funds. They believed it to be an ideological attack on them by the government at a time when the banking sector was mired in scandal.

Industry funds believed they had good reason to think it was an attack. Under the previous Labor government, a panel in the Fair Work Commission had been given the power to select which funds would be named default providers. But it had sat idle since the FSC, the lobby group representing the retail fund sector, won a 2014 court case to dismiss the Shorten-appointed group of experts on the basis it was not independent. The Turnbull Government's minister for employment, Michaelia Cash, had the power to appoint new panel members, and the industry and not-for-profit funds called for the default selection process to be restarted, but the government declined to restart it and offered no explanation as to why.

A month after the Fraser review was dismissed out of hand by the government, ISA decided it was time to launch its fox-and-henhouse advertisement. There were billions at stake, and ISA was prepared to smear the government as willing to let the big banks engorge themselves on the retirement savings of Australians. Bernie Dean, the head of marketing at ISA, reluctantly wrote to Turnbull to say that ISA was dismayed at the government's failure to listen to its arguments about the correct policy settings for super funds, and would start broadcasting the ad.

ISA spent close to $4 million on the ad and on purchasing slots to broadcast it. During weeks when parliament was sitting, it played back-to-back on Sky News, which is permanently switched on in every parliamentary office on Capital Hill. The government couldn't escape it. Turnbull wasn't just exhausting political goodwill by preventing a royal commission: the government was now seen to be actively helping the banks get their hands on even more money.

When Doris the hen is devoured by the foxes, the viewer is left with a simple message: 'Banks aren't super'.

The Liberals decided it was time to bite back. The party's acting federal director, Andrew Bragg, cobbled together a counter-campaign looking to drag Labor into accusations of misspent industry fund money.

Trawling through Australian Electoral Commission (AEC) data on donations, the money trail was easy to find. Over a decade, about $50 million had trickled out of the industry funds into the coffers of the Labor Party. On the face of it, this seemed to be a bona fide scandal: retirement savings held by union funds were boosting the ability of Labor to wage war against the Liberals. The Coalition seized on the figures.

However, when the funds explained the transfers of money, the matter seemed much less clear cut.

First of all, industry funds often made payments to union groups, but the payments were for extremely non-scandalous matters. When funds needed to communicate to their industry employees, they took out advertisements in union magazines or paid fund managers to go to worksites and talk to members and workers about how best to manage their superannuation. These payments, because of the electoral disclosure laws, had to be flagged with the AEC.

All super funds needed to advertise, whether it was to let their members know of developments with their services or to attract new members to their funds, the latter of which would help build economies of scale and drive lower fees for all savers. While a payment to a union magazine had to be declared, no such transparency measure was required for newspaper or television advertisements.

And with many industries, such as trucking, which is typified by sparsely situated and disconnected workers, unions would need to be paid to send representatives out to ensure employees were in control of their nest eggs, their life insurance and their personal details held by the company.

More controversial, however, was the practice of union-appointed directors of industry funds donating their director salaries back to their union. At about $40,000 a year for their services, union-appointed super fund directors kicked back the fees to their union organisation. Rather than pocketing the fees for themselves, the union directors were bound by their duty to the workers they represented at the fund level. Their directorship was a service on behalf of members to ensure the fund was being run correctly, not for the benefit of their own CVs or their bank accounts.

In contrast, independent directors on super fund boards, or even employer group representatives, would take their salaries home. Only in rare cases, such as the example of jailed Health Services Union leader Michael Williamson, did union officials pocket their director's fees.

For Andrew Bragg, both instances of kickbacks were enough of an opening for a smear campaign against the industry funds.

Bragg had come from humble beginnings before he became the top office-bearer for the Liberal Party. Born in the regional Victorian town of Shepparton, he had worked at the SPC cannery, packaging fruit. Moving on to bigger things, prior to his stint as acting director of the Liberal Party he represented the financial and wealth management industry at the FSC, where he was head of policy.

The FSC was the opposing lobby group to Industry Super Australia. Bragg was given a wide remit there, and the group's chief executive, Sally Loane, would even allow him to speak for her on important topics when the media came for comment. This was probably because Bragg was a far more effective communicator than Loane, who was later shown by the royal commission to have a poor grip on the intricacies of financial regulation.

In his new role as head of the Liberal Party, Bragg launched a website called 'The Fair Go' that sought to pillory the union funds over their handling of member savings.

According to the AEC disclosures, the CFMEU was the biggest recipient of super fund payments, receiving $12.4 million over the decade to 2017 from First Super, Cbus and other funds. Close behind was United Voice, a union representing cleaners and other low-paid workers, which was paid $10.1 million by Hostplus and AustralianSuper. The Australian Workers' Union, formerly led by Bill Shorten, was paid $1.8 million by AustralianSuper, Cbus, AustSafe and others, while the Transport Workers Union received $7.1 million from a single fund, TWU Super.

If it was war the industry funds wanted, the Liberals decided it was war they would get. The battle expanded in May 2017, when APRA, responsible for ensuring standards in the super sector, was called before parliament for an otherwise routine oversight hearing.

'I have some questions about some of the integrity measures in the superannuation industry,' Liberal senator Jane Hume told APRA's head of super, Helen Rowell. 'I should give you a heads-up that I used to work in this industry. I have great respect for the organisation I worked for and the people I worked with, but I have some concerns that some industry players, potentially, pose threats to the reputation of those who are doing the right thing.'

A dirt sheet was being passed around the parliamentary offices of Coalition members that detailed allegations made about the chief executive of industry fund First Super, a man called Bill Watson. First Super was a small fund chaired by the boss of the CMFEU,

Michael O'Connor, who was one of the most powerful union figures in Australia. The dirt sheet said that Watson had been sacked from his post as chief executive of Sydney Ferries between 2001 and 2004 after a corruption investigation by the state's anti-corruption body, the Independent Commission Against Corruption (ICAC).

Hume used this information to attempt to bait the APRA executives into attacking Watson over his fitness to serve as director of the $2.6 billion super fund, should the allegations prove true. 'I can name the superannuation fund if you like,' she said. 'I have parliamentary privilege. I am just concerned I might end up in concrete boots. First Super is a fund that has been backed by the CFMEU, a union that is subject to countless lawsuits due to its blatant disregard for the rule of law. First Super has an executive [who] is subject to those claims. Is this something that APRA is aware of?'

APRA refused to engage in the discussion without knowing all the details of the allegations, and the attempted smear failed to shift Watson from his position. When I asked him for a response to the claims, I was provided within minutes with a signed letter from ICAC commissioner Irene Moss clearing him of any wrongdoing. Because the accusations were made regularly against him, Watson kept the letter within reach at all times.

After taking questions on notice from Hume, APRA later responded that two investigations and an independent audit had found 'no grounds to deem the executive not to be fit and proper'. APRA said it had been made aware in 2009 of complaints about the executive, and that Watson's previous fund had also investigated the allegations. It had determined that the 'matter was dealt with' in 2010. Another investigation in 2013 by First Super, assisted by an independent auditor, had also cleared him.

The government wasn't satisfied with APRA's response to the industry funds, and pressured it to investigate the fox-and-henhouse ad to find out if it constituted misusing member savings. The regulator dutifully complied, and wrote to the boards of all fifteen industry superannuation funds that were party to the ISA outfit to find out if they had been involved with the TV campaign.

ISA chief executive David Whiteley had to publicly defend the campaign as the nervous funds sweated on the potentially damaging outcome of the investigation. He claimed the ad had been the 'third stage' in an information campaign for industry fund members, following ads about the cross-selling of super products in bank branches and at workplaces. 'We're now informing members that there are armies of bank lobbyists placing pressure on parliamentarians. The public has a right to know of the lobbying activities of the major banks,' Whiteley said.

While the government was baying for blood, it would be let down by APRA's final ruling on the ad. APRA found that the marketing campaign was backed by research aimed at recruiting members to give the funds greater scale, and that when the ad aired, lo and behold, the industry funds gained more members. APRA couldn't rule on the politics of the ad, but found it was a cost-effective means of recruiting more members to the funds, which would help create economies of scale for the trustees.

Down but not out, the government tried another route. The minister in charge of passing legislation requiring the funds to install independent directors, O'Dwyer, began circulating information designed to skewer the industry fund sector over its complex network of businesses, which were all staffed with Labor heavyweights. With nearly $1 trillion worth of superannuation assets washing through the industry fund network, the Liberals were trying to connect the dots on where member savings were being directed.

At the top of the food chain was Industry Super Holdings, a giant investment vehicle co-owned by the largest industry funds in Australia. It was chaired by Labor's godfather of super, Garry Weaven, and owned the online news site The New Daily and the commercial lender ME Bank. It was also the holding company that owned ISA.

Arrows on the government graphic connected Industry Super Holdings to Industry Fund Services, which provided administration services to the funds, and to the sector's international infrastructure and asset manager, IFM Investors. Then there was IFS Insurance Solutions, a super fund responsible for managing lost super savings, and another that looked after defined benefit schemes.

The government was privately claiming that the graphic had helped persuade Senator Nick Xenophon not to take Labor's side during the argument over the legislation. The Liberals wanted to make it public in a bid to turn people's opinion against the industry funds, so staffers set about pushing the document out through the media.

It found its way into my inbox. Having covered the superannuation sector for years, the connections the Liberal Party was seeking to make were, I thought, mostly uncontroversial. Just like the major banks, which owned superannuation assets, infrastructure managers and insurance companies, the industry funds were free to own a number of different companies that could provide the services needed to fulfil the funds' trustee duties. The document was either a case of the bleeding obvious, or a misguided attempt to sully the Labor-aligned directors of the various businesses. When it landed in my inbox, I wasn't exactly sure what I was supposed to do with it. There were certainly questions to be raised about the links between senior Labor figures, the superannuation funds and the shared investment vehicles owned by the sector, but without any further information than what was already public knowledge, the document was more or less a statement of fact.

After a few days of not knowing what to do with the document in question, I received a call from O'Dwyer's office asking me not to do anything with the graphic. Perhaps they knew me well enough to have realised I would write about the fact that they were attempting to drum up opposition against industry funds by connecting the dots between the holding company, rather than simply recite their conspiracy theory about the connections between the businesses, which by this time was already well known.

Despite the government's best efforts, nothing would stick on the industry funds. They were largely immune to bad press, and further inoculated against poor public sentiment. And why shouldn't they be?

During the period there had been countless bank scandals but the industry fund sector—at this point in charge of almost $700 billion in assets—had not been involved in any sort of scandalous behaviour. The bank-run funds, which controlled the same amount of savings, faced terrible headlines on a revolving basis. What was more, industry funds were delivering for their members hand over fist and leaving the retail sector wallowing in their wake.

When the government was backed into a corner with the royal commission, the Liberals saw an opening. They would task Kenneth Hayne, now the most powerful investigator in the country, with trawling through every aspect of industry fund governance and find what they hoped would be a killer blow.

Government MPs waited again, with bated breath.

The political power play was a curtain-raiser for the royal commission, and the industry funds were deeply paranoid about what Hayne might unearth. As the commission moved on to its examination of the nation's superannuation sector, the counsels assisting the commission had at the forefront of their minds the need to be seen to give industry funds a hard time.

The scandals in the bank-run funds were well known, and information gathering on them would be fairly straightforward. ASIC and APRA had been chasing the for-profit sector for years over an endless list of indiscretions. However, to avoid any accusations of bias, Hayne would need to be seen to be taking the scalpel just as liberally to what had been until this point the better-behaved half of the super sector. Industry funds were inundated with a flood of subpoenas to produce information for the royal commission.

Union fund directors instantly perceived unfairness. While the commission had served wide-ranging notices to produce information about the super funds' sponsorships of union events, training and marketing deals, it had not asked for equivalent information on the funds' relationships with employer associations.

One director of an industry fund complained to me that financial dealings with employer group associations were often larger than the funds being spent on payments for union sponsorship. This was being completely overlooked by the royal commission, according to the industry funds subjected to Hayne's request for information. Indeed, the employer group directors had often been more problematic than the funds' ties with unions. ASIC had been targeting default fund arrangements between employer groups and super funds to see if there were any incentives being kicked back to bosses for choosing certain funds as default managers.

Union directors were also far more qualified and savvy than their employer counterparts. Former ACCC boss Graeme Samuel once told senators during an inquiry into superannuation that employer representatives were outgunned in boardroom discussions by union-appointed directors. During his time reviewing Cbus's corporate governance in 2015, Samuel found representatives from the Master Builders Association 'were far less capable of representing the views of their organisation' than union representatives such as former ACTU president Ged Kearney and CFMEU national secretary Dave Noonan. Kearney and Noonan had spent their working lives arguing for their members in a high-pressure, politically intense setting. Master Builders Association appointees, on the other hand, were insulated from negotiating these issues in their day-to-day jobs.

The industry funds believed themselves ready to face anything, but didn't think they couldn't handle an unwieldy royal commission if it was beholden to a government intent on damaging just one side of the sector. So it was with much anticipation by the funds that counsel assisting the royal commission Michael Hodge, QC, took the stand at Melbourne's Federal Court in August 2018.

In his opening address, Hodge laid out the land as the commission picked apart one of the most powerful, but least transparent, financial industries in the world. The superannuation sector, for all its power, operates in the shadows. Money is compulsorily taken out of workers' wages to the tune of more than $50 billion a year and shunted into funds that employees may not even be able to name. The money is locked away for up to half a century until the workers' retirement. During this period, workers may not ask any questions of their fund. It is a system defined by disengagement, and super funds operate largely with impunity.

'And so we have the underlying question of this module which arises from the terms of reference,' Hodge said. 'What happens when we leave these trustees alone in the dark with our money? Can they be trusted to do the right thing? If they can, does that mean that the current regulatory system is adequate? If they can't, what must be done to protect Australians' retirement savings and to what extent do the entities that own or control the trustees, who are not obliged to act in members' best interests, act in ways that are ultimately detrimental to members, even if they do not technically cause the trustees to breach the trustees' duties?'

For three decades, the superannuation sector had been a lightning rod for partisan politics and ideological trench warfare. Now it was about to be put through the most thorough examination of its existence. All of Canberra was tuned in. You could hear jaws dropping across the nation as Hodge instantly chalked up the first win to the industry fund sector as he said no witnesses would be called from Cbus.

With its three board members nominated by the militant CFMEU, Cbus summed up everything critics of industry super hated about the union side of the super system. This was a fund that had been singled out by O'Dwyer for poor behaviour. However, after hammering it with requests for documents relating to a money trail between its savings and the unions, the commission was satisfied Cbus was acting in members' interests.

It wasn't for lack of investigation. The royal commissioners probed Cbus on the $7 million in donations made over a five-year period to unions. These donations had been carried out with no formal processes or requirements for tracking whether the agreed services had actually been delivered by the people that received the money. Instead of the royal commission examining the kickbacks, Cbus had already done the hard work for them. The fund had commissioned KPMG to do a review of the practices three years earlier, in 2015, and following the report had put in place a system where it could check that the money was being well spent.

Cbus was let off the hook, but in reality it had been preparing for the worst. Chairman Steve Bracks (a former Labor premier of Victoria), chief investment officer Kristian Fok and marketing boss Robbie Campo had all been forced to provide witness statements to the royal commission, and right up until the end of the week before the hearings, the fund had hired lawyers to coach the executives on how to handle themselves in the witness stand. Some of these lawyers were the same ones who had spent time training Shorten when the former Australian Workers' Union boss had been called to give evidence at the 2015 trade union royal commission. At Cbus, the staff had been under assault by requests for information on tight deadlines focusing on a few key areas, including the fund's partnership agreements with unions and employer bodies, credit card spending by executives, and Fok's investment choices.

In the end, there was nothing damning to pin on them.

Then, in a further bombshell dropped just moments into the start of the fortnight's examination on superannuation, Hodge said the lack of glaring misconduct was much the same in the rest of the industry fund sector. 'On the whole, it is our view that the commission's review of documents identified fewer examples of types of conduct of the industry fund trustees that raise questions … compared with that of the retail funds,' he said. 'In a number of cases, though certainly not all, the conduct of the industry funds which we have identified as warranting consideration during the oral hearings is very nuanced.'

Before it had even started publicly grilling executives, the royal commission had essentially told industry fund conspirators to pack it in. Union officials around the country breathed a collective sigh of relief.

Not one for giving up easily, O'Dwyer remained patient. Passage of her legislation targeting the sector would depend on there being enough of a scandal in the industry funds to encourage senators to support the bill, and with some of the country's biggest industry funds scheduled to appear in the next few days, including AustralianSuper, Hostplus and Energy Super, O'Dwyer maintained the faith. No one who was put on the stand at the royal commission was let off lightly.

After NAB executives were questioned on the stand, AustralianSuper chief executive Ian Silk was the first industry fund executive to be questioned.

If O'Dwyer was Captain Ahab, Silk was the government's white whale. He was the first high-profile chief executive to sit in the witness box at the royal commission. The banks and wealth management bosses had made junior staff climb out of the trenches and appear in person at the inquiry. Silk was also one of the most powerful financial executives in the country. AustralianSuper was the nation's largest super fund, and one of the best-performing. Silk's $140 billion worth of savings was bigger than the country's sovereign wealth fund, the Peter Costello–chaired Future Fund.

With the company sourcing its directors from peak bodies, such as ACTU president Michele O'Neil, AustralianSuper would be one hell of a Moby Dick for the government to harpoon.

To add to the excitement, Silk was also to be questioned over his fund's involvement in the fox-and-henhouse ad, and the investment of member savings in The New Daily. The website, funded by a number of industry funds, had attracted the ire of the government for its carriage of pro-industry-fund news and analysis—albeit alongside other not-so-fawning news about industry funds and a range of political, sports and entertainment news.

As soon as the moustachioed Silk took his oath and began to answer questions, the mood of the royal commission changed completely. Months had been spent by the commission's counsels coaxing executives to provide simple answers to simple questions. At every point, bankers had bloviated, obfuscated, deviated and meandered through their answers, which were spoken in complex legalese to avoid any admission of wrongdoing. It was a breath of fresh air when Silk answered questions straight to the point.

AustralianSuper had paid $2.3 million to help set up The New Daily, which aimed to focus on personal financial news and information to energise members into taking control of their superannuation. It would also provide a valuable source of free news for members amid the carnage in the traditional media industry, which was bleeding reporters and sounding increasingly shrill. The website was initially paid for out of the fund's $1.50-per-week membership fee, which goes towards administration and marketing. The cost worked out to about 20 cents a year for each of AustralianSuper's 2.2 million members. At that cost, setting up The New Daily was cheaper than mailing a single document to fund members through the post. The website was eventually sold to the jointly owned Industry Super Holdings vehicle, of which AustralianSuper is also a shareholder.

Silk didn't think the meagre price tag for setting up the website was any reason to be careless with the cash. 'Two million dollars is serious money in anybody's language. For a member-focused organisation, we don't splash money around lightly,' he said.

AustralianSuper had painstakingly considered The New Daily before launching it, discussing the website at board level and commissioning research as to whether it would help engage their members with their savings. It was never included in the fund's investment portfolio and did not return a financial dividend to the fund, but its shareholding in Industry Super Holdings had been 'written up' by 30 per cent over the 2017 financial year, which was a positive.

Still, Hodge wanted to know if The New Daily—which had a charter of editorial independence—was spreading industry fund propaganda.

'In the sense of advocating in relation to the positive features of industry funds,' Silk said, 'the difference between the best funds and the poorest funds is literally life-changing for a lot of people. To advocate for superannuation, in particular for the best superannuation funds, the funds that produce the best returns for members, is in the DNA of industry funds, and we were happy to see The New Daily do that. Not be a thoughtless cheerleader for industry funds, but where there are merits of those funds, and where people are best served by being members of those funds. We think it's important to point those features out to people.'

This sort of advocacy was no more clear than in the fox-and-henhouse ad. For the benefit of the public gallery, the ad was played in full at the Federal Court. Silk explained that it had been 'squarely directed' at crossbench senators and politicians, and was made with the intention of derailing the government legislation aimed at reforming the superannuation system. He said the proposed changes could lead to members of AustralianSuper moving to a bank-run retail fund and a decrease in new members joining the fund, which could jeopardise the retirement incomes of members of AustralianSuper.

He then launched into a full-scale defence of the necessity of the ad. Members would be tens of thousands of dollars worse off in retirement if they left his fund, and Productivity Commission data backed this up. The enterprise bargaining system had ensured that the more than two million Australians in the fund were having their savings carefully looked after, often without any knowledge of the expertise being deployed for their advantage. Without the ad, millions of everyday Australians could unknowingly wander into cross-selling, gouging and rorting of the bank-run super funds, Silk said.

'I don't want to interrupt you, Mr Silk, but is the point you're trying to make that your fund generates higher returns than a bank fund?' Hodge said.

'Well, that is the case,' Silk said.

In the end, Silk was able to show that the advertisement, which took $500,000 of AustralianSuper funding, was conducted within the limits of the 'sole purpose test', which requires money to be spent in the best interests of members. He was able to back up the strategy with reams of research papers, focus-group data and documents deliberating board decisions.

The fox-and-henhouse ad also achieved its aim. The legislation, which Silk believed would threaten the retirement savings of the millions of Australians who enjoyed the benefits provided by industry super funds, was stalled in the Senate and going nowhere fast. 'But it's a battle that has been won, not the war,' Silk said.

Indeed, there were more skirmishes before the industry funds could expect to survive the fortnight. Another big target of the government was soon to take the stand. The $40 billion fund Hostplus, which looks after the savings of some of the poorest-paid Australians from the hospitality and tourism industries, was due for its appointment with the royal commission. Hostplus maintained strong connections with the United Voice union. One of the union's nominated directors on Hostplus was Tim Lyons, a Labor stalwart and former assistant national secretary of the ACTU who in 2015 led an ill-fated attempt to topple the ineffectual ACTU national secretary at the time, Dave Oliver.

However, Hostplus generally only made headlines for the right reasons. It was the best-performing fund on a one-, three-, five-, seven-, ten- and fifteen-year basis, and its chief investment officer, Sam Sicilia, was one of the few industry fund figures to be routinely interviewed by the financial press for his expertise. Even Scott Pape, the so-called Barefoot Investor, who doles out simple financial advice to help ordinary Australians, was a fan of the fund.

Still, Hostplus chief executive David Elia kitted up for the examination of his career. Again, even when there appeared to be questionable use of member savings, Elia reassured the commission it was directed at protecting the fund from an onslaught of external factors that didn't have members' best interests at heart.

Maybe that is a polite way of putting it. Elia had to explain just how Hostplus found $260,000 of its members' own savings every year to spend on tickets to the Australian Open tennis slam in Melbourne. Those tickets and that money went towards wining and dining 120 chief executives and employer representatives who had a relationship with Hostplus. It was the fund's annual 'flagship entertainment event'.

On its face, this was an out-and-out scandal, but, as Elia attempted to explain, it was done with only the best of intentions. Despite being a leader of the sector, Hostplus was always at risk of having its default fund status taken away by employers who would then take their workers' savings to other higher-cost funds, including ones run by the banks. Hostplus had once lost a contract with one of the largest hotel chains in the country because Elia did not have a good relationship with its chief executive, he said. Bosses, it turned out, weren't choosing Hostplus because it was the best place to store their employees' savings—the bosses wanted to be feted in return, under threat of taking away their contracts. If this happened, Hostplus would lose its economy of scale.

It was a constant battle Hostplus had with other funds in the market, particularly those of the major banks and wealth managers. A 2012 review of the super system by the PC had found that bosses could be enticed to sign over their workers' savings to banks in return for special deals on financial products and accounting services. Former ASIC executive Jeremy Cooper's review of the super system two years earlier had also warned against retail funds providing 'bundled services' to employers in exchange for superannuation assets.

'Unashamedly, unashamedly, we utilise entertainment [and] corporate hospitality in order to strengthen the relationship we have with our employers,' Elia said. 'I wish I didn't have to do it. But the reality is it is a competitive landscape.' The money came out of Hostplus's $1.50-a-week administration charge, not members' investments, and worked out to about 1 cent a week per member. 'It's not an insignificant sum of money, but it's done for the right purposes,' Elia said.

It was an undeniably sleazy deal, but plundering a few hundred thousand dollars a year looked like child's play compared to the bigger rorts, worth billions annually, in the bank-run sector. Plus, in this case the scandal appeared to fall back onto dodgy bosses. In an ideal world, wouldn't a company choose the best-performing fund in the country to handle the savings of its employees? It was the bosses paying the superannuation, after all.

The Australian Open tennis schmooze was the heaviest hit the royal commission could land on the industry funds. As more representatives from the union-backed side of the superannuation system appeared for questioning, the more it became clear that they were operating on a different wavelength from the banking executives of previous rounds. Much of the time, the bankers could barely be trusted with their responses. It didn't seem like they believed the answers they were giving, either. Not only did the industry fund executives say what they believed, but you got the idea they also believed what they said.

Such was the case when Scott Wilson, the chairman of the $7 billion Queensland-based fund Energy Super, appeared in the Federal Court. He was there to explain why Energy Super had decided not to proceed with a planned merger with a rival fund, the $14 billion Equip Super—especially when the merger had been found to be in the best interests of its members. Energy Super had been beset by stalling membership and increasing costs and fees. The potential merger would have saved members $20 million a year, with much of the benefit coming from reduced investment costs.

Small funds refusing to merge was such a problem that APRA had even created a hit list of almost thirty funds it wanted to either find a partner or face a forced marriage. Being stuck in a small fund with high fees and poor investment returns could see a saver tens of thousands of dollars worse off at retirement compared to a member of a fund with proper scale.

There was just one problem as Energy Super and Equip headed to the altar: Equip was notoriously anti-union. Wilson told the royal commission that Equip chairman Andrew Fairley had told Energy Super director Mark Williamson that allowing union-nominated representatives to sit on the board of the merged fund would sink the deal. 'We've worked for years to get rid of them and we're not going to reopen the practice,' Fairley allegedly said.

The union directors of Energy Super would not allow the merger to go through if Equip wouldn't allow worker representatives on its board. Who would argue inside the fund for the interests of the members? Energy Super had a long and proud history of engaging with its workers all over the Sunshine State. What was more, it was delivering better returns for its members than Equip. 'If we can't be guaranteed that an anti-union employer-based fund is going to allow us to have union representation on their board going forward, what's going to happen to our members in Far North Queensland? What's going to happen to our members in Cairns and Townsville?' Wilson begged.

For the union movement, super is a sacred workplace right that was won by the workers and their representatives in the 1980s. 'When we talk about superannuation funds, the interests of unions and the interests of members of the funds are so aligned as to be indistinguishable,' Wilson said before launching into a rally cry for the sector. 'It's what we do. We look after members' money through the accumulation and into retirement.'

The industry fund sector had its week in the dock, and was given a clean bill of health. There were some issues with behaviour in the sector, but they appeared to be mostly minor, and there wasn't much evidence of misconduct to recommend anything remotely resembling a civil or criminal charge against the sector.

If there were any lingering doubts about whether the royal commission was holding open the door to make findings of bad behaviour by industry funds, Hodge made it clear. 'Not open,' he said. 'For the avoidance of doubt … the preferable conclusion on the relevant evidence is that the conduct was not misconduct or conduct falling short of community standards and expectations.'

The government had been waging war against the union funds for years, and now the most powerful financial inquiry in the country's history had barely grazed the cheek of the industry funds. The chickens could sleep easy in the henhouse. The fox hunt had only just begun.

10

THE BIG RORT

As AustralianSuper chief executive Ian Silk stepped off the stand at the royal commission, most onlookers were of one mind: there seemed to be little, if any, misconduct to be found in the industry fund sector.

Kelly O'Dwyer was not on the same page.

I received a text from one of her staffers: 'Hi mate, are you writing on Ian Silk in the RC today?'

'Yep I'm in the RC at the moment. What's up?' I texted back.

The staffer went on to tell me that Silk was misleading the royal commission: there was no legislation targeting default superannuation. Any bill before parliament aiming at removing restrictions on enterprise bargaining agreements would apply equally to all funds, whether industry, retail, corporate or public sector. 'There was no proposal & is no proposal on default. It's very misleading,' the staffer's text said.

I said I'd received their message and just had one question: 'Is Kelly going to say anything about National Australia Bank?'

The staffer responded: 'Thinking on it, I'll come back.'

I thought it was a pertinent question. Silk had sailed through his examination. He'd taken the stand on the Thursday afternoon of the first week of hearings on the superannuation sector and was finished and free to leave later that same afternoon. It had been a breeze.

By way of comparison, NAB wealth management executive Paul Carter took an oath on Monday morning the same week that Silk would later take the stand. It wasn't until Thursday afternoon that NAB's superannuation chairman, Nicole Smith, facing questions on the same fees-for-no-service scandal, was allowed to step down from the stand. That was anything but a breeze. Over four gruelling days of examination into the issue, the bank obstructed the process every way it could. The inquiry into the issue then continued into the following week, when the royal commission made the surprise decision to drag NAB's head of consumer banking, Andrew Hagger, to the court on Monday to face the music. His appearance would ultimately see the high-powered executive shown the door of the nation's fourth-largest bank.

However, O'Dwyer was not as interested in NAB as she was in Silk. I had received no approach from the minister for financial services' office in the four days of examination of NAB.

Both publicly and privately, O'Dwyer was at pains to stress she wasn't ideologically attacking one side of the sector with legislation. This was true: the minister had been instrumental in bringing forward sensible policies looking to end fee gouging across industry and retail lines. Still, there were things that gave the industry funds reason to believe she personally disliked them.

In one private meeting between Silk and O'Dwyer's office, the AustralianSuper boss sat down for what he believed would be a routine meeting only to be presented with a portfolio of documents. The documents were a number of newspaper articles in which Silk had been quoted, and roughly highlighted on them were the parts of his quotes where he disagreed with government legislation or policy. Silk was befuddled. 'Yes—you're the government,' he told them, implying that they were wasting their time trying to regulate the public comments of a fund manager when they should have had bigger fish to fry.

O'Dwyer's office was not interested in massaging the reporting of NAB. It was interested only in serving up warm slices of white whale.

After a few moments of deliberation, the staffer responded to me: 'Re NAB and RC, we want to leave the RC to do its job and the Minister doesn't intend to comment along the way.'

O'Dwyer was a former NAB banker herself, although in an entirely different part of the bank from the scandal-plagued superannuation division. But as the royal commission tugged at NAB, the thread holding its reputation together had begun to unravel. The further the commission looked into the retail fund sector, the clearer it became that the bank-run superannuation sector was sitting on one of the biggest piles of corporate wrongdoing ever to be unearthed. One of the senior editors on my newspaper would describe it later as the biggest heist in Australian history.

Everyone knew bank funds delivered poorer outcomes than industry funds, to the tune of about 2 per cent a year. In terms of investment performance there were industry funds, then daylight, then the retail funds, the latter leaving savers tens of thousands of dollars out of pocket. Explaining the reasons behind the difference in performance was difficult, but the Productivity Commission had given it a decent crack. Over the course of its three-year review of the default superannuation system, it made a series of important findings.

As PC deputy chairwoman Karen Chester described it, the super system had been transformed into an 'unlucky lottery' for many Australians. Millions of members were being defaulted into fifty funds that persistently underperformed. This was a quarter of all super funds. Because default funds are tied to the employer, not the worker, the number of multiple accounts in the system had exploded as workers changed jobs. One in three accounts in the system was now an unintended multiple. It was a boon for the industry, which was taking in an extra $450 million a year in administrative fees charged to multiple accounts.

On top of this, excessive fees and insurance premiums on the ten million lost and forgotten accounts in the system were costing savers $2.6 billion every year, hitting younger savers and low-income workers the hardest. A typical worker with two accounts would be more than $50,000 worse off at retirement than a saver with a single fund.

While some were shunted into underperforming funds, others were dudded by rampant fee gouging. The thirty largest funds in the system were collecting $600 million a year in fees charged to the youngest savers and those with the most meagre balances in their accounts of less than $6000. Rather than cut down on the fees in the retail fund sector, money was being spent on unnecessary bells and whistles, such as smartphone apps.

The industry fund sector didn't get let off lightly by the PC. There were more than 100 smaller funds, many of them union-backed industry funds, that lacked the scale to deliver the best outcomes for their members; many fund directors did not have the right skills; and mergers between funds had been scuppered because union and employer directors did not want to lose their jobs.

Still, the biggest industry funds were shown to be delivering the best outcomes for savers, while the retail fund sector produced 'significantly' worse returns. It did not name them directly, but the PC found the big four banks and AMP were far and away some of the worst handlers of Australia's savings. A handy chart in the PC's draft report mapped out the investment returns of each fund, which were identifiable only by their size and whether they were industry funds or retail funds. The returns were also painstakingly customised. Each fund was ranked against an investment performance benchmark it should have achieved based on the assets into which it was investing.

Funds would often complain that they were delivering lower or more 'conservative' returns because that was what their members wanted. If you invest in safer assets, returns are lower. The PC showed that even when member savings were invested in safe assets such as cash, they were still worse off in a retail fund than in an industry fund.

At the bottom of the PC's comparative performance chart were five huge lumps. Anyone with half a brain could identify these as the funds managed by Commonwealth Bank, Westpac, ANZ, NAB and AMP. These five huge malignant lumps on the nation's super system needed to be excised from any responsibility of looking after member savings.

Even while the PC could identify who was performing badly, it had trouble explaining exactly why this was happening. One problem was the regulator responsible for the sector, APRA, which was terrible at collecting the data necessary to examine the funds properly. This only sought to raise further questions. For example, how could APRA properly regulate the sector when it wasn't even asking the funds for the right information?

Another issue was that the funds were tight-lipped. When they did hand over data to the PC, it was likely only because they believed the statistics would reflect well on their business. If they didn't hand over the data, well, you can draw your own conclusions.

Fifteen per cent of all the super funds that were asked to complete surveys for the PC's review simply ignored the request—they were usually smaller funds. Of the 117 funds that did respond, only five were able to provide an analysis of net investment returns by asset class—a very basic data file that each super fund should have on hand. Only 17 per cent of funds could provide information on management costs for investing in Australian shares, the most basic asset every super fund would be investing in.

These failures came despite 80 per cent of super fund chief executives touting that their fund did a regular performance analysis, which would, of course, rely on an analysis of net investment returns by asset class. If the chief executives did have the analysis, then why weren't they handing it over? And if the funds didn't have the analysis, then how were they still in business?

Only twelve funds handed over data on expenses outsourced to related parties—the small number of returning forms was itself a red flag about hidden costs in the system. When the PC told funds it would publish the names of those that didn't return its survey, one fund returned it with just its name and the dollar amount of assets under its management—no other details.

Industry fund First Super, which had been attacked by Liberal MPs over its governance standards, was among a number of funds that did not bother to respond to the PC's governance survey. One would have thought it would have taken the opportunity to avoid further attacks. Instead, the PC was forced to go to private agencies, such as the industry consulting group SuperRatings, to buy data that had been given to the company by funds—they would often submit performance data in a bid to win awards for good performance. The pointy heads in the PC then had to spend countless hours stitching together private data and the bare-bones information they had managed to extract from the sector to paint a picture of how different funds were performing.

Despite the lack of reliable data, the landmark PC inquiry managed to conclude that the retail funds were indeed far worse at managing nest eggs than their industry fund rivals.

There were several reasons for this. Fee gouging was one. The PC found that just ten retail funds, run by Australia's biggest banks and listed wealth managers, were charging 90 per cent of all advice fees in the super system, at a total of $1.4 billion a year. This was costing their members an average of $341 a year. On top of this, an extra $400 million in grandfathered trailing commissions was being siphoned out of the retirement savings of hundreds of thousands of members, with many likely to be unaware they were being slugged the fees.

Another factor was that retail funds were either incompetent or deliberately terrible. Why was it that different funds that invested in the same instruments, such as the share market or unlisted property, gave savers remarkably different returns? Retail funds and industry funds were investing in many of the same areas, but the former were often outsourcing the investment management to their own subsidiaries, which delivered dismal returns. About 60 per cent of the retail segment did not provide performance-for-fee data on related parties or investments to the PC. What were they hiding?

The sub-par performance of the banks and wealth managers was laid out for all to see, but only the royal commission had the power to fill in the rest of the story.

Just a week before NAB executives Paul Carter and Nicole Smith were due to face questioning at the commission for the superannuation round of hearings, the company made a surprise announcement. The bank would be refunding $67 million to customers who had been charged hundreds of dollars in fees for the opportunity to access a financial adviser, even if they didn't use the adviser's services.

The bank had stumbled on the problem in 2016 after Carter decided to merge NAB's various superannuation trustee businesses from three into one. In this way, NAB's super division would be centrally owned and operated under the bank's MLC brand. The super trustee was called NULIS, and the merger would allow the company to kill off a number of old super products by moving customers into a simpler number of saving streams. The merger created a $100 billion mega fund.

However, in some of NAB's products, members were being charged a 'planned service fee' of between 0.44 per cent and 1.5 per cent of their account balance. The fee was charged because a financial adviser was made available to provide general advice about super, investment options or insurance arrangements. It was charged to members whether or not the adviser actually provided any advice and was described as a 'fee for access' to that advice, whether or not access was ever sought. It was a nifty little fee buried in mountains of disclosure papers that few customers ever looked through.

The only problem was that NAB did not tell customers they could opt out of the automatic fee once they put the 'business super' product into a 'personal super' account after the customers left their job. It sounded awfully similar to the fees-for-no-service scandal that had ensnared wealth giant AMP just months earlier and resulted in the turfing of several executives from the company.

As it announced the compensation plan, NAB was at pains to stress, behind closed doors to the media reporting on the issue, that this was definitely not a fees-for-no-service problem, despite it appearing to have all the hallmarks of charging people fees without providing any service. It was a confusing discussion. Why not just acknowledge it and move on?

As the royal commission pulled NAB's executives into the dock, counsel assisting Michael Hodge encountered the same confusion.

Paul Carter spent most of his four hours on the first day of the hearings arguing about the difference between a 'fee' and a 'commission'. It was an important difference, because if Carter was proven incorrect and NAB was charging a fee rather than a commission, the bank might have to refund hundreds of millions of dollars in wrongly charged fees. According to financial laws, a commission doesn't need to have any exchange of service—it is a kickback for kickback's sake. However, the law requires that fees come with a service attached.

So what exactly were customers getting when they were automatically charged the so-called 'planned service fee'? At a rate of up to 1.5 per cent of assets, the fee was enough to push it into the hundreds or thousands of dollars per customer each year.

Even the supposed promise of an opportunity to 'access' an adviser seemed a rough deal. A customer was only ever able to receive 'general' advice, such as basic information about investments and insurance. This was distinct from 'personal' advice, which is information tailored to a specific individual based on what would be in their best interests.

When NAB announced the refund, it could not tell me how many customers, if any, actually used the services made accessible by the planned service fee. The bank did not collect that kind of data. It knew that only 2 per cent of its 305,000 super customers who were charged the fee called up the bank to cancel it, and painted this as proof that 98 per cent of customers valued the service fee. Seen another, more accurate way, it was evidence that those 98 per cent were probably unaware they were being charged the fee.

After a lengthy battle with ASIC, NAB appeared to have finally buckled to demands to refund the fee to its customers.

Still, Carter was forced to defend another of the onerous and useless fees NAB charged its super customers: the so-called 'adviser contribution fee', which was distinct from the planned service fee. This second fee sucked up as much as 6 per cent of a saver's super contributions, but was also the subject of unclear definitions. It seemed to be an inherently useless impost on customers. When a saver deposited money into their super account, a financial adviser could take up to 6 per cent of the cash in return for doing nothing.

Carter stressed that the adviser contribution fee was not a 'fee' but a 'commission'. He claimed this was also the case with a third fee, the 'employer service fee'.

In all cases, customers may not have received anything resembling a service in exchange for these fees, but Carter would not budge on the value provided by NAB for charging them.

'What I'm trying to understand is: why do you say that the adviser contribution fee is a commission?' Hodge probed.

Carter fumbled through his answer: 'My rationale is that it doesn't mean—just because a commission is being paid, it doesn't mean that services aren't being provided. That is my—That is my understanding.'

'No, that's right,' Hodge said. 'But there's an important difference, isn't there, between a commission and a fee for service, which is if it's a commission and you don't provide services, then MLC can say and does say, "We don't have to refund the money if we don't provide the service"?'

Carter agreed. 'Yes.'

The language acrobatics deployed by Carter were just an attempt to shield NAB from further compensation claims. The bank was addicted to the easy streams of money, and wasn't about to let go of them easily.

Despite the FOFA laws banning the charging of new grandfathered commissions in 2013, members of two super funds run by NAB had paid $358 million in the commissions over the five years since they'd been banned.

NAB also took terribly to laws introduced in 2013, passed by the Gillard Government, that required companies to handle default super savings in a cheaper, more effective way. These so-called 'MySuper' laws required default member savings to be shifted into low-fee, simple products where the money would be protected from fee gouging and poor returns. Funds were given until 2017 to comply.

While the industry funds completed the transition nearly instantaneously after the sector found it to be in their members' best interests to do it as quickly as possible, the retail funds dragged their heels. By belatedly moving the assets into lower-fee vehicles, they managed to extract as much profit as they were legally allowed before they had to comply with the thrifty rules.

The royal commission showed that NAB had been so slow to make the legally required transfer, and that as late as four years after the reforms were passed it still held more than a third of all its savings in the high-fee products. Nicole Smith, the chairman of the bank's superannuation trustee NULIS, insisted the glacial pace—just 5 per cent of assets were transferred every quarter in 2014 and 2015—was 'the right time frame' because of the complexity of the task.

A report by Rainmaker Information found that retail super funds were collecting up to $1.8 billion over four years by leaving customer savings in legacy products with higher fees instead of transferring them to cheaper products. In 2014, assets trapped in legacy products that were owned by NAB accounted for just $17 billion of the total $73 billion worth of legacy assets across the entire industry.

While that whole-of-industry figure had shrunk by almost half to $41 billion over the following two years, NAB had only managed to reduce its amount by $3 billion to a total of $14 billion. It was slower than a snail's pace. Then, by mid-2016, NAB was considering slowing down the transition even further and not moving the remaining money across into low-fee funds until March 2017—the ultimate eleventh hour.

'Did that seem striking to you?' Hodge asked.

'I don't recall thinking at the time it was striking,' Smith said.

Along with being legally required to act in their members' best interests, super trustees are required to ensure MySuper funds have appropriate economies of scale. Smith said she couldn't recall whether the bank even considered that its MySuper members would have been better off if they were all transferred into the cheaper MySuper fund, which would have brought greater scale.

NAB was taking such poor care of its members that it was even informed by an independent ratings agency, Chant West, that its MLC Super Fund MySuper and MLC Staff MySuper funds were ranked sixty-sixth and forty-fourth in the country. This put them in the worst-performing quarter of MySuper funds.

The retail sector had long argued away accusations of terrible performance by citing their inability to invest in so-called 'illiquid' assets. These included things like commercial property and toll roads and infrastructure. They were more expensive to invest in, but you'd get more bang for your buck. Retail funds argued that the rival industry fund sector only had the ability to invest in illiquid assets because they had the benefit of a steady inflow of savings from members, and this was because they controlled the enterprise bargaining system, which guaranteed a steady stream of cash. Retail funds argued that they could be a victim of savers moving money around at will, which meant they couldn't tie up funds into longer-term investments even if they wanted to.

It was a junk claim. Any fund with more than $5 billion could invest in illiquid assets, according to the PC. NAB had more than $100 billion at its disposal.

Chant West even found that NAB's funds were not suffering from an inability to invest in high-returning infrastructure, which would have increased the bank's miserly performance. Instead, NAB was fiercely reluctant to forgo any money and give its managers extra cash to invest in higher-earning assets for its members. Several documents showed NAB's investment portfolio managers had complained to executives that they were unable to meet targeted returns without a larger investment budget, but NAB refused to hand over any money.

Then, every year, NULIS was paying a dividend of more than $100 million a year back to NAB. It was siphoning profits out of its fund members to contribute to the bank's bottom line and help top executives reach their profit targets.

Some NAB customers opted to have their savings held all in cash, which generally generates a return of about 2 per cent a year. For this,

NAB charged them a management fee of 1.85 per cent a year, which essentially ate away any return the members would have accrued. They would have been better off if they had taken their savings out of NAB's superannuation division and put them in a bank account instead.

The more parts of NAB's super division that were examined, the more distasteful behaviour was uncovered. And the bank could not pretend to feign ignorance, because the knowledge of the scams went right to the top.

Indeed, the planned service fee debacle had been known to the bank for quite some time. Despite first finding the breach in 2014, it took NAB close to a year to decide whether to compensate customers who had been wrongly charged the fees. Then, the bank put an estimate on the refund of about $35 million—half the $67 million bill it would later announce before it was drawn before the royal commission. Even this was downplaying the scandal. The total would blow out to nearly $90 million when interest was included.

At first, NAB couldn't work out which division would have to put forward the money for the refund. Was it the superannuation trustee, of which Smith was in charge, or the MLC wealth management division, of which Carter was the boss? Neither wanted to pay it out of their division.

'That's hopelessly conflicted, isn't it?' Hodge asked.

'Yes,' Smith answered. 'There is a conflict for the administrator in terms of the revenue.'

The true scale of the scandal and the cover-up was still coming.

When the royal commission got wind of discrepancies between what NAB knew about the fees-for-no-service issue and what the bank was telling the corporate regulator, it plundered the company for information. NAB baulked at handing it over on the basis of legal privilege, at first giving the commission just thirty-one documents relating to the issue. Then, just as the commission was about to sit, it flooded the counsels assisting with a further 3000 documents.

Next, NAB's top-tier legal counsel, Neil Young, QC, attempted to keep secret the bank's correspondence with ASIC over the issue.

The regulator had not been at all happy with how NAB had been behaving after it unearthed the scandal. In attempting to squirrel out of liability, the bank had argued that the issue wasn't that it had been taking money from customers to which it was not entitled: it was that it hadn't told customers about the benefits of the planned service fees. Access to NAB's website, already publicly available to all, was one of those purported benefits.

After Commissioner Kenneth Hayne dismissed Young's arguments, it soon became clear why the bank was attempting to keep the documents secret. In painful detail, they revealed how NAB had attempted to mislead the corporate regulator over the scandal.

NAB had caught the AMP disease. Once again, the cover-up, not the crime, was the larger wrecking ball for banking executives.

It was half-past beer o'clock on Friday 21 October 2016.

Just a week away, on Thursday 27 October, NAB would be announcing a bonanza $6.5 billion annual profit. But the mind of NAB's chief spin doctor, Nathan Goonan, wasn't on the pub, and it wasn't dwelling on the billions of dollars in profit the fourth-biggest bank in Australia was set to unveil.

Instead, Goonan's mind was on a more sinister issue—the looming launch by the corporate regulator of a report into what had become one of its most important investigations: fees for no service. By pure coincidence, the report would be released on the same day as NAB's annual results. The big four banks and AMP were all about to be shamed by the report, which had calculated each company's respective bill for its fees-for-no-service issue.

ASIC had been kind enough to show the banks a draft copy of the report so they could check facts before it was released. Goonan knew that with a total of just under $17 million, NAB wasn't the worst of the bunch, according to the information the regulator had collected. He tapped out an email to NAB boss Andrew Thorburn: 'At this stage, having seen the report, our thinking is to be reactive from a communication perspective given … NAB is seen as just one "in the pack", rather than called out as an outlier.'

Over the weekend Goonan's email sparked a series of interactions between NAB's top brass, including Thorburn, head of wealth Andrew Hagger, and chief operating officer Andrew Cahill. ASIC didn't know it at the time, but NAB hadn't given it the full picture. The figures undershot what the bank itself knew: the real bill was about twice as much—$35 million.

The NAB executives wanted to keep the bank in the middle of the pack. 'I trust your judgement on this one,' Cahill said after Hagger put the strategy to the executives on the Saturday. 'I think the chief is probably keen to discuss on Monday to ensure Thursday goes as smoothly as possible.'

He was right—Thorburn was interested. 'I am sure you are working through all the right detail and will be all over it,' he told the men on Sunday. 'The main piece I would like to see is our proposed media response to what is likely to come out.'

NAB had been in conversations with ASIC for months over the amount of fees it had found were charged to customers where no service had been provided. In late 2014, NAB had discovered it had charged customers an adviser service fee despite there being no adviser to offer services. Then, in 2015, it found it had charged the planned service fee for basic general advice services to superannuation customers who had no financial adviser who could provide those services.

And it knew more than it was letting ASIC know. An earlier email from NAB's head of regulatory affairs, Andrea Debenham, on Wednesday 19 October, had told Hagger and others that ASIC was about to release its fees-for-no-service report. The regulator knew about the adviser service fee but at this point wasn't aware of the planned service fee. Debenham asked the executives whether NAB should 'pre-emptively' tell the regulator all it knew. If NAB did this, it would increase its tally in the ASIC report from $17 million to the estimated compensation at the time of $35 million.

The next morning, on 20 October, NAB corporate affairs adviser Chris Owens urged the bank to be upfront with the regulator, its customers and other stakeholders, noting it was 'the best long-term strategy' for the bank. Unfortunately, his advice fell on deaf ears.

Goonan, who was acting executive general manager of corporate affairs, compiled a report into Project Rio, the name given to the strategy aimed at protecting the bank against ASIC. It was attached to the email he sent Thorburn on the afternoon of Friday 21 October, and also recommended a 'reactive' approach.

After running over the plan during Saturday telephone briefings with Cahill and Carter, Hagger wrote to Thorburn saying that the so-called reactive approach was 'still our plan', but that in the interests of 'openness and transparency' he would call ASIC commissioner Greg Tanzer to brief him on the planned service fee issue.

In the early morning of Tuesday 24 October, Hagger joined other members of the board of National Wealth Management Services, which is the administrator for NAB's superannuation funds, and helped approve the full $35 million compensation bill for the fees-for-no-service issue. This essentially formalised what the bank knew. The proper response for Hagger now would be to pass the information to ASIC before it released its report in two days' time.

About 10.30 a.m., he stepped out of the meeting to call Tanzer. After talking to Tanzer he sent a note of the conversation to Thorburn and other NAB executives. Strangely, it didn't say anything about him telling Tanzer about the new $35 million figure.

That was because Hagger hadn't mentioned it.

On the Friday night, after the dust of results and the ASIC report had settled, Hagger contacted Carter wondering when and how NAB should tell ASIC about the bigger compensation bill. 'What a big week it was,' he wrote in an email sent about 9.30 p.m. 'There's several ways to do it and there will need to be an education process with ASIC. Let's compare notes.'

Documents tendered to the commission indicate that NAB finally gave ASIC the new $35 million figure the following week.

In 2018, after four days of gruelling testimony by Carter and Smith, the royal commission made an unexpected change of plans. In a twist, Hagger would now be forced to come to the Federal Court to answer questions about his involvement in the scandal.

Hagger was a very senior member of the Australian banking community, and had been suggested as a potential replacement for Thorburn when the chief executive eventually left the bank. Now, his rising star looked as if it was about to crash to earth. Misleading ASIC is a criminal offence.

Over four uncomfortable hours in the commission hot seat, Hagger struggled to recall details and gave rambling responses as Hodge attempted to extract straight answers out of him. Executives from NAB had already sucked up four of the first five days in the fortnight of the superannuation round of public hearings. With Hagger taking the stand, NAB entered its fifth day of examination.

'Look, in the end it's a matter for you and the commissioner, Mr Hagger,' Hodge told the dithering banker. 'I'm not going to interrupt you when you talk, but if I ask you a question and then you begin saying a whole lot of other things in order to try to justify your position that are not in answer to the question, this is going to take even longer than it is already taking.'

When Hagger was asked about the phone call to Tanzer and why he did not tell the ASIC commissioner that NAB's wealth division had just finalised the bigger compensation bill for its fees-for-no-service tally, he explained that the bill also needed to be approved by Smith's division, NULIS, the following day.

Did Hagger seriously think NULIS might decide on less than full remediation for its super members? Hagger laughably responded that he did not want to 'pre-empt the trustee board discussion'. He attempted to claim innocence, and that he had left the door 'very wide' for Tanzer to ask questions about the fees-for-no-service issue.

Of course Tanzer hadn't asked about the issue—he didn't know there was any reason to be suspicious about NAB's estimates. Why would NAB hide information from ASIC?

'I want to be absolutely clear on this,' Hodge said. 'You regard the way that you dealt with ASIC as being open and transparent?'

'Yes, I do,' Hagger responded.

By this point, the revelations of NAB's tawdry behaviour were spiralling out of the control of the bank's army of spin doctors. The head of the communications team dealing with risk and regulatory issues, Joanna Ball, was left scrambling. She had accompanied executives to the Federal Court over the fortnight and, like her bankers on the stand, proved difficult in answering questions whenever my colleagues and I published stories.

On the second day of the hearings, my colleague Ben Butler and I had published an article saying that NAB could face criminal charges over the probe by the corporate regulator. Documents submitted to the royal commission outlined ASIC's thoughts on NAB's 'suspected offending'. According to the documents, ASIC's investigation related to multiple alleged breaches of corporate laws and the regulator was still yet to decide whether to strike a deal with the bank, pursue civil litigation or go for criminal prosecution.

The claims were enough to force Thorburn out of the shadows. The chief executive flooded the media, conducted hasty interviews with reporters, and relayed NAB's version of events via video to staff and customers across the social media platforms Twitter and LinkedIn. He said he wanted to make it 'very clear' that the bank's people had not been involved in criminal acts.

In the depths of the Federal Court, Ball set out to argue with reporters, including Butler and myself. Her main gripe was that *The Australian* was not carrying the arguments put forward by executives on the stand as much as it was presenting information that sided with the royal commission's accusatorial approach.

We weren't the only ones fed up with the behaviour of the bank. As the scandal unfolded, a senior ASIC member told me: 'We're gonna get those fuckers.' At nearly every point over the three-year investigation, NAB had frustrated, embarrassed and humiliated the corporate regulator.

A month after Hagger was told by Commissioner Hayne he was free to step down from the stand, ASIC filed its lawsuit against NAB. It said that NAB's superannuation trustees, NULIS Nominees and MLC Nominees, had misled super customers and deducted $33 million in fees from 220,000 savers without providing them any services. On top of this, a further $67 million had been taken from another 300,000 super savers where members didn't receive any services. Among dozens of alleged breaches of the law, there were twenty-one counts of making false or misleading statements under a provision of the ASIC Act, section 12DB. That section of the law had the potential for the bank's actions to be considered a criminal act.

All in all, ASIC accused NAB of breaking the law seventy-seven different times while undermining faith in the superannuation system.

Two weeks later, NAB showed Hagger the door.

The royal commission had caught and skinned one fox. It had taken five days, but the damage had been done.

Other foxes would prove easier to trap. This time it would be Commonwealth Bank and its superannuation subsidiary, Colonial First State.

While NAB was pilloried for its slow transfer of super members into low-fee MySuper funds, examination of CBA showed that it had barely made the effort to start the transfer. The head of Colonial, Linda Elkins, was brought back to the commission for her second appearance. Earlier, she had made headlines when she agreed that CBA was the gold medallist in charging fees-for-no-service. This time, the bank was a gold medallist in acting in its members' worst interests.

The MySuper transition had been flagged by the government well in advance of the deadline to complete the transfer. In fact, the wealth management community had been put on notice about the laws, which would come into effect from 2014, as early as 2011. Although companies had to complete the transfer by 2017, they were not allowed to accept any new members into high-fee funds from the start of 2014.

It was some surprise, then, when CBA found out in early 2014 that it was still defaulting thousands of customers into the high-fee legacy products. This was a criminal offence under section 29WA of the Superannuation Industry Supervision Act, and punishable by a fine.

The bank initially told the regulator there were 13,000 criminal breaches—one for each member it failed to move on time—but later increased the number to 15,000. CBA told APRA it had broken the law in a breach notice filed on 19 March 2014. However, instead of rectifying the error, the bank saw an opportunity to profit from the mistake.

At the time of the MySuper transfer, CBA's financial advisers were worried. When members were transferred into MySuper products, the advisers would lose the opportunity to charge lucrative fees and commissions for the sale of products. While the MySuper reforms clamped down on fee gouging, funds were still allowed to offer 'Choice' products. These were overly complex and riddled with unnecessary bells and whistles, and dodgy financial advice would trick customers into buying them.

Documents revealed that one adviser, Michael Williams, had asked Chris Micallef, CBA's corporate super relationship manager, if it was true that '$188k plus insurance commissions could be lost if we do not get them to change or confirm their investment option.'

Micallef responded: 'Yes, if there is no trustee instruction from the member (i.e., an actual investment choice of some sort held by the trustee), providers will have to transfer the balance to a MySuper option. In both cases advisers will then lose any grandfathered trail from those movements.'

Under pressure from its financial advisers, CBA then went about misleading customers to get them to stay in the company's First Choice Super fund rather than allow them to move easily to the low-fee MySuper product. The bank instructed its call centre operators to tell superannuation members that a recent change to legislation 'required' the company to confirm the customers' 'investment option'. It was a bald-faced lie, as the legislation required nothing of the sort.

Members were also sent letters containing similar information to the phone call script.

However, the bad advice from CBA didn't end there. Under the threat of better-performing funds and lower revenue on its own MySuper products, it hatched a plan to trick customers into signing away their savings to the bank when they walked into a branch. It would do this by making people think they were receiving personal financial advice about how they would be better off in one of CBA's super funds.

The issue was that personal circumstances weren't being considered, and the branch tellers weren't authorised to give such advice.

In August 2017, CBA's head of compliance, Larissa Shafir, proposed four steps to try to make sure the bank could keep selling its super products through its branches without having to provide personal advice. This was the so-called 'Project Everest' strategy. When ASIC got wind of the plan, it proposed to slap an enforceable undertaking on the bank to end the cross-selling. CBA's head of retail, Matt Comyn, who would later go on to become chief executive, called ASIC commissioner Peter Kell to try to get the watchdog to drop its threat of an enforceable undertaking in return for the bank putting out a media release. The paltry offer failed.

Then, CBA tried to get a handle on discussions about the dealings ANZ was having with the corporate regulator. ANZ was in trouble for the same superannuation cross-selling issue. At the lobby group for the wealth management industry, the FSC, the banks were openly discussing their manoeuvres to try to circumvent the regulator. Emails tendered to the royal commission showed Colonial First State head of legal Lisa Rava knew specific details of ANZ's bargaining position with ASIC over the scandal.

Just as the commission wrapped up its examination of CBA's superannuation business, Colonial First State paid a $300 million dividend kickback to CBA for the second year in a row. The payment brought the total profits paid by the superannuation arm back to the bank's bottom line to close to $1 billion over the three years. They were profits that came directly at the expense of the members in the funds. Customers in Colonial funds had lagged behind the average not-for-profit industry fund by about 2 per cent a year for the past five years.

If there was a way to obtain a slice of Australia's retirement savings for their own profits, the banks would try it.

Most superannuation members are in the dark about what is being done with their savings, but at AMP, its own superannuation trustee executives were in the dark about what the company was planning to do with the savings under its control.

AMP was the country's largest retail super fund, with $120 billion in savings. The more the royal commission examined its trustees, the more it became apparent that they didn't actually have any role in managing the superannuation they were legally required to look after. AMP's super trustees lacked the power to set the level of fees their members were charged, lacked the ability to set investment return targets, and had trouble getting different arms of the AMP conglomerate to agree to common measurements of investment performance. For instance, any changes to the fee structure of the funds' MySuper products had to be approved by the broader AMP holding company, as they would affect the profitability of the overall AMP business.

Part of the business model of AMP and its complex web of investment and management arms was to keep the trustees unaware of decisions being taken by the rest of the business. AMP's two trustees, AMP Super and NM Super, bought services from, and paid management fees to, a host of related parties inside the AMP conglomerate, including AMP Life, AMP Capital and NMMT Limited. Rather than the trustees deciding on what fees were charged, various proposals were brought to the trustees' offices from AMP's many divisions and the head of the super business, Rachel Sansom, would then be asked to rubber-stamp them.

But not all plans were brought to Sansom, including a strategy to drag out the MySuper transition in order to keep up to $87 million worth of profits from older high-fee products. For a number of products, AMP was planning to wait until mid-2016, just before the 2017 MySuper deadline, to transfer the majority of the assets. In the case of its so-called Super Leader product, it was planning to withhold 85 per cent of assets from the low-fee fund until after mid-July 2016.

Again, the interests of financial advisers were being put before superannuation members.

AMP employed the most financial advisers of any Australian company. A 'heat map' report compiled by PwC for AMP, but which was not shown to AMP's super trustees, warned that up to 50 per cent of financial planner revenue was 'exposed' to the introduction of low-fee MySuper funds.

Despite being one of the largest super managers in the country with one of the most recognisable brands, AMP was one of the worst performers. Its super product tailored for savers born in the 1950s ranked 49 out of 63 comparable products on net outcomes and 59 out of 63 on fees. For savers born in the 1960s, AMP's product ranked 27 out of 34 for net outcomes and 31 out of 34 on fees.

Its performance was atrocious. But the various AMP businesses lobbied for even worse outcomes. AMP Capital pressured the boards of AMP Life and AMP Super to lower their investment return targets as they were concerned they wouldn't be able to achieve them.

'This has happened a number of times, AMP capital has asked for a lower return target?' Hodge asked at the commission.

'Yes,' Sansom said.

In most cases, AMP's trustees, which are required to act in the best interests of members, did not have a say in the running of their own businesses. Generally, they collected members' money, which was then poured into investment-linked policies issued by AMP Life and managed by AMP Capital and AMP Services. NM Super, handed over the cash to NMMT Limited for investment services. The spider-web of related parties decided on the fees, costs and performance targets, which were then given to the trustees to approve.

AMP even had policies which meant the super trustees were not told about 'significantly underperforming' investments for more than five years. The royal commission heard a case of a 58-year-old woman who had invested her retirement savings in a cash management trust with AMP and was being charged so many fees she was losing money on the investment. Member statements revealed that in 2015 the customer, with almost $90,000 in savings, made an investment return of just 0.47 per cent. Three years later, that return had sunk to negative 0.39 per cent, meaning she was being charged more than she was earning in returns.

'If you invest it in an interest-bearing account with AMP Bank you'll get a much higher return?' Hodge asked.

'Yes, that's true,' replied Richard Allert, the chairman of AMP Super.

'Why is it that someone who puts their retirement savings in NM Super … ends up with substantially less returns?' Hodge probed further.

'You would have to ask the client,' Allert said.

'Your position is why are they foolish enough to invest their super-annuation with AMP?' Hodge asked.

'No, that's not what I'm saying at all,' Allert said.

'But isn't that your point?' quipped Hodge.

AMP only found out about the lousy cash returns after the prudential regulator told the superannuation industry it was doing a sector-wide review of cash investments run by nest-egg managers.

If AMP was keeping its trustees in the dark, it was likely because the truth was intolerable. The entire structure of the company appeared to be predicated on sucking as much money out of savers as possible. More than $100 million in fee revenue for AMP came from almost one million customer super accounts with savings under $6000. Indeed, these ultra-low-balance accounts made up a little more than a third of all the company's member accounts. Of the more than

200 super funds in the country, AMP held the most small-balance accounts—close to double the number held by the next closest rival, industry fund REST.

Just before AMP was due to appear at the royal commission for the fortnight of superannuation hearings, its new interim chief executive, Mike Wilkins, announced that the company would be cutting fees on its MySuper products. It was the first time since the introduction of MySuper five years earlier that AMP had considered cutting fees for its customers. The announcement saw shares in AMP slide to a new record low.

The fee cut would not even bring AMP close to being a low-cost super manager. It would only make it 'one of the pack' with the rest of the fee-gouging retail fund sector, rather than an outlier.

In late 2017, ANZ announced it would be selling its superannuation business for $1 billion to a wealth management company named IOOF. Along with the savings of thousands of customers, the bank would be transferring most of its financial advisers across to the new company.

ANZ called a town-hall-style meeting, where IOOF chief executive Chris Kelaher explained the changes and reassured nervous employees. As he welcomed the crowd of ANZ employees to his own business, one attendee told me there was just one question that reverberated among the staff members: 'Who the hell is this guy?'

Over the coming months, as investment bankers worked through the fine details of the corporate transaction, a fair number of ANZ financial advisers either quit or jumped ship to other businesses. There was no way they would be joining IOOF. To outsiders, IOOF was a low-profile company that was barely on the radar of ordinary Australians, but to people who worked in and around the financial sector, it was notorious.

Two years earlier, Kelaher and his chairman, Roger Sexton, had been dragged before a parliamentary inquiry following significant allegations of corporate misconduct. A whistleblower had revealed misconduct within the group's research division going as far back as 2008. History now shows that ASIC stopped short of issuing an enforceable undertaking against IOOF over the allegations, but it did find a number of issues with the company's staff share-trading policies, whistleblower protection, disclosure procedures and cybersecurity.

The probe centred on allegations that IOOF head of research Peter Hilton, who had since stepped down, was front-running trades ahead of releasing research to clients. This meant he was placing bets on the likely stock movements that would occur after the publication of his investment research, potentially giving him access to wrongfully obtained profits before his clients. His wife had made trades in Adelaide Bank, Macquarie and Toll Holdings, which were the subject of IOOF research reports.

ASIC's investigation found that the information Hilton was trading on was not material, leaving his behaviour outside of the remit of the law. Essentially, IOOF's purported investment research was too lousy to be considered market-moving. The opinions weren't worth the paper they were written on.

While there was damage to the IOOF corporate name from the scandal, it never really struck home for retail investors because the brand itself has never been a retail offering in the financial services market. Rather, it has been a business-to-business brand. Since IOOF was floated in the early 2000s, Kelaher had become famous for being the Pac-Man of Australian financial services. The company had merged with or acquired a range of firms, including Australian Wealth Management, Australian Skandia and, in its crowning achievement pre-ANZ, the $670 million merger with SFG Australia.

However, to journalists, Kelaher was known as a fickle, litigious executive. Dealing with him was often a nightmare. During one phone call I had with him, I asked if he had been subpoenaed to provide an initial document for the royal commission detailing misconduct. It was a question I asked every company representative I spoke to in the early days of the commission, and they were generally forthcoming. But Kelaher rebuked me, only to then be castigated by his head of communications, who was also on the line. 'Just answer him, Chris,' she said. Of course IOOF had been subpoenaed.

When Kelaher strutted into the Federal Court for his turn to be examined by the royal commission, the back row of laptop-bearers in the courtroom knew they were in for an interesting session. The stage had been set just days before his appearance when Commissioner Hayne shot down IOOF's attempt to hide crucial documents from the commission. It was the first and only time the former High Court judge published a ruling on an application to prevent documents from being made public during the commission.

In the process Hayne demolished the repeatedly tardy behaviour of IOOF's superannuation trustee, Questor, whose lawyers had claimed legal privilege over documents the royal commission wanted. On inspection, the documents had nothing to do with legal advice; some of them did nothing more than record communications with APRA, ASIC or the Australian Taxation Office. It was an obviously bogus claim from a company that had behaved very questionably in the past, but it was clear why IOOF had tried to keep the documents secret. They detailed the intricate power play between IOOF and APRA over the way it managed the $120 billion in savings at its disposal.

Of particular concern was how IOOF sought to fix mistakes when it made an error. This was because there was an inherent conflict of interest at the heart of IOOF. The company was both the trustee of its super fund and the manager of the investment vehicle into which the super fund tipped members' money. Whereas IOOF was supposed to act in members' best interests, it often refused to do anything that conflicted with the company's own desire to make bigger and bigger profits. It even decided not to move customers trapped in a super fund that was charging them banned trailing commissions to a new lower-fee product after working out it would cost about $8 million a year to do so.

All the while, APRA had been pressuring the company to shore up its standards. In 2015, it told IOOF it was concerned about the difficulty it was having in getting 'accurate' information, and raised concerns about its 'overall culture' and 'the number and range of prudential matters' throughout the company.

One protracted battle between the company and the regulator revolved around a long-running failure to properly compensate victims of a $6 million accounting error in a cash management trust run by Questor. The error stemmed from an incident in 2009, and Questor had initially decided to make up for the loss of money by cutting the amount of returns being doled out to savers in the fund.

However, in 2013 a whistleblower had complained about the practice because it disadvantaged new investors in the fund. While outside shareholders were being compensated, the company chose to 'compensate' superannuation members who had lost money by raiding an operating reserve that was required to be held by law. This was essentially using members' own savings to repay them for a mistake the company had made. And it didn't just happen once: IOOF used a similar approach in two further fund errors, known as the Pursuit and TPS Sweep errors.

In 2016, APRA told IOOF it was not happy and it expected Questor to 'immediately replenish the super fund's general reserves' using the company's own assets, not the assets of members. But Kelaher wouldn't back down so easily. He wrote back to APRA defending the practice, saying not one member of the fund had complained.

At the royal commission, Hodge suggested it would have been impossible for members to make a demand or a complaint because they didn't know what Questor was doing. Kelaher was confident of his approach. He had even told APRA it passed the 'pub test' in his letter. 'In terms of the so-called pub test, which in these circumstances is a proxy for members' best interests, it is the board's view that the test has been passed,' he said.

Kelaher wouldn't be caught bowing to anyone—including the royal commissioners. In documents provided to the commission, IOOF claimed APRA had 'no material concerns' about the way it ran its businesses, when the truth was that APRA was concerned the whole company was riddled with cultural failures.

Did Kelaher meet with APRA to discuss issues affecting the fund? 'We have a dialogue with APRA. It's active, it's robust. They raise concerns, we respond,' he said.

This answer prompted Commissioner Hayne to interject: 'Do I take the answer to be yes?'

Just before Kelaher's appearance at the royal commission, IOOF had made a stunning turnaround in its behaviour with the prudential regulator. APRA had long been pressuring it to split its investment management business from its superannuation trustee, in order for the two companies to better act in their customers' interests. IOOF called a board meeting at short notice, a few days before Kelaher was due to take the stand, where they resolved to remove him from the board of the super trustee and investigate separating the roles.

However, when the royal commission asked IOOF to provide board documents showing proof that the discussions had taken place and were being acted upon, the company could only manage to hand over barely legible hand-scrawled notes on scraps of paper. A company with a $3 billion market capitalisation recorded its board meetings on handwritten notes scribbled by—well, it was hard to tell.

'It looks like the handwriting of our company secretary,' Kelaher told Hodge. 'It looks like them. I'm not a handwriting expert.'

Despite the company finally appearing to buckle to the requests of APRA, Kelaher denied this was proof of poor behaviour at IOOF. Indeed, it was 'a matter of indifference' to him if the trustee and manager roles were split, he said.

'You don't share the view of APRA that there are legitimate concerns about these structures?' Hodge asked. 'It's just ultimately, as a matter of practicality, easier to make the changes rather than having to keep dealing with the complaints?'

'Yes,' Kelaher said.

With his brash and flippant responses, Kelaher's examination triggered a panicky selling of the company's shares, which had slumped 2.7 per cent by the time he stepped off the stand. Investors had a right to be worried. Over just three hours, Kelaher had repeatedly brushed off the concerns of the prudential regulator over conflicts of interest, said seven times he was not 'qualified' to answer questions, and called on the benefit of 'hindsight' nine times. If he reckoned that dipping into people's retirement nest eggs to compensate them when his own company stuffed up passed the pub test, the only questions seemed to be what pub does he drink at, and what on earth are they putting in the beer. It seemed it was time to change the kegs at IOOF.

For its part, APRA had at least been trying to change the taps on offer. A June 2017 internal APRA memo dealing with a prudential review of IOOF revealed that the regulator's staff had questioned the 'fitness and propriety' of the company. 'Since December 2015, APRA has identified a number of instances where IOOF have failed to adequately identify conflicts of interest and either avoid or appropriately deal with them,' APRA staff members Juliette Lee and Anthony Davies told their general manager, Stephen Glenfield.

Following Kelaher's car-crash testimony, attention turned to the $1 billion ANZ super transaction, in which the bank was selling its superannuation business, OnePath, to IOOF. How could ANZ have knowingly shunted 700,000 OnePath superannuation customers into such a rogue outfit? A few days later, this question would be examined at the royal commission.

On the stand, OnePath chairman Victoria Weekes said the ANZ trustee was still yet to meet with the board of IOOF to satisfy whether the deal would be in the best interests of members. Documents showed that OnePath had been considering several media reports that outlined IOOF's approach to gouging superannuation members. OnePath's legal advisers had also prepared a paper identifying the issues raised in those reports.

'Has the board yet had a presentation from IOOF?' Hodge asked.

'No, we haven't,' Weekes replied. She said OnePath had originally wanted to meet with the IOOF board in March but decided to put the meeting off until it believed 'the time [was] right'. ANZ had scheduled a board meeting for late December, when it would formally make a decision on whether to proceed with the deal.

Just days before the scheduled meeting, the decision was made for them. In the Federal Court, APRA lodged a lawsuit against IOOF. Kelaher and IOOF chairman George Venardos, chief financial officer David Coulter, company secretary Andrew Vine and general counsel Gary Riordan were not fit and proper people to run a superannuation company, APRA claimed.

It was a day of disaster for IOOF. Its share price was smashed, plunging 35 per cent in a rout that wiped $900 million off its market value.

This was exactly what a fox hunt looked like.

On the last day of the fortnight of superannuation hearings, Kelly O'Dwyer got back in touch. She said she had something important to tell *The Australian* newspaper.

Government MPs had been preparing themselves to see strips torn off the union-backed industry funds and were gobsmacked at how little or no damage had been done to the industry fund sector. In fact, the sector came out of the fortnight mostly as an example of prudent management and as financial companies that acted in the best interests of their members. If there was a problem, industry funds generally moved to rectify it as soon as possible. Every decision appeared to be taken with caution, and double-and-triple-checked that it would be in members' best interests.

Meanwhile, the banking sector had been covering up the big Australian rort. In its world, superannuation members came dead last. It was other people's money, but the fund managers saw it as theirs for the taking. On top of this, ASIC was about to launch a lawsuit against NAB and, later, AMP. What had begun as an attempt to throw dirt at the industry funds had resulted in just the opposite. It was humiliating for the Liberal Party, which had campaigned strongly on the supposed scandals in the industry fund sector.

Down at the Federal Court, Ben Butler and I received a call from O'Dywer. This time, she wanted to go on the record.

'The behaviour of some of the superannuation sector revealed during the hearings of the royal commission is disgraceful,' O'Dwyer said. 'Without doubt the most egregious misconduct identified by the commission in the past fortnight has been in the for-profit and bank-owned sector of the superannuation industry, where hundreds of millions of dollars have been wiped from the retirement savings of hardworking Australians who have received seemingly nothing in return.'

It was stating the obvious, but it was a serious admission from the government.

The next week, back in Canberra, O'Dwyer would repeat her statement at a breakfast function at Parliament House. Attending were Reserve Bank governor Philip Lowe, ASIC boss James Shipton and a bevy of senior ASIC regulators. O'Dwyer was telling them what they had already known for a long time but had only become reluctantly apparent to government MPs all too late.

Soon after the round of hearings, Industry Super Australia chief executive Bernie Dean decided to indefinitely shelve the fox-and-henhouse advertisement. He had spearheaded the campaign in his previous role as head of marketing at ISA. A few weeks later, just before Malcolm Turnbull was dumped as prime minister, the government quietly dumped the independent directors legislation targeting the industry fund sector.

The industry fund sector didn't need the ads anyway. They could have just broadcast the royal commission's superannuation round on repeat: there could be no better proof that banks weren't super.

The industry funds were rapt with the situation. Over the following months, tens of thousands of Australians starting pulling their savings out of the major banks and putting them in industry funds. Inflows into AustralianSuper doubled compared to the previous year.

Amid the celebrations, ISA called a cross-sector meeting in Melbourne, where the funds discussed the royal commission. Dean had a stern warning for them: industry funds must remain vigilant. They could be proud of what they had achieved, but they mustn't drop the ball. When the major banks survived the GFC, it ushered in a period of hubris and complacency. The banks' success ultimately ended in their crushing defeat.

The industry funds had won the battle, but the war would go on.

11
DOCTOR'S ORDERS

Imagine a situation where every individual pharmacy in Australia was owned by a particular pharmaceutical company. And imagine that in each pharmacy, the doctors on staff were only allowed to sell a small number of drugs that were manufactured by the pharmaceutical company that owned the pharmacy.

A customer would enter the pharmacy and list their ailments. No matter what the affliction was, the doctor would prescribe the pharmaceutical company's drugs, regardless of whether or not they were properly designed to target the illness.

Imagine, in this situation, that the pharmacy didn't have to disclose that this was the case, and that every drug prescribed was sold under the impression that it was the right cure for the customer.

It's actually not that hard to imagine. Australia's financial services industry concocted that operating model for large parts of the wealth management and life insurance sector.

By 2018, life insurance sales had grown to $30 billion a year in revenue. It is a massive business, equal to more than 1 per cent of Australia's annual gross domestic product. And it was being sold dubiously by Australia's major banks, because the country's biggest banks and wealth managers had created instruments known as 'approved product lists' for life insurance policies. These lists were given to the banks' financial advisers, who were then only allowed to sell policies that had been approved by the bank. Unsurprisingly, the bank's own life insurance policies were often the only policies financial advisers were allowed to sell. Customers who were being shunted into these policies were none the wiser.

For a product as important as life insurance, it's a problematic strategy.

Australians purchase life insurance to guard against bad luck. In many cases, it should probably be called death insurance. The policies, costing thousands of dollars a year, provide a payout to a customer's family in the event of the customer's untimely death. They allow a bereaved family to pay off a mortgage, continue to pay bills, and keep the kids in school.

Other forms of life insurance protect customers against ill health. If you get injured at work, your income is protected. If you suffer a bout of mental illness rendering you unable to work, you can expect to continue to get an income. If you become totally and permanently disabled and can't work in your current job or retrain in a similar line of employment, you are guaranteed to be looked after by the insurance company.

In all streams of life insurance, a customer's personal circumstances are vitally important for designing the right sort of policy. Their working conditions, their family and dependants, the value of their mortgage and their liabilities all need to be taken into consideration when designing cover.

However, Australia's banks believed their own products would suit each and every customer who walked through their door, irrespective of the complexity, differing terms and conditions, and varying levels of benefit of each different life insurance policy.

Financial advisers with Westpac subsidiary BT Financial Advice had access to just one insurer on their approved product list: Westpac Life. Suncorp allowed its financial advisers to sell only Suncorp-branded life insurance. Commonwealth Bank and its Colonial First

State dealer groups gave their advisers just three insurers to offer customers: policies from the bank's own subsidiary CommInsure, and rival companies TAL and Asteron. NAB Financial Planning had just two insurers on its list, one being its own MLC Life.

Going back to the pharmaceutical company, imagine the doctors at the pharmacy were exempted from laws that require medical workers to act in customers' best interests when they are selling drugs. While other doctors could be taken to court and sued if surgery went horribly wrong or if the doctors were negligent, the ones employed by the pharmacy would be immune to such charges.

This is also not so hard to imagine, because the life insurance industry was exempted from provisions in the Insurance Contracts Act of 1984 that protects consumers from the insurance industry. Life insurers didn't have to comply with laws about misleading and deceptive conduct, unconscionable conduct, harassment, coercion or the requirement to act honestly and efficiently when handling insurance claims. They were legally given the go-ahead to act however they wished in the sale of products that touched on extremely complex aspects of human life, such as trauma and death.

The exemption may have been justified if life insurance was a fringe product rarely taken up by customers, but it wasn't. In Australia, if you have superannuation it is more likely than not that you have a life insurance policy. Life insurance is provided to superannuation members on an automatic opt-out basis. More than 70 per cent of Australians gain life insurance this way. Every year, they hand over $15 billion in superannuation fees to life insurance companies for the provision of opt-out insurance. Most are unaware of the fee-draining policies until they are injured or became mentally unwell, and make a claim on their policy.

On the face of it, it makes sense. Superannuation is there to guarantee financial resilience in retirement. If you are injured during your career, there is no way you can look after yourself financially if you can't return to work. It's part of a holistic approach to protecting the financial wellbeing of Australia's workforce.

On the union-backed industry fund side of the super sector, funds strike deals with life insurers for contracts worth hundreds of millions of dollars. These go through careful due diligence to ensure the products are appropriate for savers in their funds.

However, on the bank-run retail side of the sector, many lenders and wealth management companies owned their own life insurance divisions. The contracts to provide life insurance to their members were signed over without any due diligence and without regard to the cost or benefits of the insurance. It was easy, legally mandated money for the ticket-clipping super sector.

When the GFC hit, the life insurance industry was completely unprepared. Soon, many workers who weren't retrenched during the economic crisis found themselves under intense pressure. They were working longer hours but with no prospect of pay rises. Stress levels rose dramatically.

At the same time, more and more employees became aware of the life insurance benefits they were paying for through their superannuation. Workplace law firms began advertising on billboards. If you were sacked or injured at work, the law firms could help you access your insurance. Meanwhile, mental health conditions started to be more openly discussed in society. Australians became more aware of the mental battles millions were facing on a daily basis.

The life insurance industry had painted itself into a corner. In a gambit to secure the lucrative superannuation contracts and win business with retail customers, life insurers had dramatically cut prices at the same time as competing to offer the most generous policy benefits.

When the number and severity of claims started to increase following the GFC, life insurers suddenly realised their businesses were unsustainable. They were paying out far too much money in claims compared to the revenue they were dragging in. Under pressure to restore profitability and protect executive salaries, there was only one way for them to stop the losses. Rather than risk losing new business by increasing policy prices, the industry believed it could simply cut down on the number of claims it approved—in any way it could legally do so.

The situation looked like a pile of wood covered in gasoline, waiting for a spark.

In 2016 Dr Benjamin Koh, the chief medical officer for Commonwealth Bank's life insurance division CommInsure, blew the whistle on what he believed was rampant wrongdoing inside one of the country's biggest insurers. CommInsure was accused of using out-of-date medical definitions of heart attack to deny otherwise legitimate insurance claims.

Heart attacks are one of the biggest areas for life insurance claims. CommInsure was asserting heart-attack survivors didn't register high enough levels of troponin in their blood after the incident to warrant a payout. The human body produces the protein troponin during a heart attack, but CommInsure's test relied on a decade-old medical definition that hadn't kept pace with medical knowledge. It was too high a hurdle for victims of heart attacks to pass, and many genuine survivors were being denied claims.

The heart-attack refusals were just the tip of an iceberg of several damaging accusations Koh would raise through Fairfax Media journalist Adele Ferguson. It was the second high-profile scandal to engulf CBA in a matter of years, following the revelations of the financial planning disaster that saw hundreds of thousands of customers ripped off by dodgy advice, and it was enough to push the opposition Labor Party to start calling for a royal commission into the issue.

Koh claimed senior CBA employees had deleted doctors' medical opinions when those opinions were too favourable to the customers. When he sought to elevate his concerns about the heart-attack definitions and the bank's purported deletion of adverse medical findings, he found only roadblocks. The bank didn't want to know and wouldn't do anything about it.

Koh was rightly concerned. He emailed a cache of documents to his private email account for protection if anything went awry. In doing so, he breached the company's internet policy, he was later told. CBA used the slip-up to fire him.

The scandal was incredibly damaging for CBA, and it forced ASIC to launch a review of claims handling across the sector. ASIC also began a probe into CommInsure, and a parliamentary inquiry was established into the life insurance industry. The sector was huge but had rarely been examined closely.

CBA updated its definition of heart attack to one that was published in 2014, and claimed it was innocent of just about every other aspect of the media allegations. A year later, ASIC's review of CommInsure ended by clearing it of any wrongdoing, but the regulator was hamstrung by the exemptions the law granted the company for distasteful behaviour. There was no legal basis for ASIC to take enforcement action against CommInsure, even where it wanted to.

'The claims-handling part of life insurance is either exempted or treated very lightly under the law, and we don't think that is justified going forward,' ASIC deputy chair Peter Kell said. 'If the exemptions were removed it would allow us to look at aspects of claims handling where we don't currently have a straightforward legal remedy.'

It was a Pyrrhic victory, of sorts, for CommInsure. The company also clung tightly to a review by consultancy Deloitte that had been released a month before the ASIC review that cleared it of any 'systemic' wrongdoing. CBA chief executive Ian Narev said at the time the report '[painted] a good picture' of the division and showed a business 'vastly different to how it has been portrayed in parts of the media'.

The company was enthused by the Deloitte report even though the narrow review of a small number of claims led to further payouts of $320,000 to customers whose claims had been either denied or incorrectly paid. Each time a journalist wrote about CommInsure from that point onwards, they would receive a call from a CBA employee asking if they had included the fact that Deloitte had cleared the bank of any 'systemic' wrongdoing. One time this happened to me, even when I had included the review's finding in the article. CBA spin doctors were quick to claim CommInsure's benign bona fides, arguing that its employees were sick of poor media coverage when they had done nothing wrong.

As the royal commission began its investigation into the life insurance sector, it was clear the whole story would now be told.

Helen Troup, the former boss of CommInsure, was called to the stand to help the inquiry decide whether the company had done anything wrong. Counsel assisting the commission Rowena Orr got straight to the heart of the matter: CBA had not been completely innocent in its outdated heart-attack definitions. Indeed, the bank had full knowledge of just how outdated its 2005 definition was.

In one example, CommInsure had denied the claim of a life insurance customer who suffered a heart attack. When the customer claimed to the Financial Ombudsman Service (FOS) that the company had misled them over the definition, CommInsure covered up advice it had received from a doctor backing up the customer's claim. When it was taken to FOS, CBA was asked to supply information about what the doctor had told the bank about the customer's condition. The doctor's medical opinion had found in favour of the claimant, but when the bank submitted the documents it blacked out this information. Then, when FOS asked for an explanation of what information had been redacted by CommInsure, the company simply did not respond. Eventually, when FOS found in favour of the customer, CBA rebuked the ombudsman and said it did not have the jurisdiction to make such a finding.

Not only was it dismal behaviour from the nation's largest bank, it also flew in the face of rules regulating interactions with FOS, which are required to be open and honest.

CommInsure's 2005 definition of heart attack required customers to register troponin levels twenty times higher than normal. When the bank's own head of life product and strategy, Dr Sally Phillips, recommended a change to a more lenient 2012 definition, the company ignored it. CommInsure failed for a decade to update its medical definitions in line with medical opinion, despite many other companies in the market managing to keep their products up to date. When the company did finally backdate its definition of heart attack, it did so only because it had worked out that remediating customers would be millions of dollars cheaper than it had previously estimated.

It wasn't just heart attack where CommInsure was cutting corners in a bid for bigger profits. The company also knocked back a claim from a woman who had breast cancer by relying on a two-decades-old medical definition that it refused to backdate. CommInsure rejected the customer's application on the basis that her surgery had not resulted in a complete removal of the breast. The surgery, CommInsure claimed, was not 'radical' enough to warrant a payout.

CommInsure was relying on a 1998 medical definition for the claim that was made in 2016, insisting it would only be paid for a full mastectomy even though the policy document did not say this anywhere. The woman had paid for the CommInsure policy since 1996. The claims denial came despite numerous letters from doctors confirming the diagnosis and detailing the invasive surgery she had suffered.

CommInsure even knocked back the claim when it didn't actually tell customers what it thought 'radical' breast surgery constituted. A doctor had told CommInsure that if the woman's cancer had occurred twenty years ago when the policy was taken out, treatment would probably have resulted in a mastectomy, but it was now current practice for the condition to be treated with less invasive surgery and radiotherapy.

While ASIC had trouble taking CommInsure to court over its behaviour, it attempted to tackle the company for misleading customers by denying a payout for reasons that were not included in the product disclosure documents. Instead of ASIC pursuing the company for a maximum fine of $8 million for misleading advertising, which CommInsure was not exempted from, the company agreed to make a measly $300,000 payment to a community benefit program for the transgressions. It did not even have to acknowledge any wrongdoing when it made the payment.

'Did ASIC take any enforcement action against CommInsure in relation to any of these advertisements?' Orr asked.

'I'm not sure if enforcement action is the correct term,' Troup said, 'but we did come to an agreement in terms of how to close the matter.' She couldn't remember how the $300,000 figure was decided. Still, CommInsure executives believed they had been suitably punished.

'At the end of the day, Ms Troup, did CommInsure come out of this process thinking that it had been punished or brought to book?' Commissioner Hayne asked.

'Yes we did, sir,' Troup said. Customers who were wrongly denied claims may think differently.

While CommInsure had campaigned vigorously against any admission of wrongdoing for years after the scandal broke, Troup had now changed her tune. The way the company had treated its customers when they were at their most vulnerable was a source of embarrassment, she said.

Orr was curious as to why Troup was now willing to concede the company had misled customers, despite fighting the accusation for years. 'What is different?' Orr asked. 'I don't understand the difference between CommInsure's position at this time and your evidence in the royal commission today.'

Troup responded: 'I think at that time we were still defending our position. Sitting here now looking at their position I can see how ASIC's position is legitimate.'

Orr asked, 'CBA was not prepared to acknowledge that, and has never publicly acknowledged that at any time before today?'

Troup said, 'That's right.'

CommInsure was also found to be ripping off the bank's own superannuation members. A review of the company's policies by actuarial firm Rice Warner, aired during the royal commission, found the company's premiums were extremely uncompetitive. Some policies were 132 per cent more expensive than the market average. Despite this, Commonwealth Bank's super division, Colonial First State, never sought a better life insurance deal for its super members. It never even put out a tender to see if there was a better deal.

'On balance, the decision that's been made has been to negotiate with the incumbent insurer,' Colonial First State boss Linda Elkins told the commission.

Luckily, by this time the rest of the superannuation sector had begun to cotton on. Just eighteen months after the CommInsure scandal broke, the company had lost at least five high-profile contracts held with various super funds. The industry funds that had dropped CommInsure included Vision Super; HESTA, which looks after the needs of Australia's health and community services workers; the transport and logistics fund TWU Super; education and community worker fund NGS Super; and professional services fund CareSuper. In total, these contracts were worth more than half a billion dollars per year in revenue for CommInsure.

Denying legitimate heart-attack claims turned out to be bad for business if you were a life insurer.

Rather than being there for customers when they needed it most, life insurers saw a customer claim as an assault on their bottom line. The companies were meant to be in the business of paying insurance claims, but given the way they operated you could be forgiven for believing they were putting more resources into denying claims.

Australia's biggest life insurer, TAL, appeared reluctant ever to pay legitimate claims. In one case, a nurse who worked in intensive care (who can't be named for legal reasons) took out a life insurance policy with TAL in 2009 that was designed to protect her income if she was unable to work. The nurse cared for a partner who suffered a mental illness, and witnessed a violent incident in her own home. She was later diagnosed with generalised anxiety and depression and made a claim with TAL a year after buying her policy.

TAL, operated by a Japanese multinational, worked out what it was on the hook for and calculated that a total of $800,000 would need to be paid to the woman depending on whether or not she could return to work. The company then quickly began to look for ways not to pay the claim. Claims-handling staff began a fishing expedition, plundering the nurse's old medical records.

There were very few rules regulating what access life insurers had to medical records, and doctors often handed over complete patient histories. It was all signed off in the small print when you bought a policy.

TAL discovered the nurse had taken a few days off work in 2007 and then a further ten days in 2008 and 2009 due to stress. It also gained access to records of her attendance at a counselling service. The company was looking for any evidence of pre-existing medical conditions, and believed it had scored a get-out-of-jail-free card. The nurse hadn't disclosed these brief periods off work when she bought the policy. Her doctors informed TAL that some of the leave was taken to look after her partner, and the other days were not related to her diagnosis at all. TAL didn't care. It told the nurse she should have informed the company, her life insurance claim was rejected and her policy was cancelled.

The nurse was in shock and went straight to FOS to complain. After losing its battle with FOS, TAL was eventually forced to reinstate the policy and pay her claim, but it would take until 2013, three years after the claim was first made, for this to happen.

Employees in TAL knew it was ridiculous blocking the payout. One worker even described it as a '100 to 1 shot' to win against the nurse, but the company proceeded to fight FOS anyway. 'FOS are clearly going to put us to the sword on this,' a member of TAL's complaints resolution team emailed a colleague. In one exchange, TAL's internal lawyer warned that 'every facet of TAL's decision is rejected' but went on to recommend continuing to fight the claim. 'In my view there is nothing to lose by pressing on but ultimately it is a decision for the business,' the lawyer wrote.

After FOS found in her favour, the nurse received a payout and believed the ordeal to be over. Little did she know that TAL was just gearing up. Bruised from its loss at the ombudsman, it hired a private detective, at a cost of $20,000, to follow her every move over the next four months. It was paying her close to $3000 a month for her income protection policy and wanted to know what she was doing with her time.

'OMG here is another one for you,' the TAL case manager told the private detective. 'I want results.'

Unbeknown to the nurse, the private investigator watched from afar. He followed her to the local swimming pool and to cafes, and made notes of what swimwear she was wearing, what strokes she was practising, and when she touched her partner affectionately. Photos taken by the investigator were circulated among staff at TAL, and the company's employees routinely mocked the claimant. TAL even told him to gather information from her former workplace and to approach local police to discuss her.

But the company wasn't finished. By late 2013, it decided it would force the nurse to keep a daily diary of her activities. This way, it might be able to find a way out of its liability. TAL told her to keep the diary because one of her symptoms was short-term memory loss.

The diary made the woman's anxiety worse. Constantly trawling over old memories heightened her stress, and doctors agreed, telling TAL to give it a rest. The nurse was contemplating self-harm as a result of being forced to keep the diary. 'Please do not read between the lines for the medical history recorded and make ill-informed decisions' read one doctor's letter to the insurer. She became so unwell her psychiatrist warned TAL she had suffered a 'progressive deterioration' in her health that left her unlikely to be able to go back to work. 'The level of suspiciousness, feelings of oppression, loss of trust and social withdrawal have all worsened considerably,' the doctor said.

TAL's chief medical officer rebuked the concerns, and the company threatened the nurse with cutting off the payments if she stopped filling out the diary. By early 2014, another doctor told TAL she was now suffering panic attacks as a result of the bullying. Soon after, out of nowhere, TAL told the nurse it would be stopping the payments.

On top of this, it was demanding she refund close to $70,000. All the while, the company's claims-handling staff had KPIs focused on making a profit for the insurer.

In the witness box, TAL general manager of claims Loraine van Eeden did not accept that the company had made its customer's mental health condition worse. Commissioner Hayne was forced to interject when van Eeden refused to answer a question about whether she thought the company's treatment of its customer was 'heavy-handed'. He said, 'That's not the way the system works' and demanded, 'What's your view?'

Van Eeden also refused to be drawn on whether it was a lie that the company had told the nurse the diary was necessary when there was no formal requirement that it be kept. She preferred the word 'misleading'.

'Do you accept the word "lie"?' Hayne probed.

'I can't actually comment on that, based on I don't know the reason why they put it in,' van Eeden said.

'To accept that it is misleading but to hesitate or reject the notion that it is a lie is, I think, perhaps, to draw a distinction that may be without difference?' said Hayne.

'I would not say that it was a lie,' van Eeden said.

Orr interjected: 'Well, was it the truth, Ms van Eeden?'

'It was misquoted,' van Eeden said.

TAL's bad behaviour wasn't just a one-off. Another customer, a woman with cervical cancer, had her policy unexpectedly cancelled by the company when it claimed she had an unrelated 'history of depression' that had not been disclosed to the company. The depression had no bearing on her cervical cancer claim, but after the company got its hands on her medical history, a TAL manager phoned her up out of the blue to inform her that her policy would be cancelled. The cold call was played for the Federal Court. 'I certainly didn't deliberately not disclose anything,' the customer said. The case went to FOS, where it was settled for a $25,000 payment even though the customer was entitled to $45,000.

TAL's lack of respect for its customers didn't end there. When it was complying with the royal commission's request for documents, its legal team failed to properly redact documents that breached individuals' privacy.

Even the choice of van Eeden as a witness for TAL was difficult to comprehend. She had forty years' experience in the industry but had only begun at TAL in January 2017, a little over a year before her appearance at the royal commission. She was forced to apologise repeatedly for being unable to handle questions on wrongdoing that had taken place from as early as 2010. Orr even had to question why she had been chosen as the appropriate TAL worker to handle questions, considering the events in her witness statement had all taken place before her time at the group.

TAL kept van Eeden in the dark as she prepared for the witness stand. The royal commission had asked for evidence from several TAL executives, but the company refused to show the statements made by other TAL witnesses to van Eeden despite the fact that they could have been of direct relevance to the questions she was asked to answer.

Behind closed doors, TAL had briefed the *Financial Review* that witnesses from a single company being probed by the royal commission were banned from seeing the witness statements made by their colleagues.

Hayne made it clear this was wrong: 'It's important to emphasise that at no time have counsel or solicitors assisting communicated to TAL or to any other party that their witnesses should not read or discuss what other witnesses, whether from the entity or not, have said in their statements. It was then surprising to hear that Ms van Eeden had not been shown the statements made by other TAL witnesses. It was also surprising that Ms van Eeden appeared to be unfamiliar with a number of documents that the commission had foreshadowed that she may be taken to. In the case of TAL, all of the documents that were put to Ms van Eeden by counsel assisting were provided to the solicitors acting for TAL a number of days in advance of Ms van Eeden providing her evidence.'

It was clear TAL wanted to know all the information possible about customers who made claims on their policies. It would go to extraordinary lengths to find out their entire medical history, their thoughts and their most intimate and vulnerable moments. But when the royal commission wanted to know how standards at the company had deteriorated so badly, TAL didn't want its customers to know a thing.

The life insurance industry's reputation had been going up in smoke since 2016. It was only made worse when AMP was once again forced to enter the Federal Court, this time to face questioning about its life insurance division. By September 2018, the wealth management giant was a frequent flyer at the royal commission.

Since AMP had demutualised and listed on the stock exchange, its life insurance division had grown problematic. It was known as the 'wealth protection' business inside the company, but it seemed to be protecting the wealth of neither its customers nor its shareholders. By the time Hayne began to probe the division, AMP was cobbling together plans to sell its life insurance business completely.

The biggest criticism of AMP may be that by September 2018, it came as little shock to anyone when it was caught out for charging life insurance premiums to dead customers. Although it knew it had been charging fees to almost 4000 dead customers, it failed to refund the $1 million involved. AMP had even logged an internal complaint in 2016 about the practice of regularly charging insurance premiums to members it knew had died. Instead of acting on the complaint, it ignored the concerns of its own staff members in favour of aiming to refund life insurance premiums at a later date rather than stopping the charging of fees upon notice of death.

Fair play, if it indeed refunded the charges. But it didn't.

Hayne asked AMP's group executive of wealth solutions and chief customer officer, Paul Sainsbury, 'Charging premiums to life insurance to someone who's dead, that's the position, isn't it?'

'Yes, that's the way the system is treating it today for a portion of our business,' Sainsbury said.

'There was a better way to do it, which was to stop premiums on death rather than refunding them. It seems a rather obvious step, doesn't it?' counsel assisting Mark Costello said.

'Yes, it does. It was not the best way in my opinion,' Sainsbury said.

AMP didn't want its customers dead—but it certainly liked it better if they were smoking. It offered its customers three life insurance options when they were in the AMP super fund: the cheapest one was for non-smokers, and the most expensive one was for people who smoked. However, some fund members were defaulted into the third option. This 'de-linked' option was just as expensive as the rate that was charged to smokers, but it was insuring the lives of non-smokers. What was more, if you wanted to be charged less, all you had to do was tell AMP you didn't smoke and they would take you out of the 'de-linked' option and put you into the non-smoking policy.

What was the point of this third 'de-linked' option? In the case of one customer, they were being slugged an extra $400 a month to be insured under it. The customer told AMP through his financial planner that the last time he'd smoked 'was when he was thirteen and at Scouts'. AMP refused to refund the premiums, which had totalled an extra $72,000 by the time the customer realised he was being classed as a smoker. It was his own fault, AMP said, because he had failed to respond to a letter in 2013 that asked him to declare he was not a smoker. He had never received such a letter.

The member took AMP to the Superannuation Complaints Tribunal, but the company argued there were lots of reasons why members in the 'de-linked' pool of insurance were charged higher rates. In fact, the only thing a customer had to do was to tell the company they were a non-smoker and they would be transferred out of the policy.

It was a strange argument for AMP to be having. Indeed, ASIC recommends that life insurance companies do not presume a person is a smoker, given that only about one in ten Australians smoke.

However, it was an easy way for AMP to extract more money out of people who didn't realise they were being fleeced.

Just like Commonwealth Bank, AMP had never bothered to check if its life insurance products were suitable for its own superannuation members. It had last reviewed the appropriateness of using its own life insurer for its superannuation members in 1995.

Just a week before AMP once again faced the music at the commission, ASIC revealed that many companies across the wealth management industry had been taking advantage of superannuation retirement savings by automatically putting members into high-premium life insurance policies designed to cover smokers. About a quarter of all Australians didn't even realise they held life insurance through superannuation. If they didn't know they held a policy, there was every likelihood companies were defaulting them into significantly higher premiums for smokers. While the companies would make off with the loot, the rip-off would unfairly erode a member's retirement savings. With more meagre nest eggs, the taxpayer would eventually have to pick up the bill for the member's reliance on the age pension.

Even companies that appeared to be trying to overhaul the life insurance industry for the better were caught up in poor behaviour.

When Simon Swanson left CommInsure in 2009, he did so with a mission to create a better life insurance business—one that actually met customer needs. The executive established ClearView Wealth in 2010 from the merger of two companies, ClearView Retirement Solutions and MBF Life, the latter of which was purchased from health insurance company BUPA Australia. Without the problems of a legacy portfolio of insurance customers, which would constrain the company and bog it down with policies that were ill-designed for contemporary needs, Swanson would be able to offer a genuinely different product in the Australian life insurance market.

ClearView soon grew to become a $1 billion company. With the backing of a fast-growing business behind him, Swanson went about trying to reform the industry. He was one of the only executives in the market attempting to break open the pharmaceutical-company–pharmacy cartel model. 'We are very keen for the industry to finally grow up and have open approved product lists,' he told me in early 2017.

Swanson also threw his weight around at parliamentary inquiries and in discussions with the FSC lobby group that represented the life insurance sector. There, he argued for an end to the approved product lists system, which was forcing financial advisers to sell only a tiny number of the policies on offer even if they weren't in customers' best interests.

'We are asking people to be professional. They should be able to represent all the companies in the market to provide solutions that meet the needs of their customers,' Swanson told Nationals senator John Williams during a 2017 parliamentary hearing. 'I have no doubt that life insurance fulfils a vital function in our society. I also strongly believe that the life insurance industry is characterised by a high degree of mediocrity. By this, I mean that many parts of the industry are characterised by restrictive practices that stifle competition and innovation, and there are, in many instances, glaring conflicts of interest. In addition, it has been chronically underinvested in by its shareholders, as they have chosen to chase the mandated money in the superannuation system.'

In late 2017, when the FSC launched a new industry standard requiring approved product lists to offer financial advisers the choice of products from at least three life insurance companies, Swanson was the first to publicly criticise the move as too little, too late. 'Vertically integrated institutions are incapable of self-regulation and incapable of providing objective, independent financial advice,' he told me. While the FSC had been given an opportunity to demonstrate actual leadership on the eve of a royal commission, it had instead produced 'the kind of ineffectual policy expected from a conflicted industry represented by the FSC', Swanson said. But what else was to be expected from the group referred to as the Financial Services Cartel?

In many cases, big banks and wealth managers also required smaller companies to pay 'shelf space fees' if they wanted to be listed on an approved product list. Those fees were up to $650,000 per annum. 'It is just a straight bribe,' Swanson said.

ClearView seemed to be doing things differently in an industry riddled with apathy and malignancy, so it came as something as a surprise when, in early 2018, it was stopped in its tracks by ASIC over high-pressure sales tactics. ASIC said ClearView was using the tactics to sell inappropriate life insurance products to more than 1000 people in remote Indigenous communities who didn't have English as their first language. The company was put on the hook for refunds worth a total of $1.5 million for more than 16,000 customers who had been wrongly shunted into its policies.

The culprit was ClearView's 'direct' life insurance division. This area of the business conducted thousands of cold calls to sell policies. The calls misled customers about what the insurance covered, the cost of premiums, and the effect of the consumer's pre-existing medical conditions. Often, customers were signed up to policies without their consent.

Swanson moved immediately to shut down the outbound call centre and end its 'direct' insurance operations, but the brand damage had already been done. ClearView never quite looked the same.

A few weeks later, I bumped into Swanson at an industry gathering and he asked why he had never seen a report in *The Australian* about the scandal. Unfortunately, I had been on holidays at the time. 'But I would have absolutely skewered you for it,' I told him.

'I know that is exactly what you would have done, Michael,' he said.

Unluckily for Swanson, the proper skewering would take place a few months later when the royal commission began to probe exactly what had gone wrong at the fledgling life insurer.

The problems had begun early, when ClearView first took over Bupa.

Life insurance was a product mostly purchased by wealthier Australians. If you had a decent wage and the means to protect it, you would probably buy life insurance. ClearView saw an opportunity to tap an untouched part of the market: customers it referred to as 'lower socioeconomic' customers. It was a polite phrase for poor Australians.

The company geared its remuneration incentives to get its call centre staff to sell as many policies under the 'Your Insure' brand to poor people as possible. Bonuses of up to $8000 a fortnight were available to staff if they won enough business for the company. ClearView even held 'Let's rip it up' incentive days. Lucrative bonuses and prizes were a necessary part of the business.

'ClearView decided that an injection was required to stimulate the team and revive the cultural pulse,' counsel assisting Rowena Orr read from an email sent to ClearView managers. The sales drive would take place over a five-month period and would force call centre staff to compete to enter the top-third bracket of sales staff. The prize was a trip to the New Zealand ski town of Queenstown with paid travel, accommodation and entertainment. 'This is not a junket or a celebration, it's an investment. Strategic projects such as this should be seen as a necessary cost,' ClearView management told staff in an email.

The company also launched 'random' days of competition to reward with gift cards sales staff who sold the most policies. An email showed managers attempting to whip up excitement among staff: 'I'm putting a random incentive day … I want this joint pumping with belling, clapping and SALESSSSSS … LET IT RAIN WITH GIFT CARDS!!!!!'

The strategy backfired, with large swathes of poor customers cancelling the policies sold to them or letting the insurance lapse. They'd never wanted it in the first place, and had been signed up without giving consent. Why would they continue to pay?

ClearView's quality assurance staff lacked the qualifications, experience, supervision and resources to check that policies were being sold correctly. It should have been crystal clear the strategy would fail. Internal documents revealed how the company coached its staff to sell products to poor Australians differently from how it sold them to wealthier customers. Staff were told to rely on 'emotional pitch' rather than use a tone of voice that rationally explained the benefits of the policy.

Customers who couldn't qualify for life insurance due to pre-existing conditions were 'downgraded' to lesser-value products such as accidental death insurance. This is a largely useless type of policy that covers events such as falling from a ladder or losing a limb. The products were of such low value to customers that ClearView only paid out about 25 per cent of all the revenue it collected through them over a five-year period. In one particular year, it kept 99 per cent of all revenue from accidental death policies as only 1 per cent was paid out in claims.

'It was poorer people that were being targeted by Your Insure?' Orr asked.

ClearView chief actuary and risk officer Gregory Martin said the company had never meant to target the poorest Australians. 'I emphasise it was poorer, not poorest. You can't build a business on that. But that's where it was finding itself,' Martin said.

Orr fired back: 'I would say poor, you would say poorer people.'

Not only was the conduct abhorrent, it was also illegal. ClearView was directly in breach of anti-hawking laws that prevent unsolicited and pestering sales of life insurance policies. Martin couldn't remember how many times ClearView was thought to have breached the laws, but put it at between 10,000 and 12,000.

After ASIC raised concerns about the situation, a company review found more than 260,000 phone calls where it couldn't identify whether the call had complied with the anti-hawking provisions. This number was subsequently revised upwards a number of times. All up, ClearView estimated that by early May 2017 it had breached the anti-hawking provisions between 300,000 and 303,000 times over a period of just three years. Each instance was a criminal offence.

Despite the findings, the company failed to punish its head of sales for systemic non-compliance. 'None of you took any steps to discipline your head of sales over his clear intention to breach the law?' Orr asked Martin.

'We didn't take any action,' he said.

'Was that a satisfactory response?' Orr asked.

'Not in retrospect, no,' Martin said.

'ClearView never prioritised compliance, did it?' Orr said.

'The direct team did not prioritise compliance, no. This reflects a culture within ClearView Direct that was a full-on sales culture without much regard for customers,' Martin replied.

After two days on the stand, Martin was left largely speechless by the end of proceedings. 'The intention of ClearView is not to offer rubbish products to the market,' he said. 'If we had our time again we wouldn't do that business. It's just, yes, sack them.'

As the royal commission prepared to examine the life insurance industry, ASIC was feverishly at work investigating the 'direct' life insurance industry.

Outbound cold calling was a terrible way to sell complex life insurance policies. People didn't need or want the insurance and weren't familiar with the companies that were selling it to them.

As ASIC looked closer, it found a company far worse than it thought possible—and that was after it had combed through ClearView's direct business.

In May 2018, an ASIC executive sat down at their desk to tap out a note for the other ASIC commissioners. The executive had just had a meeting with Freedom Insurance, a small life insurance company that conducted all of its business through outbound calls. ASIC had found a high rate of lapsing policies, policies that were sold multiple times to the same customer, and large numbers of family members signed up to funeral insurance in a single call. It found high rates of policies sold to customers in postcodes where Indigenous customers lived, and funeral insurance being sold to very young customers.

There was also a litany of angry customer reviews of Freedom Insurance being left on websites. 'While not a basis for action, it does provide interesting insight into current practices and substantiates the issues identified in the complaints. Also suggests that misconduct is live, and that Freedom are aware of what is happening,' the ASIC executive wrote. 'Overall', the conduct was 'far worse' than ClearView. ASIC needed to serve Freedom with an investigation notice 'asap', the executive said.

Freedom was a publicly listed company with a market capitalisation of $100 million. Before it was dragged before the royal commission, its shares were trading at 40 cents apiece. Just weeks after it appeared at the Federal Court, even before Hayne handed down his final report, the shares had been obliterated and were changing hands at just 2 cents each.

Freedom Insurance was revealed to have deployed every trick in the book to hold onto each dollar it siphoned from its unsuspecting victims. The company pitted its staff against each other in a battle to convince even the most determined customers not to cancel their policies. It enticed its employees with financial rewards and prizes in the hottest boiler-room operation in Australia. Freedom even deducted the cost of an employee's 'seat'—literally the chair they sat on in the office; they had to earn it back before they won any bonuses.

Freedom's main game was the sale of funeral insurance policies—which it somewhat callously named 'final expenses policies'—and accidental death insurance. Sales of the policies had soared for the fledgling company, but so too had the number of victims calling up in vain to try to cancel them.

Grant Stewart, a Baptist minister from Melbourne, was one of the people who tried to cancel a policy that had been sold to his son, a 26-year-old with Down syndrome who had been signed up to a funeral insurance policy after he received a cold call from the company. The man was audibly disabled, had trouble understanding financial transactions and could not in any imaginable way comprehend the complex product he was pressured into buying. He relied solely on a Disability Support Pension for income.

None of that mattered to the sales staff member on the other end of the phone. In that call, which was played aloud to the Federal

Court, the staff member had asked the man if he had another family member who could handle the call after he regularly failed to make clear responses during the sales process. At one point he told the sales agent, 'I need to go.' The agent replied: 'I'll let you go in a moment' and then requested his bank details.

Stewart only found out about the policy after discovering that deductions were about to be taken from his son's bank account. When he called up the company he was confronted with one of Freedom's 'retention' agents, who attempted to block the cancellation of the policy and instantly launched into a sales pitch about how the cover was free for the first year. They said only his son could cancel the policy, and they didn't believe he would want to do that.

After the call finished, the employees mocked Stewart. The retention agent called him a 'bloody whinger' in an email to a colleague, and another staff member said the son 'sounds not normal tho'. In an online chat between retention staff, one remarked: 'I don't know what he [the father] expects to get out of it lol.' When one retention agent asked a colleague to look at Stewart's cancellation request, the colleague simply replied, 'No'. The retention agent responded with twenty-five sad faces.

Freedom employed a team of thirty retention agents whose sole job was to handle calls from angry customers and try to fob them off. The retention staff were paid bonuses to do so. Of the almost 40,000 cancellation calls—more than seventy a day—that Freedom received over the 2017 financial year, about half the callers complained they could not afford the cover and a further 28 per cent said they were cancelling because they had not wanted the policy in the first place.

Despite the number of callers wanting to cancel their Freedom policies, only a quarter of them managed to do so. More than two-thirds of the people who called to cancel were persuaded to continue it without change. Freedom wouldn't even accept a written request to cancel a policy. Customers were told they had to phone, not write to, the company to get their policy cancelled. There was no escaping the gauntlet.

Customers complained that policies were not cancelled on request, premiums were still being deducted after they had been told the policy was cancelled, and they were 'just hung up on' when they asked for policies to be cancelled. Freedom Insurance policies were riddled with exclusions and were rarely claimed upon, and the company paid out very little in claims compared to the revenue the policies brought in.

Freedom yielded to the requests of Stewart only after forcing his son to verbally repeat the word 'terminate' on a call. The royal commission heard the son's pained stuttering of the word over the recorded call.

The company drove its staff's behaviour with extreme bonuses such as luxury trips to Bali, cruises on Sydney Harbour and Vespa scooters, in competitions that pitted employee against employee—all despite a ban on conflicted remuneration, which prohibits the payment of rewards that encourage staff to sell products that aren't in the best interest of customers. 'Everyone aiming for seven lives over the first two sessions—3.5 lives [insured] per session, easy-peasy—and we'll smash 400 lives to lock in the incentive money for the last part of the day,' read one email to staff. 'Get on the phone and SELL SELL SELL,' another email read. 'Show me the money!' read another, illustrated with a picture of actor Tom Cruise yelling down the phone in the film *Jerry Maguire*.

Just before the round of hearings on life insurance, ASIC tolled the bell on outbound call centres selling crappy insurance. These centres, where policies were sold without financial advice, were just too riddled with poor behaviour to warrant their continued existence. ASIC also demanded that companies stop selling accidental death insurance, after it found the product was useless.

Hours before it appeared at the royal commission, Freedom made the snap decision to junk its sales of accidental death insurance, accidental injury insurance, trauma insurance and life insurance, but decided it would try to continue selling funeral insurance through outbound calls. This was despite the regulator's instruction the previous week for companies to cease the sale of life insurance through outbound call centres under threat of legal action. Freedom was also planning to continue to sell accidental death insurance policies but only through 'inbound' calls, despite ASIC threatening to ban the product.

The snub didn't last long. Within weeks, senior management had been completely cleared out. Two months later, Freedom announced that it lacked a viable business model. It had 'no immediate commercially viable' option to restart selling insurance products, it told the ASX.

Freedom Insurance was a business predicated on taking money from unsuspecting Australians and refusing to give it back. After the royal commission, there was no way it could keep going.

The life insurance industry was used to raking in big coin, but it wasn't used to spending that money on customers or reinvesting it in its own businesses. The inability to prudently manage their own operations would put life insurers into a potential death spiral.

There had long been a reticence among life insurers to spend scarce money on administration systems. Following the GFC, the sector had been swamped by surging costs amid a sector-wide blowout in claims. In early 2017, APRA warned the sector to invest in their own businesses to ensure they were sustainable, under the threat of firmer action if its requests continued to be ignored.

'While there are many positive examples, the less welcome legacies in some parts of the insurance sector are decades of neglected investment in systems, outdated products, poor business processes and ways of working that are not responsive to the challenges of our time,' APRA member Geoff Summerhayes told the Actuaries Summit in Melbourne. 'Legacy directly impedes innovation. The old structures and systems are no longer able to meet the needs of many of today's consumers.'

Many life insurers had old and obsolete back-office systems that have made dealing with rising numbers of claims difficult. The situation was so bad that one life insurance company had been forced to scour the market for a computer programmer fluent in Fortran, a programming language developed in the 1950s, to implement a regulatory system change. NAB's MLC Life stored customer records on microfiche, a dated technology that was formerly used to store photographs of newspaper pages. One super fund had to source a spare part on eBay to keep one of its legacy systems operational because the manufacturer did not make or supply it anymore.

About a quarter of all assets in the funds management industry are in legacy products. These products are now closed to new investors and have become uneconomic due to changes in the market or government policy. Laws require life insurance policy terms to remain constant for the duration of the policy—which is often a lifetime—although new products have been created to better reflect consumer demands and changed market conditions.

It was meant to be easy money. Australia's biggest banks all got in on the action, taking over independent life insurers in a bid to shunt their banking customers into more and more products. But things went awry, and now the sector wasn't just seeing life insurance profits becoming slimmer—they were completely disappearing. Rather than shore up standards, the banks responded by putting their life insurance divisions on the chopping block. A hasty sale would get them out of the sticky situation.

For those that remained in the sector, there was one last chance at restoring their profits without having to change their ways. Parts of the sector became increasingly interested in workers' rehabilitation, and many companies began to invest in in-house rehab resources. There was just one hitch: the law prohibits life insurers from paying for workers' rehabilitation.

At the start of 2018, the FSC launched a desperate attempt to convince a powerful parliamentary joint committee to overturn laws that banned insurers from paying for workers' treatment. They argued that it could help claimants return to work early. Allowing the companies to get a foot in the door of workers' rehabilitation would also dramatically lighten the load on the amount of money insurers would have to pay out in claims. Moreover, they would be able to conduct the rehabilitation themselves. Consumer groups and doctors were concerned.

The problem was that the FSC would have to convince the same parliamentary committee that had just finished trawling over the sector for the past eighteen months, investigating a mountain of scandalous behaviour. The committee had handed down nearly fifty proposals to improve the shocking practices found to be widespread in the life insurance industry, but the industry had either ignored or failed to adopt them. They included getting rid of conflicted remuneration, ending the practice of cross-selling, getting legal enforcement for a strengthened code of practice, restricting access to medical records, tightening access to genetic information, and more regularly keeping up with medical opinion.

Despite being given the opportunity to prove it could self-regulate in line with the wishes of politicians and consumer groups, the life insurance sector had been reluctant to reform. 'The FSC promises to give us updates on their progress with the proposals, but we go into meetings and all they want to talk about is access to workers' rehabilitation,' one parliamentary source close to the discussions told me.

The life insurance industry's attempts at self-regulation had already fallen well short of the requests of regulators and politicians. Its codes of practice—including one code made by the FSC and another by the Insurance in Superannuation Working Group, which includes the nest-egg sector—were recommended to be combined into a single mandatory code enforced by ASIC. The FSC code had not been approved by ASIC, which would give it actual regulatory teeth, while the Insurance in Superannuation Working Group code was not mandatory and was unenforceable.

In May 2018, just a few months before ClearView's Gregory Martin faced the royal commission, he told an industry conference that companies could not resort to cutting benefits or adding in more exclusions. 'We need to get on our bikes with early intervention,' he said, referring to workers' rehabilitation. 'We'll need some law changes and we need to get on with the lobbying of that.'

In October, just a month after the royal commission hearings on life insurance, the parliamentary committee denied the industry what it wanted. The government wasn't about to hand the companies any more responsibility now.

12

HOW MUCH IS ENOUGH?

When ANZ chief executive Mike Smith moved the company's headquarters out of its home in the historic Gothic tower on the corner of Melbourne's Queen Street and Collins Street in 2009, he got quite the upgrade.

In the bank's new premises, a shiny new building in the Docklands precinct, Smith was handed a palatial new office. On the top floor of the building, his new chief executive suite was more than 100 metres square. That made his personal office bigger than most two-bedroom apartments. In fact, it was bigger than many three-bedroom apartments.

The top floor, where other senior executive offices were also located, was highly exclusive. While staff had to swipe a card to gain entry to the building as a whole, they had to have special clearance to enter the floor where the senior managers worked. The new digs were fitted out lavishly. Stone imported from Turkey adorned the boardroom, in which sat a big leather desk with a price tag of half a million dollars.

Smith, who had been appointed ANZ chief executive two years earlier, had joined Australia's third-largest bank with a sign-on bonus of $9 million. That was in addition to his base salary of $3 million.

Bonuses were able to be earned on top of that. Smith's office was nearly as big as his Toorak mansion, which cost $10 million. The four-bedroom home had a heated in-ground pool and a tennis court, and space for eight cars. This was good, as Smith was a keen collector of vintage Aston Martins.

Under his leadership, between 2007 and 2015, ANZ spent billions on an optimistic expansion into Asia. From Indonesia to China, Japan and South Korea, it wanted a piece of the growing Asian economy.

But the plan proved a failure. Over the period of Smith's reign, ANZ's share price fell 6 per cent. Over the last five years of his leadership, it was the worst performing of the major banks on the local share market. Investors rejected his strategy. Still, he became the highest-paid major banking chief executive in Australian history. Over his eight years at ANZ, he took home close to $100 million. As a banker, even if you lost, you still won.

When the bank's chief financial officer, Shayne Elliott, took over from Smith as CEO, he was told he could move into Smith's old office. Elliott stood at the threshold of the gargantuan office, the size of half a basketball court, but didn't want to set foot inside and chose to sit in a smaller office down the corridor. Now, Smith's old office has been carved down the middle. On each side of the divide is a separate meeting room for all employees to use.

Just as Smith's luxurious office was dismantled, the edifice of the most powerful corporate titans in Australia was slowly demolished by the royal commission. For an inquiry that began its public hearings in March, it took very little time to careen through the top ranks of Australia's biggest financial companies. By the time its public hearings had wrapped up in November, sixteen senior executives in those companies had lost their jobs as a direct result of the revelations. Two smaller companies had been shut down, one of them with its financial services licence revoked. And Commissioner Hayne had not even handed down his findings or recommendations.

However, bankers appeared to be insulated from ever being truly punished for their wrongdoing.

As counsel assisting the commission Michael Hodge, QC, tore through the superannuation round of hearings, he made a pointed finding about NAB executive Andrew Hagger.

Hagger had spent hours in the Federal Court defending his failure to tell ASIC the truth about the company's fees-for-no-service scandal when he'd phoned up ASIC's Greg Tanzer. 'Hagger's description of the call as "open and transparent" is not accurate,' Hodge said.

A few weeks after his spell in the dock, NAB announced Hagger would be leaving the business. As he drove away from the bank's headquarters in his Maserati for the last time, he took with him a redundancy payout of up to $796,000. So long, and good luck. It was a nice little package, adding to the more than $20 million he had trousered over his decade at the bank. He had taken home an average of about $2.5 million a year in statutory pay since 2009, including $4.1 million in 2016—the year in which it emerged NAB had fleeced its superannuation members of $35 million in fees charged where no service was provided.

In 2015, NAB had even paid Hagger a one-off 'retention award' worth $550,000 that was the only such payment made to the bank's executives that year. 'Mr Hagger is important to the business and its transformation in the medium term,' NAB said at the time.

While Hagger's nest egg had been well-feathered by NAB, savers in the bank's MLC-branded super funds for which he was responsible were lucky if they received even remotely the same treatment. NAB's MLC Super Fund MySuper and MLC Staff MySuper funds were ranked among the worst performing in the country.

It was a humiliating exit for Hagger, but Australia's tight network of corporate heavyweights managed to sort things out. Just a few months later, iron ore billionaire Andrew 'Twiggy' Forrest came to the rescue. Hagger was chosen to run the family's charitable and commercial activities, known as Minderoo—a group of interests that had the backing of more than $5.5 billion in assets. The former NAB banker would become the inaugural chief executive officer of the Minderoo Foundation, along with running Minderoo's investment arm.

'I find hardship and suffering is the shortest road to wisdom,' said Forrest, whose day job was chairman of Fortescue Metals, one of the world's largest mining companies. 'The investment community at large have been really supportive of Andrew who did take a lot of the brunt for the bank on himself,' the billionaire told the *Financial Review*. 'I don't deny it was a very difficult period for him and I do admire people who come through a very challenging period because they are much richer for their experience as a result.'

Salvation came easy to some.

In late 2015, Matt Comyn, a rising star at Commonwealth Bank, received interesting feedback during a routine review of executive development at the company.

The bank gave feedback to all its senior executives. Comyn was in charge of CBA's sprawling retail division, which looked after savers, borrowers and mortgages.

However, the recommendations given to Comyn were strange. The banker was told he needed to work on his 'personal conviction'. It turned out the company believed he had to prove he could manage competing agendas. He needed to pick which battles he wanted to fight if he wanted to make it to the top of the corporate ladder. 'Calm down' was the main message he received, Comyn said.

The message was given to Comyn after he revealed his concerns about the sale of insurance products at the bank. CBA was selling thousands of insurance policies to consumers who weren't able to claim on them, and Comyn had been waging an internal fight against the useless products over the course of 2015 and 2016.

The bank wanted to continue to make the sales. It was making $150 million from the insurance each year.

Comyn visited chief executive Ian Narev to put forward his case as to why the sales should stop. He told his boss the bank was 'not treating our customers fairly'. Narev insisted it was a 'very good product' and at the end of the conversation told Comyn: 'Temper your sense of justice.' The young executive came away from the discussion confused, but didn't stop calling for the insurance products to be overhauled.

A year later Narev promised Comyn he would ask the bank's chief legal officer to conduct a review of the insurance products. That review never took place.

Comyn couldn't ask the company's board of directors to handle the issue. He figured they would just refer it back to Narev, who would ignore it and possibly punish Comyn for raising the issue with the bank's governing panel over Narev's head.

Why should Comyn trust the board anyway? More often than not, it seemed to be a protection racket for the company's profits and the executives who were raking in the most money.

CBA's board was a collection of a few of Australia's most successful and influential business executives. When the full extent of the company's failure to comply with money-laundering laws became clear, questions started being directed to them.

CBA chairman Catherine Livingstone was a lauded figure in the business community. She was both a former president of the Business Council of Australia and the former chair of Telstra. She had also chaired the CSIRO, acted as a director of Macquarie Group and Goodman Fielder, and taken Cochlear to the world as the ear implant maker's chief executive. There were few more celebrated figures in corporate Australia.

However, when she joined the bank there was no immediately clear sign that she would be holding the company to higher standards of governance.

Company boards have few tools at their disposal to either incentivise or punish their executives other than with the payment or withholding of bonuses. On top of standard 'base' salaries, executives are measured against a range of short-term and long-term incentives. The overriding concern is profit. The higher the profit, the bigger the executive bonus. With little else guiding executive behaviour, profits were put before people. And when customers came last, the banks failed to punish executives by taking away their bonuses. In fact, it was highly unusual for a company to do anything but give executives their bonuses, regardless of their behaviour.

As a CBA board director, before she was shortly promoted to chairman, Livingstone signed off on the full suite of bonuses for executives while knowing the lender had failed thousands of times to comply with anti-money-laundering legislation.

It was during the 2016 financial year that CBA had first discovered its failure to send the regulator, AUSTRAC, tens of thousands of transaction reports. Each failure was a breach of the law. Instead of punishing executives, Livingstone decided to sign off on CBA's 2016 financial year remuneration report, which gave an 'above target' strength rating to matters of risk management. This resulted in Narev being awarded $12.3 million. It was also the year during which the bank was under assault over its treatment of life insurance customers.

Dragged before a House of Representatives parliamentary committee in October 2017, Livingstone was taken to account for her actions. 'Surely it must be the case that the board has manifestly failed in relation to its duty with the remuneration report,' said the committee chair, Liberal MP David Coleman. 'You signed off on a remuneration report that found all metrics had been met, and one, that related to risk … was above target … it is very hard to see at a bare minimum that that is not extraordinarily incompetent.'

But Livingstone was not one for budging. 'On the basis of the facts that the board knew at that time, we made the right determination,' she responded.

Later, it would become clear that the members of the board had known more than they were letting on. Indeed, documents obtained under freedom of information laws showed the board had been probed for all documents relating to its oversight of the bank's anti-money-laundering compliance. There was no way CBA was in the dark about its dealings with the regulator, which would eventually lead to a $700 million settlement—the biggest fine in Australian corporate history.

When Livingstone was later put on the stand at the royal commission, she revealed the bank had attempted to recover some of the bonuses it had paid to former CBA chairman David Turner, after concluding that he had overseen a period when the bank had a disregard for prudent behaviour.

After APRA conducted a prudential review of the bank's failures, CBA asked Turner to give back 40 per cent of the director's fees paid to him over his last year at the bank—equal to hundreds of thousands of dollars. He did not agree to return any of his fees, and the bank was powerless to do anything else. Turner told another board member that 'he didn't recognise, in the APRA report, the CBA board that he knew'.

All in all, the board contended it had a limited knowledge of the compliance issues at the bank, despite this being one of the main reasons a board exists. Since 2011 CBA had never reduced an executive's short-term bonus for compliance issues unless those issues were publicly aired by the media.

Bankers were fiercely protective of their pay. The 2017 federal budget revealed the lengths to which they would go to protect their salaries.

In early 2017 Treasurer Scott Morrison paid a visit to the UK, where he held discussions with the banking regulator, the Financial Conduct Authority. The UK had been stung by the GFC far more severely than Australia had, and the government had been forced to rescue stranded lenders using taxpayer money to plug the holes in the sinking financial system, which had been created by executive largesse and excess.

When it repaired the sector, the UK government instituted a series of hard-hitting reforms. These included a bank levy, which would tax the biggest banks as a way to both temper their sense of exuberance and collect revenue in case the public ever had to pay for their negligence again. It also created an executive remuneration register, which would keep a portion of banker bonuses until well after the financial year in which they were awarded so it could more easily take back financial rewards if misconduct was later revealed.

When Morrison handed down his budget in May that year, Australia's banking sector was subjected to local versions of both policies. The banks loudly campaigned against the introduction of the sensible measures.

The major banks—CBA, Westpac, NAB, ANZ and Macquarie Bank—were expected to receive a collective bill in the order of $1 billion a year thanks to the proposed levy. The major bank levy, which applied a 0.06 per cent tax on banks with liabilities in excess of $100 billion, was forecast to rise to a total of $6.2 billion over four years.

Even starting out at $1 billion a year, the banks complained that the levy could undermine the stability of the financial system as a whole. But as they cried poor, they were also helping themselves to a fair amount of revenue just for their own executive pay packets. Those five banks paid a combined $300 million to their small senior executive teams during that financial year, meaning remuneration packages were equal to nearly a third of the estimated $1 billion impact of the government's new levy. The $300 million went to a total of just sixty-four bankers across the five companies.

CBA had paid its twelve senior executives a total of $52.4 million for the year when it was aware of the AUSTRAC scandal and the life insurance claims-handling debacle. The remuneration paid by Macquarie Group to its twelve-member executive team—more than $120 million that year—was more than twice its expected $50 million tax bill stemming from the levy. Macquarie even pushed a rumour that it was considering options for relocating overseas following the announcement of the bank tax.

The ABA warned that the cost of the levy would be passed on either to customers through higher interest rates, to shareholders by cutting dividends, or to staff by cutting jobs or freezing wages.

In his 2016 book on the financial system, *The End of Alchemy*, Mervyn King, a former Bank of England governor and renowned British economist, found high banker pay had fallen little since the GFC despite the sizeable economic damage inflicted by the financial system. 'Many of the examples of high personal remuneration, especially in the form of bonuses, in the financial sector reflect not high productivity but what economists call rent-seeking behaviour,' he said. This 'diverts talent from professions where the social returns are high, such as teaching, to those, such as finance, where the private return exceeds, often substantially, the social return.'

Banking is highly lucrative, and as the GFC revealed, it is a government-backed sport. If a bank fails, it is almost guaranteed a bailout. A 2014 study by the International Monetary Fund estimated that the world's eleven largest banks enjoyed implicit subsidies from governments of US$62 billion a year, some of which might be captured by bankers rather than shareholders.

Kevin Davis, the chief economist from the Australian government's 2014 Financial Services Inquiry, believes banker remuneration might not fully reflect the value added to the economy by the highly paid workers in the financial sector. 'Part of the reason for finance sector growth is that there is potentially lots of money to be made by bright people at the expense of others,' he said.

It wasn't always like this. In its first year of privatisation in 1997, CBA paid its top twelve executives a combined $6.6 million. By 2017, the twelve highest-paid executives earned almost $32 million, an increase in wages six times bigger than salaries in the rest of the economy over the same period.

Brought before a parliamentary inquiry into the government's new bank levy, ABA chief executive Anna Bligh was asked about the executive pay bonanza. 'There was an article in *The Australian* today that suggested that the big four banks and Macquarie paid a combined $300 million to their small senior executive teams last financial year,' the committee chair, Liberal senator Jane Hume, said. 'Does that sound like a reasonable figure to you?'

Bligh, who had attended seeking only to raise the alarm on the government's big new tax, was wrongfooted by the question and offered a non-answer.

'It sounds like an awful lot, to have sixty-four employees paid an average of about $4.5 million per employee,' Hume continued.

Bligh responded: 'You know that these are very big organisations, and regardless of what you are talking about, they do deal in big numbers. But they are big numbers in and big numbers out.'

Greens senator Peter Whish-Wilson was forced to interject. 'I think what the chair might be referring to, Ms Bligh, is that perhaps they could absorb the bank levy in their bonuses in the future,' Whish-Wilson said.

'I think that is a matter that you might want to put to the individual banks,' Bligh replied.

While excessive bonuses for bankers may not have seemed like a problem to the bankers themselves, the regulator was deeply concerned. Despite the introduction of laws giving APRA broad new powers to monitor remuneration and sack badly behaved bankers, the sector was not taking heed of the new world.

APRA chairman Wayne Byres told an industry gathering in late 2018 that the Banking Executive Accountability Regime was just one tool to regulate behaviour, and that the sector needed to take more responsibility for punishing rogue bankers. APRA's own sector-wide review of banker pay had found that while junior bankers and front-line staff faced financial penalties for acting out of line, senior executives in charge of each division were usually 'insulated' from the consequences. 'This must change,' Byres warned.

The regulator found that big banks were too heavily focused on rewarding executives for return on equity (the amount of profits being paid out to shareholders). Boards also failed to challenge executives who wanted more pay. The oversight of board remuneration committees suffered from 'insufficient documentation' given to them by executives.

'Financial organisations are adept at designing financial incentives for staff to say yes to taking risk—after all, taking risk is how profits are generated,' Byres said. 'Far less incentive exists to say no, even when it is the right thing to do for the long-term interests of the company itself. The perception in the community is that in the financial sector, particularly at senior executive level, the carrots are large and the sticks are brittle.

'It's no surprise that areas where the financial sector has been dogged by scandal have been areas where the most basic form of incentive—sales or revenue-based rewards—are prevalent: financial advice, broking, mortgage lending, insurance sales, financial markets trading. Not only are rewards generous, but there are seemingly few repercussions for poor outcomes. It's in the industry's interests that this perception changes. Without effective accountability, particularly at the highest levels, companies send a message, to both employees and the public, that they are all care and no responsibility. From a prudential perspective, this is a major concern.'

However, it was not just the banks that were hooked on bigger and bigger profits: their shareholders were also demanding fealty to the almighty dollar.

In Australia, shareholders are given the right to say no to the companies they invest in.

Under the two-strikes rule brought in under the Gillard Government, if 25 per cent of investors in a company vote against a board's remuneration report, a first strike is recorded. The next year, if 25 per cent of investors decide to vote against the company again, a second strike is notched up. This second strike allows a vote on whether to spill all the positions from the board and elect new members. It's designed to keep companies accountable for how they incentivise their highest-ranking executives. If shareholders disagree with the path a company has taken, they are able to voice their concerns. It's a small, somewhat tokenistic power given to shareholders to help steer how their money is spent.

The laws were introduced in 2011, but it took until 2016 for them to be put to the test. And the victim of the first strike in Australian corporate history? The Commonwealth Bank of Australia.

It came during a harrowing year for the bank. The CommInsure scandal had blown up in its face and was the second major disaster for the nation's largest company after the financial planning revelations just two years earlier.

However, shareholders weren't so upset about these scandals. When 49 per cent of them voted against the bank's remuneration report in late 2016, it was, curiously, because the bank wasn't focused enough on its profits.

CBA wanted to introduce a new 'people and community' measure to determine 25 per cent of chief executive Ian Narev's long-term bonus. Another 25 per cent would be tied to measurements of customer satisfaction. The other 50 per cent would be based on total shareholder return, or the profits the company was delivering.

For a bank in the middle of a public relations disaster over how it was putting profits before its customers and the public, it was a head scratcher.

The shareholders weren't interested in the public. They were only concerned about their financial returns. 'We want to see the shareholders' interests being protected by the remuneration committee, and being focused on long-term monetary benefits for shareholders, as opposed to soft measures like diversity and culture,' Australian Shareholders' Association representative John Campbell told the bank at its annual general meeting as the shareholders registered the first strike.

Following the slapdown CBA reverted to its old scheme, under which 75 per cent of bonuses were tied to shareholder returns and just 25 per cent to measures of customer satisfaction. Shareholders' interests had won out.

The victory was short-lived, however. All it would take was a few more scandals for a royal commission to be called, which would cost shareholders dearly. Ironically, they should have been more concerned about the culture in the bank than its short-term profitability.

At the four largest banks, more than half of the $212 million their 150 top managers earned during the 2017 financial year was made up of bonuses. Much of this was tied to long-term and short-term profitability metrics, and that was the way shareholders wanted it to remain.

The problem was not just small retail shareholders, made up of mum-and-dad investors—it was institutional shareholders. These included some of the biggest financial institutions in the world, such as Blackrock, which managed more than $6 trillion in funds, and Vanguard, which had $5 trillion invested in companies across the world. Sovereign wealth funds, which hold untold fortunes, were also in on the act.

NAB chairman Ken Henry, a former Treasury secretary, lamented these shareholders' focus on financial incentives above all else. He told a business lunch in early 2018 that there was an 'insufficient appetite' for including any non-financial metrics as part of the incentive plan for executive remuneration. Financial institutions were forcing the banks to put financial performance before other concerns.

'A lot of investors in Australia are in a long journey,' Henry said. 'Many of them are very close to the starting line on that journey. It's not just frustrating for boards or other investors, it's also frustrating for regulators.'

Despite his exasperation, Henry's hands were not entirely clean.

In 2016, NAB's board gave senior executives their full bonuses even though board directors were unhappy about a rising tide of breaches that had seen the bank's compliance audits covered in red ink. During that year the board's risk committee had heard for the first time about the fees-for-no-service scandal discovered two years earlier by the bank's executives.

When it was finally time for Henry to sit in the witness box at the royal commission, it took a lot of effort to extract simple answers from him. Counsel assisting the commission Rowena Orr, QC, asked whether he thought if the bank had clamped down on executive pay earlier, 'issues might have been resolved earlier'.

'Yes, they might have,' Henry said. 'Yes, indeed.'

His admissions came only after lengthy questioning, and didn't reflect favourably on the former Treasury mandarin. He appeared both flippant and stubborn in the dock. This was a chairman who had been brought to explain how NAB had gone about trying to retain money it had stolen from customers in order for its profits to be larger, despite a long-running regulatory investigation.

When Orr asked if there was any better way to demonstrate to executives that their behaviour was wrong other than cutting their bonuses, Henry answered, 'Well, we could have fired everybody, I suppose.'

When Orr wondered whether the bank's engagement with ASIC over the fees-for-no-service issue was appropriate, Henry didn't want to hold a debate. 'We've been through them,' he said.

Orr said no, she didn't believe this was the case. 'You don't,' Henry said. 'No. No. You wouldn't.'

Then Orr wanted to know why the scandal hadn't been reported to the board in 2015, when the rest of the executives already knew.

'If you're saying should the chief risk officer have said, well there may have been a breach, OK, fine,' Henry said. 'Perhaps.'

For the wider public, it was their first uncut look at Henry, who many only knew as the man who had helped steer the country through the GFC. For others who had worked with him in Treasury, it was the man they were familiar with. A female barrister demanding answers from one of the most powerful men in Australia was a set-up designed to provoke a certain response out of him.

When Orr asked whether Henry should have stepped in and sorted out the scandal earlier, he appeared not to understand the gravitas of what he was being asked. 'I wish we had, let me put it that way. I wish we had—I still don't know,' he said.

This was a royal commission, and Orr demanded a proper answer. 'I would like you to answer my question, Dr Henry. Do you accept that the board should have stepped in earlier?' she asked.

'I have answered the question how I can answer the question,' he said.

'I'm sorry, is it a yes or a no, Dr Henry?'

'I've answered the question the way I choose to answer the question.'

'Well, I would like you to answer my question. Do you accept that the board should have stepped in earlier?'

'I wish we had.'

'I'm going to take that as a yes, Dr Henry?'

'Well, you take that as a yes, all right,' he said.

It seemed that if you were anointed into the small circle of directors who were privileged to sit atop one of the country's few financial behemoths, you believed yourself to be invincible. The pay appeared to be commensurate with immortality.

However, slowly but surely the royal commission revealed that there was nothing special about these corporate titans. They were fallible, just like everyone else.

As AMP head of advice Jack Regan walked onto the stand at the Federal Court, the company's chairman, Catherine Brenner, was half a world away. From her family's skiing holiday in Japan, she picked up her laptop and tuned into the proceedings.

It was mid-April in 2018, and the royal commission was in its early stages of public hearings. Until that point, Brenner had seemed unstoppable in climbing Sydney's corporate ladder, but on the laptop she witnessed the beginning of the events that would spell the end of her career.

Within twenty-four hours of Regan finishing up on the stand, Brenner was on a late-night flight from Tokyo back to Sydney. She was drawn back to face her own fate in the wake of the revelations that AMP had charged clients fees where no service had been given, and then had lied to the corporate regulator when ASIC began asking questions.

Brenner's fingerprints were on many aspects of the scandal. Days later, she would be forced out of the company, and from there, it was a slippery slope for her to be turfed out of her other board commitments. By September, she was gone from the boards of construction giant Boral and Coca-Cola Amatil. All her corporate boltholes were gone.

Brenner had been on the AMP board for eight years in a posting that had brought her into the top ranks of corporate Australia. The former investment banker had enjoyed a meteoric rise with some assistance from her mentor, ANZ chairman David Gonski. She was known as one of the FOGs, or Friends of Gonski. Gonski was also chairman of Coca-Cola, where Brenner would later end up on the board. She had grown close to Gonski when she was appointed to the government's Takeovers Panel, which ruled on corporate mergers.

At AMP, Brenner's ambition was such that it unnerved fellow board directors. The company had long been a perennial underperformer on the stock market. Indeed, its shares were a quarter of their value compared to where they had traded at the turn of the millennium. Under pressure from increasingly irritated shareholders, the company launched a review of its chairman, Simon McKeon. He hadn't been in the post long, and his credentials as the 2011 Australian of the Year—awarded for his charitable work and his stewardship of Monash University, where he was chancellor—didn't seem to earn him any kudos with a certain faction of his fellow board members. Indeed, Brenner was pressuring her fellow directors to install her as chairman, saying that only she could gear up the company to make more profits, more quickly.

When he became aware of the putsch, McKeon abruptly stepped aside as chairman just two years into the role. If he didn't have the support of his colleagues, he didn't want to stay. Brenner was appointed as chairman shortly after, but the promotion would sow the seeds of her demise.

Almost instantly, she went about pressuring the company to take short cuts in the pursuit of profits. She leaked to the media that some institutional shareholders had called for AMP chief executive Craig Meller to be sacked, saying that while she was happy with the group's current strategy, 'I just want to get Craig and his team to do it a little bit faster, if possible.'

The problem was that AMP didn't really have a strategy to earn money in any respectable fashion. Its financial advisers were a continual source of headaches, with dozens forced out of the industry by ASIC over the sale of dodgy advice. Its life insurance business was scandalous, with salespeople cancelling policies and signing customers up to the same product just to earn hefty bonuses in an illegal manoeuvre known as 'churning'. Its superannuation business was underperforming and only really existed to sell contracts to the other underperforming arms of the AMP conglomerate. Its funds management business was also lousy. Its products would not be recommended by any independent financial adviser because they were instruments used mainly to dupe customers into handing over as many fees as possible.

Any reasonable adviser inside AMP could see the writing on the wall. Soon, hundreds a year would be walking out the door for greener pastures at rival organisations.

When the royal commission published a series of documents outlining the negotiations senior board members were undertaking with ASIC as AMP misled the regulator over its fees-for-no-service scandal, it was clear Brenner would have to go. She tried to hold on. Gonski even reportedly counselled her to defend her position, which had grown to be seen as obviously untenable to anyone outside the circle of her company director friends.

The small pool of Australians chosen to sit at the top of company boards usually look after each other's backs. According to Bronte Capital founder John Hempton, a meticulous independent investor who helped blow the whistle on widespread fraud at US pharmaceuticals group Valean, the club of corporate directors is more like a cartel than a competitive group of experienced business leaders. With the major companies in Australia steered by just a handful of directors, the situation has become one of 'You scratch my back, I scratch yours', Hempton told an ASIC gathering in 2018. Directors on one board will argue for better remuneration, and other boards will follow by pushing up their executives' pay.

Famous American investor Warren Buffett uses the phrase 'ratchet, ratchet, bingo' for directors who sit on various remuneration committees and drive up one another's salaries. 'It's pretty obvious what's wrong with incestuousness. Incestuousness means the compensation goes up,' Hempton said. 'There are directors in this market on four or five boards taking home half a million dollars. Do you really think they want to rock the boat?'

Taking away bankers' pay is the only way to send a message that their behaviour is not right. Although CBA was slapped with a $700 million penalty for its anti-money-laundering breaches, the bank's chairman responsible for overseeing governance standards kept all of his pay.

Fines levied against companies are a roundabout way of targeting poor behaviour. More often than not, shareholders or customers are the ones who pay for the penalties. Meanwhile, taking money away from a bank only serves to reduce its regulatory capital, meaning taxpayers will be relied upon more heavily to rescue a lender if it gets into trouble.

Corporations cannot be sent to jail, although individuals can be. Individuals can have their money taken away from them. 'Referring to "banks", which are nothing but legal entities with a banking licence, as if they are real things is unhelpful,' wrote my colleague Adam Creighton. '"Banks" are collections of workers in buildings using computers to make and oversee contracts between borrowers and lenders that are enforced by the courts. If we want executives' behaviour to improve, penalties for poor behaviour need to fall on them.'

For Shayne Elliott, this was a bridge too far. In the dying days of the royal commission, he penned a note to Commissioner Hayne.

In the letter sent on 7 December, just a week before shareholders voted against ANZ's own bonus plan with a strike against its remuneration report, Elliott warned Hayne against a proposal that banks explain why they make cuts to executive salaries. 'It will often be difficult to articulate who is responsible for compliance and conduct issues where roles have changed over time, and to fairly represent the position in a communication about remuneration outcomes,' Elliott said. 'Executives may be less willing to take on senior roles in banks, particularly in divisions which are perceived to be at greater risk of compliance incidents.'

The banks had long argued that big pay packets were the only way to attract talent at their companies. They were operating in a global environment and wanted to attract the best executives from across the world. Big pay packets to lure bankers away from the US and Europe were a part of that deal.

However, the problems with banking scandals were not unique to Australia. Banks across the globe had failed to comply with the law. In a 2017 speech, Bank of England governor Mark Carney calculated penalties against banks across the globe since the GFC had hit US$320 billion. 'A series of scandals ranging from mis-selling to manipulation have undermined trust in banking, the financial system and, to some degree, markets themselves,' Carney said. The 'crisis of legitimacy' had left just 20 per cent of British voters believing their banks were well run, compared with 90 per cent in the late 1990s.

When CBA ousted Narev in the wake of the money-laundering scandal, it scoured the globe for a suitable replacement. In the end it settled on Comyn, the executive who was in charge of the division of CBA that had produced the most scandals. 'The easy answer for us would have been to appoint an external person,' Livingstone told the royal commission. 'To find an external person globally at that level who has not been involved in some regulatory event is almost impossible. And I don't mean that as a joke.'

AMP was also forced to look for a new chief executive when Meller was forced out after the fees-for-no-service scandal. Luckily for the company, it found a global candidate who agreed to come on board. But if AMP wanted to send a message about paying its executives the right incentives, it certainly had a strange strategy. The Asia-based Credit Suisse private investment banker Francesco De Ferrari signed on to the top job with almost $18 million in possible performance bonuses on top of a maximum $8.3 million annual salary. He would win $6 million worth of shares if he got the stock price higher than $5.25 by early 2023. To get over that hurdle would be a herculean task. De Ferrari would need to more than double the company's share price in just under four years. The pressure to engineer a heroic share price performance would be intense. It was a confusing move for a scandal-ridden company.

De Ferrari was appointed the new boss by AMP's new chairman, David Murray, who had replaced Brenner. Murray was himself a controversial figure. He had been chief executive of CBA for thirteen years, and was respected in the business community. He was also the inaugural chairman of the country's sovereign wealth fund, the Future Fund, and had steered the government's 2014 Financial System Inquiry.

Murray was also known for speaking his mind and shooting from the lip. In 2016 he took a swipe at ASIC's campaign to improve corporate culture in Australia, labelling it an 'absolutely impossible' idea. 'It's anti-competitive, it's inefficient, and to be perfectly candid there have been people in the world who have tried to enforce culture; Adolf Hitler comes to mind,' he said. He was forced to walk back his Hitler comments a day later, but remained steadfast in his opinion of the corporate watchdog.

Shortly after he was named AMP's new chairman, Murray gave a speech criticising former ASIC boss Greg Medcraft's six-year tenure. ASIC was 'an organisation not focused on its main job, which is to be the cop on the beat in the financial sector'. He was particularly scornful of Medcraft's enthusiasm for 'tracker mortgages', where loan rates followed movements in the Reserve Bank's cash rate. Medcraft saw the products, which are popular in many overseas jurisdictions, as a way to help restore trust in the banking sector. They would do away with the problem of banks copping flak for withholding the RBA rate cut and failing to pass on the savings to customers.

'The chairman decided to tell the industry it should have tracker mortgages,' Murray said. 'If I was at the Reserve Bank, I'd say "Excuse me, keep out of monetary transmission". If I was at APRA, I would say "Keep out of credit".'

It was clear what Murray thought of the regulators. Plus, by the time of his appointment, AMP was being circled by ASIC for potential criminal prosecution over its lies to the regulator during the fees-for-no-service blitz.

It was hefty language for a chairman supposedly responsible for rebuilding the company's shredded reputation, let alone one negotiating with the regulator over an impending court case. But AMP wasn't going to simply roll over.

In December 2018, ASIC launched legal action against AMP to force the company to hand over documents related to the fees-for-no-service scandal that the company was claiming were covered by legal professional privilege. These documents went to the heart of exactly what the company's most senior-ranking executives knew about the scandal, and what they had told Clayton Utz, the independent firm that had been tasked with providing a report on it to ASIC. That report had been doctored beyond recognition by AMP.

Why wouldn't AMP hand over the documents? After all, most of the executives involved in the scandal had been forced out of the business already—there was no one left to protect. One company source said AMP did not want to make the documents public because after the scandal broke and the company's share price was smashed to smithereens, five separate class actions had been lodged against AMP. If the documents were made available, there was every certainty it would lose the class actions. Not only would it be humiliating, it would likely affect the bonuses to be paid to the executives who were left.

There's another Warren Buffett line he likes to tell his followers: 'You only find out who is swimming naked when the tide goes out.' AMP had a large financial interest in keeping its misbehaviour as opaque as possible. Transparency would cost it dearly.

13

LAST GUNSLINGERS IN TOWN

Every day when Westpac interest rate trader Colin Roden went to work, his job in the bank's treasury department was simple enough. He managed the company's interest-rate exposure to domestic and macro-economic risks with its bank bill holdings.

It sounds tricky, but essentially the job involved sitting in front of a computer screen and attempting to make numbers go up and down during a very specific time of day.

In Australia, billions of dollars' worth of business and home loans each year have their price set according to the bank bill swap rate (BBSW rate). It's a key interest-rate benchmark designed to reflect the demand for bank bills, which are debt instruments traded between the lenders.

In the Australian bank bill market, billions of dollars changed hands every day, mostly during a ten-minute auction just before 10 a.m. Following the trading period, financial companies across Australia would have a reference rate to price a range of financial instruments.

Each day, Roden would ensure Westpac's holdings of bank bills weren't leaving the bank open to having too much expensive debt to repay, and that it wasn't going to be caught wrongfooted if interest rates went the opposite way to what the bank expected.

Because of his fine work balancing Westpac's exposure to the BBSW rate, Roden was handsomely rewarded to the tune of millions of dollars in bonuses. He was one of the highest-paid bankers at the company.

The bonuses were not handed out recklessly. Roden single-handedly brought in close to $1 billion in extra revenue for the bank in a period of just a few years. All seemed to be going well, according to his glowing annual performance assessments.

That was until 2016, when ASIC started chasing the big four banks over alleged rigging of the BBSW rate. In a series of sensational lawsuits, it achieved penalties collectively totalling $120 million from Commonwealth Bank, NAB and ANZ over claims that star traders in the banks' market divisions were continually manipulating the BBSW rate. Westpac was the only major bank not to settle the claims outside of court.

Because Westpac had chosen not to settle, the Federal Court case—which ran separately but concurrently with the royal commission—gave the public an inside look into one of the most intense parts of one of the world's biggest banks. What was revealed was not at all edifying, but it was certainly colourful.

Court documents revealed reams of instant-messaging chat records between traders across the major banks. Each trader had an adopted personality and nickname. There was Col 'The Rat' Roden and his colleague Sophie 'The Perfumed Steamroller' Johnston, Daniel 'The Bench' Park and Patrick 'The Sheriff' Stokes. CBA traders included Garfield 'Bad Kitty' Lee and Mark 'The Powerful Owl' Hulme, the latter nicknamed as such because he had a propensity for swooping on the market.

These traders were exchanging hundreds of millions or billions of dollars in bank bills each day. Because of the huge sums of money the financial instruments were worth, the traders could make huge profits or losses for their respective treasury departments.

While 'managing financial and economic risk' was ostensibly the job description of these traders, the role appeared to be something else entirely, according to ASIC's investigation. They would either flood the market during the ten-minute window, dumping bank bills onto the trading floor in a bid to push the BBSW rate down, or they would withhold bank bills and buy up instruments in a bid to artificially constrain supply, lifting the interest-rate benchmark.

It grew to be known as 'fucking' the rate set. Indeed, Justice Jonathan Beach was forced to spend quite some time getting his head around what economic role was exactly being fulfilled by the traders who wanted to 'fuck' the rate set. Philip Crutchfield, QC, the lawyer arguing on behalf of ASIC, argued that the word 'in this context' meant to manipulate the BBSW rate. 'And Mr Roden used it a number of times,' he said.

Indeed, it was a regular part of Roden's vocabulary. One day, he told a colleague he was 'going to fuck the rate set'. In another conversation, he appeared to regret fucking the rate set. 'I knew it was completely wrong but fuck it I may as well, I thought fuck it. We've got so much money on it, we just had to do it, right,' he said.

Justice Beach's job was to decide whether Westpac had rigged the interest rate, but the transcripts threw more confusion on exactly what the bankers were doing with it. 'Clearly, the fuck word and its derivatives are not terms of art in the finance industry,' Beach wrote in his deliberations. 'Nevertheless, their use in otherwise polite conversation appears to have been well understood by the colourful interlocutors. It has been used as both a transitive and intransitive verb. It has been used in an active sense and a passive sense. It has been used in the past tense and the future tense. It has been used as an adjective. It has been used as a noun including as a verbal noun. Someone even tried to use it as an adverb.'

The job of these traders was thoroughly detached from reality. They appeared to be sitting around forcing a set of numbers to increase or decrease each day, so it was little wonder the language they employed was in its own fantasy world.

Westpac's traders regularly discussed the BBSW rate and the vast quantities of money that were at stake. After one big day of trading in

April 2010, Roden was waiting on the Reserve Bank's monthly decision on interest rates to learn whether he'd made the right bet. 'We'll find out very shortly whether or not we win the lottery,' he told Johnston down the line to the London desk. The RBA didn't move the cash rate, and Roden was elated. 'We made about 12 million bucks today … that's what you'd call a good day,' the Rat told the Perfumed Steamroller.

The good news followed a 'massive rate set' that had seen him buy $2.5 billion worth of bank bills from other banks. NAB were 'scum' and 'deadshits'. As for Goldman Sachs, 'I hate those fuckers as well,' Roden said.

Suitably, the traders' remuneration was also detached from reality. Because of the huge sums of cash involved, minor adjustments in the BBSW rate had the ability to massively affect profits. Remuneration for the traders was also at stake depending on how they performed. In one of the transcripts (internal logs of computer messaging systems and phone calls made by and between traders), the wife of a CBA chief dealer of interest-rate swaps, Grant 'Barnsey' Barnes, told their children 'Daddy's very sad'. Barnes had just told her he had lost out on a big bonus because ANZ and Westpac traders had rigged the BBSW rate out of his control. He told his wife it 'just gets worse' and he was 'down a mil'. 'Oh, another mil, two days in a row,' his wife responded.

Barnes told her he had 'lost a massive chunk of my position at rate set the last couple of days and usually that's when I make all my money. ANZ are just basically manipulating the market at rate set time. There's nothing I can do about it. They'll probably end up getting in trouble with ASIC at some point. But at the moment they're not, so I just wear the pain on the other side.'

The couple agreed they couldn't 'be banking on any bonus' in September and that would affect the renovations they were planning on their house. 'But that's all right, this may be what we need to just make us focus on ensuring that we don't go crazy on this reno,' Barnes's better half said.

London School of Economics anthropologist David Graeber shot to fame in 2013 by describing the phenomenon of 'bullshit jobs' in rich countries. 'Huge swathes of people in Europe and North America spend their entire working lives performing tasks they secretly believe do not really need to be performed. The moral and spiritual damage that comes from this situation is profound,' he wrote.

In Australia, the financial services sector had grown to be either the biggest or second-biggest contributor to the economy by 2018, depending on the measurement used. You would think this was due to the underlying demand for services by Australia's population, but it wasn't. A large degree of the growth was attributable to the immense amount of revenue it was dragging in, often not through an increase in the number of products on sale—although this did expand significantly—but through the entrenched monopolisation of services.

With a lack of competition between financial services providers to drive the price of products lower, banks and wealth managers ratcheted the cost of services higher and higher. By 2018, about $1 in every $10 being spent in the Australian economy was captured by the financial sector. That's double what it was in the 1970s.

With rivers of gold flowing into company coffers, banks employed an unusually large number of workers to engage in increasingly obscure and unnecessary work. Paying lots of money to rig a key interest-rate benchmark is just one example.

A study released in early 2019 by *Industrial Relations: A Journal of Economy and Society* found that nearly one in ten workers think their job is socially useless. The survey of 100,000 workers also found that people in the private sector are far more likely than those in the public sector to believe their job serves no valuable purpose: 11 per cent versus 3 per cent.

Graeber wrote that areas such as financial services and consulting were rife with employees turning up to work only to earn money, with no higher purpose. 'Say what you like about nurses, garbage collectors or mechanics, it's obvious that were they to vanish in a puff of smoke, the results would be immediate and catastrophic,' Graeber said.

The banking royal commission revealed how Australia's banks, wealth managers and superannuation funds were looting as much out of their customers as possible, but with so little in the way of purpose for banking employees, it also showed how companies plied their workforce to do the companies' bidding. With little meaning in their everyday work, employees—from top-ranking executives to lowly front-line staff—had to be incentivised to keep the racket going.

Because it worked so well, the companies were not going to give up their rewards easily.

In the early 1990s, John Symond introduced the country to mortgage broking, bringing much-needed competition to Australia's banking sector. Aussie John, as he came to be known, helped break the strangle-hold of the major banks on the price of home loans by forcing lenders to compete for customers. His catchphrase, 'At Aussie, we'll save you', was more or less true.

For a time, at least. Over the next two decades, the use of mortgage brokers exploded. By 2018, one in every two loans being written by a bank came through a mortgage broker rather than through its own branches.

However, as brokers grew in size, so did the benefits they attempted to squeeze out of customers. When Productivity Commission chairman Peter Harris began investigating the financial sector, he found that some brokers were earning a $6000 trailing commission for an average home loan of about $350,000. The kickbacks created 'perverse incentives' for brokers to prevent borrowers from switching banks into a better deal. They also meant that if a broker sold just one loan a week, he or she could take home a salary of about $250,000 for doing a job that a comparison website could do.

Harris said the trailing commissions offered 'no evident link to customer best interests' and should be banned from the mortgage broking industry. This would threaten nearly $3 billion in kickbacks earned by brokers each year. Under the scheme, brokers were receiving an average upfront commission from banks equal to about

0.6 per cent of the value of a loan, and a trailing commission of just under 0.2 per cent of the outstanding value of the loan each year. To get bigger bonuses, brokers shunted borrowers into larger and larger loans in a bid for bigger and bigger commissions. The kickbacks added about $4600 to the cost of the average home loan for a customer as some of the other money would be paid by the bank, according to UBS estimates.

Meanwhile, mortgage brokers were enjoying the spoils of their victory over consumers. Mark Bouris, who owns one of the largest broking networks in Australia, Yellow Brick Road, gave an insight into the party being enjoyed by brokers when he told Commissioner Hayne his response to the inquiry's initial request for information was incomplete 'owing to the interruptions caused by the festive season'.

Not only was the broking industry hooked on trailing commissions, it was also lush with soft-dollar bonuses that included prizes such as entertainment, cruises, trips and other non-cash rewards for selling mortgages.

It wasn't just brokers who were in on the home loan bonus drip feed. People called 'introducers', who could be anyone from a teacher to a gym owner, were paid huge sums to recommend customers to a bank. When NAB found a fraud ring of bribe-taking bank managers and other employees in western Sydney, a subsequent review discovered that its remuneration structures were driving the bankers to write hundreds of millions of dollars in dodgy home loans. While introducers, who received a commission of up to 0.6 per cent of the loan, were supposed to come from the ranks of professions including financial planners and lawyers, the royal commission heard that those involved in the western Sydney scam included a gym owner and a tailor. NAB's review of the fraud ring found that bankers were also 'double-dipping' on bonuses by duplicating and postdating deals.

Outside the mortgage sector, other financial industries were rife with prizes and bonuses to reward employees for meaningless work. The life insurance sector was paying hefty bonuses to financial advisers who did very little in the way of advising.

While new laws had sought to clamp down on the amounts life insurers could pay in upfront and trail commissions—in 2018 it was 80 per cent for upfront commissions, falling to 60 per cent over the following two years—more than $6 billion in these commissions had been paid by just a handful of the country's largest institutions over the five years to 2018. Westpac, which allowed its financial advisers to sell only its own BT Financial–branded products, paid out $640 million on commissions. This money was paid to its financial advisers for advising customers to buy the only product on their approved product list. Suncorp, which like Westpac only gave advisers its own policies to sell, paid out $590 million in commissions.

Front-line sales staff were also handsomely rewarded. As outlined in Chapter 8, the royal commission heard how sales staff at Sydney-based life insurer Select AFSL pushed funeral insurance policies onto thousands of Aboriginal customers using non-financial rewards to encourage their call centre operators to sell as many products as possible. According to the recorded sales calls played to the commission, staff were generally, if not exclusively, British backpackers on working holidays. The punishment of socially hollow work was offset by the prospect of prizes to help energise the backpackers, who had little reason to care if customers wanted the product, understood the product or said no to buying the product. A paid trip to Las Vegas was on offer to the backpacker who sold the most policies. Under its points-based demerit system, Select AFSL sales agents could engage in two unethical sales, or two instances of illegally providing personal advice, every six weeks without being sacked, as demerit points were reinstated at the end of the six-week period. Employees were told it was 'every salesman for themselves' when competing for a $6000 Vespa scooter, a cruise on the *Pacific Pearl* to the Sunshine Coast with a $75 daily drinks package, and a paid trip to Las Vegas with a $500 cash card.

During the royal commission it was revealed that Bank of Queensland's franchise bosses did not receive any salary from the company and were rewarded only with income based on commissions.

On top of this, bankers were offered annual prizes such as a BMW, travel vouchers and a waiving of the IT fee the bank charged its franchisees if they sold as many loans as possible. As described in Chapter 7, a champion regional bank manager at Commonwealth Bank subsidiary Bankwest whose target-beating lending won him a trip to Hayman Island later left the company after he was found to have allegedly overvalued loans and fudged figures.

Top executives at the major banks also had their beds feathered with special treatment. Even though they were raking in some of the largest salaries in Australia, that wasn't enough to sate them.

In April 2018, Strike Force Napthali, established by NSW State Crime Command's Financial Crimes Squad, raided several buildings in connection with an alleged kickback scheme that penetrated the highest ranks of NAB. At the centre of the scheme was a curious company called the Human Group, which had been providing 'executive services and event management logistics' to NAB for about a decade.

NAB chief executive Andrew Thorburn's long-serving chief of staff and closest confidante, Rosemary Rogers, was connected to the suspected fraud. She resigned after a whistleblower complaint was lodged about a corporate fraud arrangement that was siphoning millions of dollars out of the bank. It involved receiving commissions in return for NAB rubber-stamping inflated invoices sent by the Human Group.

It was hard to know exactly what the Human Group actually did. The company was largely obscure or unheard-of to the rest of corporate Australia, but it developed close relationships with senior leaders of NAB. The Human Group boss Helen Rosamond helped run NAB's so-called Enterprise Leader Program, which provided training for the bank's top 200 executives. It ran the sort of corporate spirituality retreats that might seem more at home in Silicon Valley than in Sydney, but the financial services industry was increasingly looking towards such services. This sort of corporate cultural trend has seen high demand in Australia for 'thought leadership' and 'chief imagination officers' despite little evidence of the value of such jobs or requirements.

The Human Group organised getaways for executives in regional NSW, leadership meetings in San Francisco, and the hiring of helicopters and other arrangements. On its website, it listed Qantas and UNICEF Australia as corporate partners, but Qantas had never used services provided by the group and the logo used on the group's website was the airline's logo from the 1980s. The trips—which cost the bank on average over $10 million a year—included numerous first-class getaways, including a trip to Dubai where executives were flown first class from Australia and then helicoptered into a desert oasis for a 'corporate retreat.'

Thorburn was drawn into the debacle after it turned out he had taken a luxury holiday to a private island in Fiji, to a resort that was owned by Red Bull co-founder Dietrich Mateschitz and only accessible by private jet. That trip came with the gift of a Thermomix, an expensive household appliance, and it was all allegedly organised by the Human Group.

If you were in the financial services industry, you were going to be looked after. The rewards and remuneration kept you believing that no matter how banal the work might be, you had the power of alchemy.

If the bankers were rewarded so handsomely for their deeds, perhaps it made them believe in what they were doing. But as soon as the royal commission began asking questions, it was clear the bankers lacked the answers to justify their behaviour.

When Commonwealth Bank private wealth division executive Marianne Perkovic was put in the dock to answer questions about charging fees where no service had been delivered, she demurred, to say the least. She had to be asked the same question a dozen times by counsel assisting the commission Michael Hodge before she gave a proper answer to it.

'Is the reason why you are dissembling in the way that you are dissembling because you are trying to pre-emptively explain why it took more than two years to notify ASIC of this breach?' Hodge asked Perkovic.

True to form, she dissembled through her response, saying, 'I'm trying to, yes, I'm trying to, um, sorry, I'm just trying to explain to you, in this two-year period before we actually identified that we actually had a problem with ongoing service fees, as to what we were solving for with the information that was in front of us in a broader context of the business.'

'Ms Perkovic, I do not regard that as answering counsel's question,' Commissioner Hayne said. 'Please ask the question again. I want you to listen to it and I want you to answer it as directly as you can.'

All Perkovic could muster when the question was repeated was another long-winded non-answer.

'The answer to my question is "yes", isn't it?' Hodge said.

'Yes,' Perkovic finally agreed.

The banks wanted everything to seem as complicated as possible to cover up the fact that they were not doing much for their customers. To illustrate this, Thorburn climbed on to the stand at the royal commission and, with his job on the line after a series of scandals, expounded on the virtues of the bank's overarching goals. These included its 'purpose' and 'vision', which were meant to be distinct from each other—apparently, a purpose should be for fifty years and a vision should be for five years.

Hodge was confused. 'The bank must have always had a vision and a purpose?' he asked.

'Well, in the last two years the purpose and vision have been—We never had a purpose,' Thorburn said. 'Our chairman and myself led that work inside the company to work out what is our purpose. And I think it was very thorough and very disciplined. We went back and looked at a lot of artefacts and there have even been books written about the bank and why we existed. So we've got to go right back to where we are at our best. So the purpose was new. It was approved two years ago. The vision was renewed this year.'

'It sounds so complicated when you say it, but you're a bank,' Hodge said. 'Presumably your purpose is to be a bank?'

'Well, yes, but,' Thorburn stuttered, 'yes, but you need—what is a bank and what does it do?'

Hodge quipped: 'It seems like, as a bank, your purpose would be to take deposits and lend money and to do that as well as you could. Is that oversimplifying what you should be doing?'

Thorburn agreed. 'I think that's the functional activities of a bank.'

It was a revealing piece of dialogue between the commission and the NAB chief. NAB had put a lot of effort into telling its customers it was different. In 2011, it had spent millions telling Australians it was 'breaking up' with the other major banks. It was of some surprise, then, just a few years later in 2016 to hear NAB's spin doctors trying to keep the bank as 'just one in the pack' when it came to the company's fees-for-no-service scandal.

Two years later and the bank was still stalling on remediating customers, if the protracted testimony of NAB executives Paul Carter, Nicole Smith and Andrew Hagger at the royal commission was anything to go by. Despite having to repay about $100 million in fees charged to its superannuation customers where no service had been given, the executives drew the ire of Hayne for bloviating rather than providing direct answers to questions.

All this was coming from a bank that boasted of being 'customer-centric'.

During the time NAB had been dealing with ASIC over charging fees for no service, the bank had been preoccupied with maintaining its reputation and overhauling its public image. In August 2016, two months before it spent mountains of effort plotting to massage its compensation figures due to be published by ASIC, it was also busy touching up its executive ranks. 'Personal Banking' was renamed 'Consumer Banking' and Hagger had his role changed from 'Executive, Wealth' to 'Chief Customer Officer' of the retail division. NAB appointed two other 'Chief Customer Officers' to its business and corporate divisions.

When Hagger was forced to account for the bank's habit of charging fees for no service, he said it was not the chief customer officer's role to ensure that services had been delivered for its customers. 'We had a fundamental belief, which I still hold today, that customers tend to know whether service has been provided or not,' he said.

While NAB was busy attempting to discover exactly what a bank should be doing, the financial services industry had a strong network of lobbyists working to convince politicians and the public that they were acting in the best interests of society. The Financial Services Council is the peak lobbying and policy development body for the life insurance, for-profit superannuation and wealth management sectors, and has a very visible presence in Australia's financial regulation debate. It had spearheaded a campaign against the introduction of Labor's FOFA reforms, and then worked to undermine them once they were passed into law. The wealth management sector was pouring millions into the FSC to put an arms-length face on convincing the public that harmful practices were vital to consumers.

When FSC chief executive Sally Loane was put on the stand in September 2018, it became clear that the lobby group wasn't just representing the worst habits of the sector, it didn't appear to understand the implications of the positions it was putting forward. Loane's lack of knowledge of the FSC's own flagship life insurance code of conduct, and the insurance law that underpinned the regulations it was fighting against, was revealed in an uncomfortable few hours of examination at the royal commission. A former newsreader turned corporate relations professional who collected hundreds of thousands of dollars for her work at the FSC, she was unable to explain the lobby group's own position on a section of the Insurance Contracts Act that allowed insurers to reject a claim for unintended non-disclosure by customers. Taken to the FSC's endorsement of changes to the law in 2013 by counsel assisting the commission Rowena Orr, and asked what the FSC's current position was, Loane said, 'Look, I'm sorry, I don't have the up-to-date detail of when we said that and what we think now.'

Orr asked, 'And you don't have a current position on that yourself?'

'Not myself, no,' Loane replied. 'I don't know the detail of that but I can certainly provide that detail to you.'

Loane was also asked about the lobby group's position on 'fishing'—a practice where life insurers trawl through medical records of customers to find information that could be used to deny a claim. Evidence before a parliamentary committee had found entire medical records had been handed over by doctors. Despite the FSC's position being attached to her witness statement, Loane was unable to answer the question.

'Do you know what reference to "no fishing" is?' Orr asked.

'No I don't. This was put together by a member of my staff who is, his entire job is to deal with the code,' Loane said. 'I've been trying to spend every minute with him to understand the detail of his work.'

'Are you unable to explain this document that you've annexed to your statement?' Orr asked.

'I'm sorry that I have neglected and not understood this particular detail,' Loane responded.

Orr was also unable to get the FSC's position on reforms in the UK that seek to limit insurers' ability to knock back claims with non-disclosure of information when the customer has acted in good faith. 'I want to put it to you but I expect you'll be unable to answer. Are you aware of that?' Orr asked.

'No I'm not,' Loane said.

'Does the FSC have any view?' Orr asked.

'I don't have a view on that. I am unaware but I can certainly find out,' Loane said.

Again, Loane was unable to explain the purpose of the $6 billion in commissions the life insurance industry had paid to financial advisers over the previous five years. The industry had fought tooth and nail to keep the lucrative commissions, but under examination Loane could not explain what benefit the payments were actually delivering to customers. 'I really couldn't say with certainty,' she explained. 'These are commissions paid to advisers for essentially selling their products.'

Orr put it to Loane that 'the whole point of paying commissions to financial advisers is to influence the advice they give'.

'It would certainly mean they are paying for their products to be sold, yes,' Loane responded.

The FSC under the leadership of Loane had been an intensely vocal critic of any move to establish a royal commission. Countless times, she had argued that a royal commission would only undermine faith in what was one of Australia's most important industries.

In reality, the royal commission showed the financial industry for what it was. At nearly 10 per cent of the country's gross domestic product, the financial sector had become bloated. It was a bubble inflated by useless fees, harmful kickbacks and commissions, and sustained by a lobbying network that at every point tried to keep the grift going.

When the government in 2018 introduced new laws seeking to ensure financial advisers had minimum education requirements such as a bachelor's degree, the industry claimed such laws would destroy the sector. Nearly half of Australia's 25,000-strong workforce of financial advisers would be expected to leave the industry because of the new 'professionalisation' standards.

This is what it had come to. When greater professionalism in the industry was demanded, workers saw it was easier just to leave the job. The jig was up. There was no reason to stay in the job when the bonuses dried up. Employees raking in untold fortunes by swindling customers with meaningless products was not going to be situation normal anymore.

If the industry shrinks, then the only thing that is evident is that it was too bloated to begin with. The only thing the royal commission undermined was the industry's claim that what it was doing was in the best interests of the customer. It had been working for itself, and itself alone, all along.

14

THE WATCHDOGS THAT DIDN'T BARK

Royal commissions tend to go places that no one expects.

In 1980, Australian prime minister Malcolm Fraser established a royal commission into the Federated Ship Painters and Dockers Union, a notoriously criminal outfit that controlled the country's ports. They held sway over nearly everything that came in and out of Australia. This was enough to irk the government, but many members of the union, including at its highest ranks, were also engaged in a wide array of criminal activities.

The Liberal government of the day was encouraged to launch the royal commission after a number of media reports detailed serious misconduct by members of the union. In 1981, during the Costigan royal commission, all eleven Painters and Dockers officials in Victoria had criminal records (with an average of twenty-three convictions each) and nine had served prison sentences.

Its own members were not beyond the reproach of the union. Victorian secretary Jack 'Puttynose' Nicholls was found dead in his car with a suicide note nearby on the day he was meant to appear before the royal commission to answer allegations that he'd been involved in the murder of his predecessor, Pat Shannon, in 1973. According to one of Puttynose's mates, the secretary was about as likely to commit suicide as he was to take ballet lessons.

Headed by Frank Costigan, QC, the royal commission soon uncovered gross amounts of social security fraud, compensation fraud, theft, extortion, the handling of massive importations of drugs and shipments of armaments, and all manner of violence and murder. Despite the public outcry for action against members of the Dockers, many of whom went around Melbourne with impunity as they killed and stole, the commission was decried as a politically motivated witch-hunt by Labor and the union movement.

It was easy to see how it was painted as a show trial. The Liberals had a longstanding battle with the union movement. Constant airings of violent dealings in the Dockers would probably serve to secure Fraser a re-election, based on pledges to clamp down on union intransigence.

But not everything went according to plan. It's why there's an adage that you should never hold a royal commission unless you already know the outcome.

Costigan began to uncover corporate Australia's biggest little secret, and Fraser was caught off guard. Along the course of its investigation, the royal commission stumbled upon one of the most infamous tax scams in Australian history. There was a widespread practice of asset-stripping of companies to avoid tax liabilities, and it was facilitated by members of the Painters and Dockers Union. Thanks to the Dockers' reputation for criminal bastardry, wealthy businessmen outside the union stooped to harness the unionists' criminal prowess to achieve their own questionable ends.

The tax scandal was known as the 'bottom of the harbour' schemes because some tax records were thrown into Sydney Harbour to be destroyed, and it brushed up on some of the governing Liberal Party's nearest and dearest supporters. In a rort that stretched back decades, about $3 billion was estimated to have been stripped from government revenue each year thanks to the tax avoidance scheme—a cost of about $600 for every working Australian, in 1980s prices.

The trick was that before a company's tax fell due, the group would be stripped of all its belongings and profits and then transferred to the directorship of a person who had little interest in its past dealings.

In many cases, this person was a member of the Dockers Union, who would collect a fee along the way for his part in the scam. The company would then be bankrupted and sunk to the metaphorical bottom of the harbour, out of the reach of the Australian Taxation Office. One man identified by the commission had been named a director of 2000 companies.

While Fraser had hoped to shut down a rogue element of the union movement in an exercise that would hopefully ricochet across to a few prominent Labor politicians, the tax dodge became the centrepiece of the royal commission.

The Spectator wrote in 1983 that in the context of the tax scheme, the Painters and Dockers were 'far too thick' to understand what was going on and began to look like innocent bystanders. 'Trade unions may be corrupt, but only amongst themselves,' the magazine wrote.

Meanwhile, the Liberals started becoming the victims of their own inquiry. The tax schemes were employed by some very powerful corporate Australians, many of whom were connected to the party. More importantly, they were among the Liberal Party's biggest donors. Media mogul Kerry Packer, whose own magazine *The Bulletin* had been instrumental in forcing the Costigan royal commission, was even enmeshed in the scandal.

Under pressure over the tax avoidance revelations, Fraser's government, through its treasurer, John Howard, was forced to introduce retrospective legislation ending the rort. Some in the party never forgave Fraser. Then, when Labor leader Bob Hawke came to power, he shut down the royal commission before it finished its inquiry.

The whole endeavour serves as a reminder to governments that if they start to ask tough questions, they might not like the answers they get.

After months of ugly revelations at Kenneth Hayne's royal commission, the chairman of the banking regulator made an unusual interjection into the debate about standards in the financial industry.

At a Sydney business luncheon in July 2018, APRA chairman Wayne Byres gave an address ostensibly to declare that APRA's mission of shoring up standards in the $1.7 trillion mortgage sector had been accomplished. This was a curious enough claim, but it was just the pretext for a secondary, more curious spiel.

Byres went on to tell the crowd that it was about time consumers took more responsibility for themselves when engaging with a financial company. 'It is important that the concept of caveat emptor remains in the system,' he said. Caveat emptor is Latin for 'buyer beware'.

'Regulators cannot be everywhere overseeing everything. It is important the community understands that,' Byres said.

He was right. Regulators could not be everywhere. But his comments, though lauded by the *Financial Review* as a 'timely reminder' of the financial industry's reticence to be held responsible for its own failings, were met with reservation by the industry Byres was meant to be policing.

A few days after the comments were made, Westpac chief executive Brian Hartzer told a luncheon that the concept of caveat emptor did not absolve banks from selling dubious products. Indeed, Westpac had been slowly culling the products it had found to be directly in contravention of good customer outcomes. By July 2018 it had reviewed 320 products and made over 150 changes, cutting the number of products on sale by more than half.

'Almost all financial services products involve an element of risk,' Hartzer said. 'When you buy a term deposit, when you buy a share in a company, when you buy a bond, you are taking on some risk. If you inadvertently end up in a situation where nobody can ever take a loss, that will dramatically end up changing the economics for everyone. It is a topic that deserves to be highlighted. At the same time, we absolutely agree that we should not lend money to people who clearly can't afford it. We should not put people into investments that are unsuitable.'

While the main thrust of Byres' argument was correct—of course APRA was not an all-seeing, all-powerful regulator—it missed the point. The problem wasn't that APRA wasn't across every instance of misconduct all the time: the truth was that the regulators were often nowhere to be found at all.

In his interim report handed down just a month after Byres' comments, Commissioner Hayne made it clear who was responsible for failing to punish much of the misconduct unearthed by the inquiry. 'When misconduct was revealed, it either went unpunished or the consequences did not meet the seriousness of what had been done,' he said. 'The conduct regulator, ASIC, rarely went to court to seek public denunciation of and punishment for misconduct. The prudential regulator, APRA, never went to court.'

Nowhere was this absence of court action more evident than in the $2.7 trillion superannuation sector.

In March 2014, APRA had been given a stunning breach notice by Commonwealth Bank's superannuation arm, Colonial First State. While it had been aware of changes in the law requiring it to create low-fee MySuper accounts to handle the savings of its least engaged members as early as 2011, CBA had failed to make the proper arrangements by the deadline and had pushed 13,000 customers into its high-fee legacy products. The bank later discovered the number was actually 15,000. Each one was a criminal offence. (See Chapter 10 for a detailed examination of this.)

APRA had all the evidence it needed to take the bank to court, get remediation for customers, and send a message to the rest of the industry that this type of behaviour would not be tolerated. But that was not what happened. APRA didn't even demand that the customers be transferred immediately to the low-fee fund. Instead, the regulator oversaw a process that allowed members to be transferred over more than three years, during which time Colonial continuously broke the law. Call centre transcripts, which showed how customers were misled into choosing the high-fee fund, were even reviewed by APRA, but the regulator gave CBA the tick of approval. It asked the bank to appoint an independent consultancy to review the process of transferring the members, and after twenty-four updates from Ernst & Young on the remediation, the breaches of the law ended three years later, in September 2017. On that date, APRA officer Nick Johns emailed Colonial thanking it for sending a copy of Ernst & Young's report. 'We have no further queries and consider this item closed,' APRA said.

Colonial boss Linda Elkins admitted to the royal commission that the call centre communications with customers were misleading, but APRA didn't seem to care. Brought into the witness box at the Federal Court, APRA's head of superannuation, Helen Rowell, refused to admit the communications were misleading, saying, 'I think … more complete communication to the members would have been desirable.'

Taken to another misleading call centre script, she said it did not 'provide complete information to the member to enable them to make their choice or decision'. Michael Hodge, QC, asked if that was an acceptable outcome from APRA's perspective. 'It's not desirable,' Rowell said.

'It's not desirable? Surely it's unacceptable from a regulator's perspective?' Hodge shot back.

'It would be preferable if there was a complete disclosure to the members,' Rowell said.

It wasn't just CBA that got off lightly. APRA was aware of other, smaller breaches of the same law requiring members to be moved to low-fee MySuper funds, but never prosecuted any company for the crime. In fact, there was a whole range of poor behaviour in the super sector that APRA never sought to clamp down on. It was as if the companies were the prisoners in the scene towards the end of *Monty Python's Life of Brian* when they are lined up before they are marched off to be crucified.

As each prisoner comes forward under instruction from the guard, they are asked whether they are there for crucifixion, to which they dutifully reply that they are. Good, responds the prison guard, who then sends them out the door, to their left, to collect one cross each.

That is until one responds, with a straight face, that he's not there for crucifixion but to be set free. He says he's been told he hasn't done anything wrong and can live on an island somewhere. The guard is momentarily confused, but tells him, 'Jolly good, and off you go.' The prisoner laughs and confesses he is only pulling the guard's leg and he actually is there to be crucified, and he is sent out the door to his left to collect his cross like the other prisoners.

APRA seemed a bit like the guard who was fooled by the straight-faced prisoner. Even when super funds told APRA they were guilty of the crimes, it let them go free. Even when APRA was aware of poor behaviour in the superannuation sector it wanted to end, funds simply ignored the regulator. And when super funds dismissed APRA's concerns, it did nothing to clamp down on the intransigence.

A year before the royal commission began, APRA had created a hit list of about twenty-eight funds that had underperformed across most or all of a range of different metrics. They were charging high expenses and high life insurance fees, reporting poor investment returns, and suffering large levels of outflows of cash or churning of member numbers. While about two-thirds of the funds subsequently engaged by APRA either worked to address the issues or struck up deals to merge with better funds, the remaining third refused to take on any of the regulator's demands and dug in their heels.

The original hit list included bank-owned for-profit funds, not-for-profit funds and both public and non-public funds. When those funds refused to engage with APRA, the regulator didn't take any further steps.

One industry fund, First Super, even launched a public campaign defending its position as it faced pressure from APRA to merge. The $3 billion fund generated very good investment returns but its membership, which included 64,000 workers in timber, pulp and paper, furniture and joinery businesses, was ageing and employed in dying industries. As its membership dwindled, sooner or later First Super would be hit with ever-increasing costs to perform the same duties.

'The big funds, some regulators and some media commentators would like Australians to believe that only funds over a certain size can possibly compete in the market,' First Super chief executive Bill Watson said as he celebrated small super funds in the wake of the royal commission's examination of the sector in August 2018. Feeling emboldened by the failure of the commission to damage the industry fund sector, First Super took the moment to revel in itself. While APRA preferred to keep its regulatory approach behind closed doors, here was an example of a fund publicly rebuking it.

As the Productivity Commission began investigating the superannuation system as part of its landmark 2016 review, questions were asked of Rowell's appetite for action. APRA knew who the bad funds were, so why not pick one retail fund, one industry fund and one corporate fund and take all three to court over failing to act in members' best interests?

Rowell is said to have slapped down the idea: 'That's not how we operate.' Under her stewardship, APRA was a behind-closed-doors operator. However, this was proven to be an ineffectual way of operating.

More, APRA had a blind focus on ensuring only that super funds did not collapse, allowing the companies to engage in less-than-ideal behaviour as long as it didn't threaten their prudential stability. This was entirely misguided: the taxpayer already underwrote the risks in the system.

When it handed down its final report, the PC shot down APRA and ASIC for their failure to protect the nest eggs of working Australians. It said the roles of the regulators were unclear, they were too slow to act, they needed to take more legal action, and they should be more focused on members' interests.

'Members would have a realistic expectation that government and regulators would ensure their fund is looking after them, but this expectation would have been sadly misguided—with no regulatory disposition nor effective mechanism in place for weeding out underperforming funds and products,' the PC said.

'It is clear that strategic conduct regulation with deterrence intent—where public enforcement action in response to material member harm is undertaken to deter similar behaviour by others—has generally appeared either largely "missing in action" or been "too little too late". The "behind closed doors" nature of APRA's supervisory activities means that there is little potential for demonstration effects.' These effects would have included court action or public denunciation of poor behaviour that would have both cracked down on misconduct and sent a message to other funds contemplating stepping out of line.

Rather than allowing bad funds to continue to operate in the market, the commission urged the regulators to make the funds prove their 'right to remain' in the system. To ensure this would happen, the PC proposed a tough hurdle known as an 'elevated outcomes test'. At its core, the test would force APRA to continually monitor the performance of super products as measured against a benchmark target that was customised to a fund's own asset allocation. This way, funds would not be unfairly punished if they had a more conservative investment strategy, but would face regulatory action if they failed to deliver performances on par with better-performing funds that were investing in the same instruments.

The royal commission revealed that many retail funds continued to outsource management to their own divisions even when they knew their own divisions were long-term underperformers. However, when APRA was given the opportunity to adopt the elevated outcomes test, it squibbed it in favour of a far weaker proposal. Launching its member outcomes rules in November 2018, a month before the PC finalised its proposals and as Kenneth Hayne was drafting his final report for the royal commission, APRA gave funds guidelines that incorporated soft investment return targets that appeared to allow laggards to set dismal targets and game the system.

'The regulators appear focused on funds and their interests, and not on whether members' needs are being met and their interests unharmed,' the PC said. At its core, the commission said, the 'caveat emptor approach that has guided much regulation to date is both inappropriate and inadequate'. For anyone who cared about shoring up standards, the laissez-faire attitude wasn't going to cut it anymore.

Under pressure while being hammered by the royal commission and the PC, APRA needed to put a head on a spike. Luckily, it had a big, smiling face in mind. In fact, it had five candidates. In December 2018, it filed a Federal Court legal suit against IOOF's managing director Chris Kelaher, chairman George Venardos, chief financial officer David Coulter, general manager legal, risk and compliance Paul Vine and general counsel Gary Riordan. They were not fit and proper people to run a superannuation company, APRA said.

Finally, APRA was publicly denouncing poor behaviour. In its statement, it said the IOOF directors had 'each demonstrated an inability to properly identify and appreciate conflicts of interest; a lack of understanding of obligations under the SIS Act [Superannuation Industry (Supervision) Act] and the general law; and a lack of contrition in relation to the breaches'.

Behind closed doors, APRA had been demanding IOOF shore up its standards since 2015. A few days after the suit was filed, Kelaher and Vernados reluctantly agreed to step aside from the company while the court case was underway. Public actions were finally getting results.

Interest-only loans had surged to a heady 18 per cent of all outstanding mortgages and were a 'ticking time bomb' according to financial regulators, which have put in place severe curbs on lending and are now requiring banks to check more regularly with borrowers who may have no plans to pay down their loans.

The preceding sentence describes a situation that sounds familiar, but it was actually the situation in the UK in 2018, where the Financial Conduct Authority had, since 2012, taken extraordinary steps to rein in loose standards in the banking sector after finding that interest-only loans, which don't require repayment of a loan's principal amount for a period of generally five years, had helped to fuel a housing boom before the 2008 GFC.

Back in Australia, it couldn't have been more different. APRA ditched its own crackdown on interest-only loans in December 2018, getting rid of the restriction that these loans had to make up—at most—30 per cent of all new lending (double the level the UK regulators were uncomfortable with). APRA's rule had been in place for only eighteen months.

When the royal commission triggered a tightening of lending standards in the banking sector that then fed through to falling house prices across the nation, financial watchdogs grew increasingly concerned. APRA decided to declare its mission of restoring stability to the financial system accomplished. The temporary cap had done its job, and if banks wanted to start lending out interest-only loans again, APRA believed deposits would now be larger and borrowers would be able to repay their mortgages.

But in comparison to the UK's financial watchdogs, which had learned the lessons of the crash, APRA was shown to be asleep at the wheel. The Australian regulators had waited until interest-only lending accounted for nearly 50 per cent of all new loans in the market. And it wasn't just fringe operators hawking the risky products, which have the capacity to trap people in large loans they have little ability to repay—about half of the loans in Westpac's $400 billion portfolio were held on an interest-only basis.

The UK has continued to demand higher standards of its banking sector, with one eye on the time bomb of hundreds of billions of dollars' worth of loans due to mature in coming years when those loans switch from interest-only to principal-and-interest. At that point, monthly repayments will jump by about 50 per cent, and customers who are already under financial stress, or close to it, will find themselves unable to afford repayments.

In Australia, regulators threw in the towel on higher standards out of a fear the local property bubble was bursting. More than $300 billion of interest-only loans in Australia are due to expire over the few years to 2023, and without the ability to refinance into another interest-only loan, APRA and the RBA are worried about a large-scale rise in loan defaults. However, rather than ensuring the longer-term resilience of the financial system by requiring a permanent lift in standards, the regulators decided it was easier to keep borrowers in a perpetually revolving line of credit in which they are never expected to repay their loans.

Many of the borrowers are investors, with more than three-quarters of interest-only loans being taken up by property speculators by the start of 2017. Under negative gearing laws, investors could deduct the interest payments from their tax bill, meaning they were hardly paying a dollar out of their own pocket on the loan, and then flip the property when they were happy with their price gain.

APRA's ditching of the rule came not long after the Reserve Bank showed interest in ensuring the housing bubble didn't inflate too much further. In a speech in April 2018, assistant governor Chris Kent said the value of interest-only loans as a product had its limits: 'For housing investors, the key motivation for using an interest-only loan is clear. By enabling borrowers to sustain debt at a higher level over the term of the loan, interest-only loans maximise interest expenses, which are tax deductible for investors.' They also helped fuel surging house prices across Australia, which has left the country with the second-highest rate of household indebtedness in the world.

After the royal commission shamed the sector over its nonchalant approach to compliance with responsible lending laws, the banks withdrew from the lending market. Loan applications became more thorough and credit decisions were often overturned by wary banks. But APRA now appeared less concerned about whether the banks were complying with responsible lending laws than whether the sector was simply lending or not.

The intervention was also bungled from the beginning. Since introducing the 30 per cent interest-only cap, borrowers barred from the APRA-regulated sector had flooded into the shadow non-banking sector where there were no limits. Over the eighteen months the rule was in effect, the shadow banking sector grew at its fastest pace in a decade.

Standards are even lower in the non-bank sector while interest rates are significantly higher, leaving the non-regulated industry a larger weakness in the body of the financial system than it was before the interest-only intervention. APRA had been given powers to regulate the shadow banks, but chose not to use them.

The whole episode made the government's decision to prevent Hayne's royal commission from any investigation into 'macro-prudential' policymaking by financial regulators seem prescient. However, the intervention was emblematic of the approach the regulator had always taken towards the banks. APRA was too late off the mark, and then it was too ready to throw in the towel when things got tough.

Just before Christmas 2015, Byres attended a meeting with Commonwealth Bank executives. He was there to deliver an unequivocal message: CBA's financial success had made it arrogant.

The bank had presided over the biggest housing boom in history. Its profits were soaring and executives were reaping the reward. But APRA had that year launched a secret prudential review of CBA's risk management framework and found several large gaps. Byres wanted to warn the bank in person about the need to overhaul its behaviour. He found a bank board that had insulated itself against criticism, and later characterised it as having been 'bureaucratic and arrogant' in the meeting.

APRA decided against making the findings of its review public, and because its failings were kept secret, CBA saw no reason to improve its behaviour. Months later, it was hit by the CommInsure life insurance scandal, and then, a year later, with the AUSTRAC money-laundering Federal Court case.

It wasn't until the camel's back was broken that APRA decided to go public, launching a transparent 'prudential inquiry' into the bank's culture and governance. That inquiry found that CBA's industry-beating profits had 'created a collective belief within the institution that CBA was well run and inherently conservative on risk, and this bred overconfidence, a lack of appreciation for non-financial risks, and a focus on process rather than outcomes'. The report also outlined how the bank had continually thumbed its nose at the regulator. CBA had shown a 'reluctance to proactively volunteer information on matters of regulatory concern' and there were 'frequent delays in compliance with regulatory requests', according to the review.

The prudential review of CBA was a watershed moment for the financial industry. Although it singled out CBA for being guilty of 'complacency' and having a 'reactive stance' to issues rather than being prudently responsive to changing tides, the rest of the financial sector was put on notice over the report. APRA would make all financial institutions mimic the cultural review and return their own findings to the regulator by late 2018.

But it was too late for the banking industry. Australia had already forced a royal commission on the sector for its decade of negligence.

When it was Byres' turn to sit in the royal commission dock, the chairman was forced to reconcile APRA's knowledge of the mounting scandals at CBA in 2016 with its lack of action against the bank. APRA should have done more to pressure the board on its pay structures, which were seen to be driving the poor outcomes, he admitted, but it lacked expertise in analysing banker remuneration. It wasn't confident to take on CBA over poor risk culture, conduct or pay matters because it didn't have 'sufficient expertise', he said. Rather, the regulator's primary interest was one of supervising banks' capital and stability.

'We didn't have a lot of expertise in remuneration,' Byres said. 'It was an area that is not the natural forte of a prudential supervisor. We were talking to CBA a lot on mortgages; mortgages are bread and butter.'

For banks, however, governance standards are one and the same with financial stability.

The world's second-largest bank, the US-based Wells Fargo, was hit by a scandal in 2016 where it had created two million customer accounts fraudulently after bank staff were pressured to sign up new customers to meet their bonus KPIs. Although there was little financial damage caused by the creation of the fake accounts, the bank was blasted with regulatory penalties, restrictions on its growth and a plunge in its stock price. The scandal also caused institutional investors to take their money elsewhere, risking the ability of the company to source funding. It was a cultural scandal that resulted in weakening the bank's financial stability.

When CBA's cultural pulse had shown signs of flatlining, APRA had neglected its duty. This included the CommInsure debacle. When

APRA held a routine meeting with CBA in late 2016, six months after that scandal had broken, Byres decided not to raise the issue with the bank. 'We went to that meeting thinking we didn't have to rub their nose in it,' he said.

APRA's job depended on financial institutions being honest and open with it. If it was too hard on the banks, it feared it wouldn't be told about important matters. It often assumed that the conduct regulator, ASIC, would be on the case. If one watchdog was thought to be chasing poor behaviour across the sector, it wouldn't make sense to double up the work. Byres even said it could be 'clumsy' to have two regulators investigating the same misconduct.

'I think what we would say is we've got another regulator that is looking at, essentially, the same facts, the same documents, the same actions, overlap of people,' he said. 'It's actually inefficient and sometimes unhelpful to have two regulators investigating the same thing at the same time.'

That may be the case, but the issue wasn't that there were two regulators turning the screws on rogue behaviour in the sector. The issue was that there was none.

In 2011, when ANZ hatched a plan to make its front-line branch staff convince customers to sign over their superannuation to the company, it knew it was a risky strategy. Under the law, ANZ branch staff were only allowed to provide 'general advice' about super. This meant they were only able to give general advice and facts about ANZ's own super fund. They could not assess whether the product was suitable for the customer or compare it to the customer's existing fund.

Still, ANZ saw a big opportunity in convincing people to roll over their retirement savings into its own funds.

The bank's own legal officers were wary of the plan, labelling the 'inherent risk' of the strategy as 'extreme'. 'It is possible that regular breaches of incidents would be seen by the regulator as "systemic", putting ANZ's licence at risk,' the lawyers' internal presentation to the bank said.

Despite warnings it could be stripped of its ability to operate as a financial institution, ANZ proceeded with the plan anyway. Why wouldn't they? ASIC was a toothless tiger.

Between 2012 and 2016, ANZ sold $2.6 billion worth of super accounts through its branches. And when ASIC came knocking, the bank was proven right—despite sitting on super savings that had ballooned to $3.6 billion by 2018, ANZ was slapped with a penalty of just $1.25 million. Its financial services licence was never under threat.

When Commonwealth Bank's CommInsure division had been misleadingly telling their customers they were covered for heart attack when in reality they were covered only for the most severe of heart attacks, the bank faced an $8 million penalty under the law. CommInsure had been pushing the misleading advertising for four years to 2016, but instead of pursuing the bank for the full penalty, ASIC decided it would make it pay a 'community benefit payment' of just $300,000. The soft touch didn't end there. As it was wrapping up its work on its investigation, ASIC's head of enforcement, Tim Mullaly, emailed CommInsure a copy of the regulator's draft media release on the matter, wanting the insurer to get back to him and let him know if 'this is sufficient to CommInsure to resolve' the investigation.

Why was ASIC, the supposedly tough cop on the beat, allowing companies to workshop its media releases?

In fact, it was a shamefully regular practice at the watchdog. After a two-year freedom of information battle with ASIC, my colleague Ben Butler unearthed a series of documents revealing the very same behaviour between the regulator and the banks. Over nearly a decade, the corporate regulator regularly bowed to demands from the biggest financial institutions in Australia to water down the language in its press releases.

The releases issued related to some of the biggest scandals to hit the sector, including a financial planning snafu that hurt the retirement savings of up to 560,000 Commonwealth Bank and Macquarie customers and sparked calls for a royal commission nearly four years before Kenneth Hayne was asked to inquire into the sector.

CBA's chief lawyer, David Cohen, was closely involved in drafting a 2014 press release about fresh licence conditions that had been slapped on the bank's financial planning arm. In his previous posting as AMP's head legal officer, Cohen had sent ASIC a two-page list of 'issues we have with ASIC's draft media release' after the regulator found the company was shunting its financial advice customers into its own in-house products 93 per cent of the time. ASIC accepted many of Mr Cohen's changes. The regulator appeared quick to buckle under pressure.

In a 2014 review of the wealth management sector, as ASIC worked on a press release about customer losses from investment platforms, a worker in the regulator's media unit emailed colleagues: 'This is one of those releases that has been drafted by everyone other than ASIC ha!' ASIC appeared to be too trusting of the companies it was supposed to be regulating.

Both APRA and ASIC stood in direct contrast to the way the ACCC went about its business. When the Rod Sims–chaired ACCC saw something it didn't like, it dragged the relevant company before the courts without so much as a courtesy call. If the ACCC lost the eventuating legal suit, it would then publicly argue for the law to be changed—if it couldn't enforce the law, it wasn't the ACCC's fault, it was up to the legislation to be able to be enforced by a regulator. Under pressure from the ACCC, the government would be dragged to the table and forced to amend the law.

ASIC took a far more 'consultative' approach to the new 'unfair contracts' law that came into force in November 2016. This law would put smaller companies on a more equal footing with big business when negotiating contract terms. The ACCC's approach to enforcing similar legislation in its remit was far more rigorous. In early 2017, ASIC deputy chairman Peter Kell said that if the regulator found 'a potentially unfair term we will work with the lender to remove or amend the term'. On the ACCC's side, a year before the contracts law came into force, it began demanding sample contracts from companies it regulated. If they were incorrect, they would be punished. ASIC considered doing this but decided not to, choosing instead to wait until the banks had reviewed their contracts and then see if they complied with the law.

'Why work with the lender? Why not just say, "Do it"?' Hayne asked ASIC's head of credit, Michael Saadat at the royal commission.

Saadat said there were too many lenders with too many contracts to be able to conduct such a big sweep. ASIC lacked the resources to go through every contract. 'If the lender is prepared to make changes in response to the concerns we have raised, that can be a quicker process than going down the road of taking court action,' Saadat said.

A lack of time and resources also appeared to keep ASIC from ensuring that dodgy financial advisers were kicked out of the industry. ASIC senior executive Louise Macaulay, who was responsible for overseeing discipline of financial advisers, told the royal commission the regulator was doing as much as it could, given its resources. While it may have seemed easy to kick bad apples out of the sector, it was an arduous process and a legal minefield. ASIC took about two years to ban a dodgy adviser, and had never attempted to fine any advisers for their misconduct.

Macaulay told the commission that investigations of adviser misconduct were resource intensive and often heavily contested by the targeted planners. Even when they were flagrantly disobeying the law, companies bogged down the regulator in legal warfare over the expulsions. 'We find even in the jaw-dropping cases, commissioner, defences are put on, material is put on that was not in the file ... to explain why the advice was good advice,' she said.

When it did ban a financial adviser, ASIC was hamstrung in sending a stern message to the rest of the industry. Australia's notoriously fickle defamation laws prevented the regulator from airing details of misconduct lest it be bogged down again in a subsequent trial over damage to a planner's reputation.

The dodgy financial adviser problem was only set to worsen. As the major Australian banks sought to carve off unprofitable or troublesome divisions such as financial planning arms, there would be an increasing number of advisers outside the ranks of the big four banks and AMP. This meant tracking bad behaviour would be much harder for a regulator that lacked the resources even to tackle misconduct in the larger, more professional firms. It didn't have the time or the money to investigate the hundreds or thousands of fringe operators in the market.

It also didn't have the time or the money to spend days in the courtroom, especially when it was up against some of the most profitable financial giants in the world. ASIC chairman James Shipton called it 'legal trench warfare'. When hit with accusations of misconduct, banks and their well-armed teams of lawyers would fight back against even the slightest suggestion of indiscretion.

And why wouldn't they? The big four banks made a combined profit of $30 billion in 2018. They could afford the best silks in town to defend the most indefensible of cases. When ASIC was weighing up legal action, it had to factor in how much of a bruising it would take during a fight. The default mode for the major banks was to 'vigorously defend' any case brought against it.

Take for instance the bank bill swap rate rigging saga. When ASIC began targeting the banks over their practice of manipulating the key interest rate benchmark, it scored several early wins. Royal Bank of Scotland paid $1.6 million to clear up allegations from ASIC, and Swiss giant UBS and France's BNP Paribas both paid $1 million over the scandal.

However, when it came to the big four Australian banks, they sought to block the regulator at every stage of the fight. ASIC filed cases against CBA, Westpac, ANZ and NAB over a drawn-out two-year period as it built its case against each lender.

Despite initially defending themselves against the claims, ANZ and NAB folded after a few months as it became clear they would spend an inordinate amount of money fighting a case during which they were likely to suffer significant brand damage. Westpac held steady and forced ASIC into a lengthy proceeding; it was eventually found guilty on a number of the allegations made in the Federal Court lawsuit, with a minor victory on several other alleged breaches of the law. ANZ and NAB were proven correct—the scandalous chatroom banter about Westpac's traders who had attempted to manipulate the interest rate was splashed across newspaper headlines for months.

CBA, which was the last bank to face ASIC action over the rate-rigging behaviour, initially said it would defend itself in court against the allegations. That was until its new chief executive, Matt Comyn, had second thoughts. By mid-May 2018, CBA was less enthusiastic about going to war with ASIC, and settled the case out of court.

Taking the big four banks to court over rate rigging was the career highlight of former ASIC boss Greg Medcraft, who had faced continual criticism over the impotence of the financial watchdog under his leadership. When Shipton replaced Medcraft in early 2018 after a storied career as a top executive at Hong Kong's financial regulator, he was determined to kick ASIC into gear. However, he soon realised why Medcraft had had such a difficult time keeping the financial sector on a tight leash.

When Shipton sat in the royal commission box, he argued that there were decisions ASIC was forced to take when it wanted to rein in bad behaviour, and it had to make these decisions only because the government refused to hand over more money to properly fund the watchdogs.

'It weighs very heavily on the regulatory choices that we have to make, because it means that we are restricted in our ability to take on matters or to pursue matters in a way that, perhaps, we would like to,' he told the commission. 'We are constrained in probably every aspect of our regulatory work. It's certainly in investigations, certainly in other matters relating to enforcement. We are constrained in our surveillance, our supervision, our important work on financial capability and other work.'

Australia wanted a tough watchdog, but the royal commission showed that the government was not prepared to feed it.

In October 2018, ASIC was due to make a routine appearance before a joint parliamentary committee. The MPs on the committee were given no forewarning of what Shipton had in store, but the executives at ASIC had been cooking up a plan to go nuclear on the regulator's funding. Rather than coming cap in hand, Shipton hauled in buckets that were open for donations.

Commissioner Hayne's interim report had been made public just weeks earlier, and in it he had singled out the regulators for failing to properly curtail bad behaviour in the financial system. ASIC was sick of being a punching bag. It had been effectively neutered by successive governments, including a particularly harsh budget cut of $140 million made by the Abbott Government in 2014. Despite rendering the watchdog impotent by constraining its funding, the government had immediately attacked it over the failures aired during the royal commission. It was demanding that the regulator put no foot wrong at the same time as freezing it into a state of inaction by squeezing it of the funding it needed to litigate against the biggest corporations in Australia.

'Now is the right time to ask whether ASIC should be resourced differently to meet the community's expectations and the unique challenges of Australia's financial system,' Shipton told the joint parliamentary committee. 'Now is the right time, and this is the right forum … to discuss whether ASIC and its peers are "right-sized". This question is not a statement, nor a demand. It is instead a question aimed at starting an important policy conversation.'

In Shipton's old stomping ground of Hong Kong, financial regulators were funded to be three times as large as Australia's in terms of how much money they were given compared to the number and revenue of the companies they sought to regulate. Just on unadjusted numbers, regulators in Hong Kong had a combined budget that was 50 per cent bigger to regulate an industry that was a third the size of Australia's.

ASIC received tens of thousands of complaints and mountains of breach notifications every year, but it had to handle this workload with an enforcement team that numbered less than one-third of the work-force of the tiny ACT police force. With ASIC's expenses close to $400 million a year, APRA running at $130 million and the ACCC budget costing taxpayers $200 million, a tripling of funding could take the expense for the main financial watchdogs to close to $2 billion a year.

Under the government's industry funding model for ASIC, the regulator's budget was constrained by the level the government decided to appropriate it in the budget, which was then paid back by the industry it regulated. While the financial industry was indeed covering the cost of regulation, the overall level of funding kept the regulator hemmed in. It could only do what it could with the level of funding nominated by the government each year, leaving it reactive to changes in the regulatory environment and pinching pennies where possible.

While the government was urging ASIC to take more action against bad behaviour, ASIC didn't have the funds to take people to court. It declared it lacked the cash to fund the expected fifty criminal and civil prosecutions to be launched against rogue executives and corporations over the two years following the royal commission.

As Shipton pulled his finger out of the levy, other departments began coming forward complaining of lack of funding. The Commonwealth Director of Public Prosecutions (CDPP) warned Attorney-General Christian Porter that it didn't have the resources to handle the case load if banking executives were about to be taken to court. While ASIC conducts prosecutions of minor criminal matters, it refers more serious matters to the CDPP. However, under the gaze of the federal budget razor gang, Porter wasn't about to dole out funds willy-nilly. 'Once the final report of the royal commission is received, the government will consider its findings and recommendations and make any further decisions required, at that point,' he said.

This position soon unravelled, and just days later the government was forced to scrounge together an extra $40 million for the CDPP.

APRA then came for the chequebook, asking for more money it said it needed to spend on installing its own supervisors inside large financial companies, and to boost its ability to respond to emerging issues such as cyber threats and the explosion of financially savvy 'fintech' start-ups that were disrupting the traditional financial sector. The requested $60 million funding boost to APRA's budget was also going to be put towards an 'enforcement review' at the regulator, where an investigation would be launched into just how it had come to be so timid when dealing with the companies it was supposed to be regulating. The government agreed to hand over the money.

ASIC also got some emergency funding. In August 2018, it was given an extra $70 million to 'embed' some of its staff inside major companies. But the top-up was not enough. It had only just recovered the Abbott Government's cuts to its budget. When Malcolm Turnbull took over the prime ministership, he had replaced the money Abbott took out in 2016, but this left ASIC in the same position it had started in. Medcraft said the problems in the financial sector caused by a regulator that didn't have the money it wanted, nor the powers it was asking for, had been 'brewing for a number of years'.

Over the past twenty years, the remit of ASIC had expanded considerably, as had the number of companies it regulated. By 2018, it had a wider regulatory remit than regulators in the UK, the US and Germany. The breadth of this responsibility increased the complexity of its operations, which required an appropriate amount of resourcing. The 2015 capability review of ASIC had found that only 15 per cent of external stakeholders believed the regulator was adequately funded.

This was one of the reasons ASIC was gun shy with court cases. It won 90 per cent of the cases it launched, but this in itself was a sign it was not willing to launch 'test' cases to clear up grey areas of the law. Litigation was expensive. And when it did take companies to court, the penalties were pathetic. Financial companies in the US and Europe can be fined billions of dollars from a single court case, but in Australia, they are slapped with wet lettuce. When enforced by ASIC, Australia's penalty regime could only draw out fines in the tens of millions, if it was lucky to have a judge willing to punish banks to the full extent of the law, but when a bank was making profits of up to $10 billion a year, as was the case with Commonwealth Bank, such paltry penalties were simply factored into the cost of doing business. Australian penalties were not a deterrent.

Even when ASIC wanted to put executives in jail, the law was ill-designed to allow it to do so. ASIC chief prosecutor Daniel Crennan, QC, argued that federal laws would have to be overhauled to allow the regulator to launch criminal cases against executives and companies, because criminal legislation differed among the various Australian states. The government would need to extend the Federal Court's jurisdiction to cover corporate crimes, and it belatedly launched a formal review of the legal system at the tail end of 2018. It also had to stump up an extra $10 million for the Federal Court of Australia to fund new judges and extra resources to handle the increased load of civil cases stemming from the royal commission.

Evidently, even if ASIC had wanted to launch criminal cases, the structure of the law precluded that from being a straightforward endeavour. The law remained out of step with what was necessary for ASIC to do its job, and the government was reluctant to hand it new powers to intervene in the free market.

The regulator had been demanding so-called 'product intervention laws' for years that would enable it to apply straight-out bans to products that were harmful to consumers. Examples of these included the insurance products Freedom Insurance was hawking and the useless credit insurance Commonwealth Bank had been selling. In 2014, the government's own Financial System Inquiry had backed in the regulator and demanded the government amend the law to give ASIC the power to intervene, but by the end of 2018, the government had still not got around to doing so. By dragging its heels, it was allowing companies to continue selling deleterious products without any threat that ASIC would be able to stop them.

Even where the government did take action, it bungled the process and complicated ASIC's work.

When Bill Shorten, as financial services minister in the Gillard Government, looked to bring in the FOFA laws, he made a significant compromise with the industry. The FOFA rules outlawed any new trailing commissions that could be charged to financial advice customers. These kickbacks totalled thousands of dollars a year per customer, and were paid in perpetuity until the customer got rid of whatever wealth management product they had bought, or if they died.

To ease the passage of the legislation through the parliament, Shorten allowed current trailing commission arrangements to be 'grandfathered', which meant advisers could continue to collect the payments on legacy products. It was thought the trailing commissions would wither on the vine and soon be banished from the industry, but the opposite happened. Portfolios of financial advice customers who were largely unaware they were continuing to be charged trailing commissions were traded around the sector by financial advisers. 'The parliament has in effect put in place a provision that enables the continuing payment of commissions that generate conflicts of interest and unnecessary costs widely across the financial system,' ASIC deputy Peter Kell told the royal commission.

Proposals to clamp down on the payday-lending sector were also victim to questionable political manoeuvres. ASIC had been lobbying the parliament to bring payday lenders under the remit of the Credit Act, which would give the regulator the power to clamp down on gouging and inappropriate products in the predatory sector.

But the government had sat on its own legislation targeting the sector for more than two years. The bill was passed among four different ministers during that time, and none managed to bring on the legislation for a vote to enshrine the proposals in law. The bill would have capped the amount payday lenders could siphon out of customers in interest charges, which were as high as 900 per cent. Customers—and they were often poorer Australians with limited access to formal credit products—were being sold into dozens upon dozens of loans with harsh terms and cripplingly high rates of interest.

Despite the urging of ASIC, consumer groups and financial counsellors, the government failed to enact the legislation. Indeed, it appeared beholden to lobbying from the payday-lending sector. Liberal MP Stuart Robert even met with payday lender Cash Converters before he was made assistant treasurer. When he was given responsibility for the legislation, it disappeared from the government's agenda.

Meanwhile, ASIC was being forced to waste its time trying to bring the sector to heel through other means, and had spent resources taking action against lenders Thorn Group and Radio Rentals, Cash Converters and Nimble in separate enforcements.

When companies don't act in the interests of consumers, public policy can be an important first line of defence to steer the behaviour back in the right direction. But the architects of Australia's regulatory policy had failed to foster vigorous competition among financial companies. There was an inherent reluctance on the part of the government to allow large companies to lose any money, and this contributed to both the misconduct and the failure to tackle wrongdoing.

After banks survived the GFC and were 'prudentially regulated against failure', profit became their defining measure of success at the same time as they were ignoring the risk to their reputation, Hayne said in his interim report. 'The law sets the bounds of permissible behaviour. If competitive pressures are absent, if there is little or no threat of enterprise failure, and if banks can and do mitigate the consequences of failing to meet obligations, only the regulator can mark and enforce those bounds,' he said.

Since the late 1990s, Australia's regulatory system had been hobbled by a disclosure-based free-market model of laws introduced after the government's Wallis Financial System Inquiry in 1997. However, disclosure may well have proved to be a failed experiment. Customers were often inundated with disclosure documents riddled with fine print that were given to them at the wrong time, generally after they had been tricked into buying something. Companies were dumping customers into products and assuming they were absolved of all responsibility because of a few dot points in a 100-page product disclosure statement.

Hayne said the Wallis inquiry 'reflected the prevailing conditions of deregulation and globalisation' at the time, together with the view that competition in financial markets would diminish the role of banks and decrease costs for consumers. However, since Wallis the opposite had happened—'banks' accumulation of wealth management businesses accelerated', Hayne said. The free market approach had only allowed the banks to become more powerful, and meanwhile the industry had exploded in size and complexity. All the while, APRA had only 200 front-line staff to monitor about 600 institutions.

In many cases, the most effective way to achieve regulatory simplicity would be to simply ban certain types of conflicts or conduct, rather than require burdensome disclosure and risk management rules that had the propensity to be uncertain or very costly. ASIC had long warned of such failures with the government's laissez-faire approach. In 2014, ASIC commissioner John Price warned that the factors behind a rise in consumer losses 'challenges some of the assumptions and philosophy underlying our financial regulatory system'. 'In particular, the assumption that underpinned much of retail financial services regulation since the Wallis inquiry—that disclosure is the best tool in almost every instance to fix market failures—has not been borne out in practice,' Price said.

When Hayne lectured ASIC on its failure to enforce the law, the regulator listened to the criticism and agreed it needed to take an 'If not, why not?' approach to litigation. When government MPs began to repeat the criticism, members inside ASIC were astounded. At nearly every point, ASIC had been hobbled by the government. Its budget had been slashed, appropriation of resources had been withheld or provided on a short-term basis, and legislation that was necessary for its ability to enforce the law had been killed off by politicians too close to the banking industry that donated to their parties.

Successive governments had let the banking industry off the leash and allowed it to run riot across the neighbourhood. When the watchdogs had failed to bark, it was because the government had muzzled them.

15

VENI, VIDI, VICI

It was the culmination of twelve months of panic for National Australia Bank boss Andrew Thorburn.

The royal commission had reached its final round of hearings, which called on the chairmen and chief executives of the major companies to give evidence as to how to fix the financial system. Thorburn was aiming to show Kenneth Hayne exactly how seriously the bank was moving forward in the post-royal-commission world.

Inevitably, the banker was asked to explain how the bank's 'introducer' scheme, which gave gym managers, hairdressers, real estate agents and others big payments for signing up borrowers to NAB loans, became the subject of a multimillion-dollar fraud ring operated out of a string of western Sydney bank branches.

'I think the first thing is that we've had the wrong incentive schemes in many cases,' Thorburn said. 'We put the bait right there for people. Right there. They stepped over the line. That's their own decision. I'm not excusing that. But we put incentive schemes in place. Not good.'

Thorburn explained that NAB had since overhauled its remuneration schemes. Banker pay was now set against variable measurements, the system was centralised, and bonus targets were diffused across a number of KPIs. More than that, bonuses were now deferred.

'It's starting to get more sustainable,' he said. 'Nothing to see here anymore' was the message he wanted to give the commissioner.

So it must have come as a surprise just two days later when he saw a story by me on *The Australian*'s front page that challenged the claims that everything was hunky-dory in NAB's lending division.

I had obtained an internal email sent by the bank's regional executive responsible for large swathes of eastern NSW and the ACT. Sent at the same time as Thorburn was being lambasted for failing to give direct answers on the witness stand, it told staff members they had to sell five mortgages and one loan refinancing by the end of the week, for which they would be rewarded with points under the bank's 'Recognise' reward scheme.

'Crank it up,' the manager wrote. 'Our pipeline is low team and we need to really knuckle down over the next 5 weeks before the Xmas lull to fill our funnel. You are our biggest introducers, we need your help right now.' This was a dramatic increase on business as usual. Under normal circumstances, staff were expected to secure just two home-loan customers a week.

The email, replete with smiley faces ostensibly to encourage staff to shunt customers into loans, was not a good look. Although frontline staff had supposedly been moved away from financial targets and bonuses under recommendations made by the 2016–17 Sedgwick review of banker remuneration, NAB's non-financial Recognise reward scheme was now being used to get staff members to flog loans.

The Recognise program was originally designed to reward bankers who 'demonstrated NAB's values' with prizes such as movie tickets and vacuum cleaners. But now it was being used in the same way financial incentives had been deployed in the introducer program.

The Finance Sector Union was livid. National secretary Julia Angrisano said she had been telling NAB for years that 'the toxic sales culture in the bank leads to bullying behaviour, a high-pressure workplace and poor customer outcomes … Andrew Thorburn says one thing in the royal commission while senior staff continue to pressure people to sell products. On the best interpretation, Mr Thorburn is being continually misled by his senior executives. On the worst interpretation, he has lost all authority within his bank.'

It seemed the early lessons of the inquiry hadn't been learned at NAB.

Indeed, when Hayne had handed down his interim findings just a few months earlier, he had singled out greed as the primary driver of misconduct in the financial sector. Selling products, he said, had become the sole 'focus of attention' for the banks rather than service, and this pushed front-line staff into chasing a bigger share of a customer's wallet to help executives win big bonuses. 'From the executive suite to the front line, staff were measured and rewarded by reference to profit and sales.'

A few weeks after his appearance on the stand, Thorburn announced he would be taking extended long-service leave after one of the 'biggest and most relentless' years in his time at the bank. It was an unusual move for any chief executive of a major Australian company. You don't rise to the top just so you can book a holiday. It was also strange timing to take leave right when the royal commission was preparing to publish its final report. According to the plan, Thorburn would return to NAB at the start of February, a week before the report's release, and then head off for another month to recover and recuperate.

Observers began openly discussing his retirement.

Less than a year after conducting the first round of public hearings for his inquiry, on the day his recommendations were due, Hayne sat in the front seat of a white government car as he made the drive to Yarralumla. It was Friday 1 February, not a day earlier or later than had been specified in his terms of reference.

At Government House, he handed over his three-volume final report to Governor-General Peter Cosgrove before heading to Parliament House to meet with Treasurer Josh Frydenberg. Frydenberg had advised that he would be holding on to the 1000-page report over the weekend before allowing the nation's media to access it on Monday afternoon. A few hours after that, it would be published when the share market closed. That way, financial traders would have time to digest the information in the report before the opening of trade on Tuesday morning.

As the former High Court justice made his way over to Capital Circle, the treasurer's office began frantically ringing around in search of a photographer. It being a Friday when parliament was not sitting, most journalists and photographers were not in the House. Luckily, *The Australian*'s snapper Kym Smith was available.

In Frydenberg's office, Hayne sat down for a photograph with the treasurer. His displeasure at being used as a prop was evident. Troubled by the lack of warmth between her two subjects, Smith asked, 'Can we get a handshake or something between you?'

Without missing a beat, Hayne replied, 'Nope.'

There had been more than 10,000 public submissions, 69 days of public hearings, and the appearance of 134 witnesses. Counsels assisting had trawled through hundreds of thousands of documents and had tendered almost 400 witness statements and more than 6500 exhibits. As Hayne left parliament, he did so without making a statement—no comment about what was in the report he had handed over. He was finished with his role in the royal commission, and returned to Melbourne.

The recommendations were about to fall somewhere in the no-man's-land between the government and the Opposition, and that land began to disappear as Labor and the Coalition started to skirmish over Hayne's recommendations.

A week before the final report was delivered, Labor treasury spokesman Chris Bowen told the *Financial Review* he would implement all the proposals. This was without even seeing what might be recommended. Both sides of politics would need a 'very, very, very good reason' not to adopt any finding, he said. 'Your default position should be if the royal commission recommends it, it shall be done.' The day before Frydenberg received the report, the treasurer pledged to do the same, more or less. 'While in principle that may be our intention, we have to receive the report and read it in a considered manner before reaching a final decision,' he said.

The game that was about to be played out was who could be seen to be acting tough enough on the sector to stand up to the lobbyists, while ensuring that none of the proposals overreached and damaged the financial system or the economy.

As a senior Labor MP remarked to me ahead of the release of the report, the focus on the implementation of the royal commission's recommendations would be unlike that of many other similar inquiries. The negative public mood surrounding the sector had been fermenting for decades, and the national media would continue to keep the recommendations in focus for years after any government commitments were made. Any diversion from the key proposals would be picked apart by the hundreds and thousands of interested parties who wanted the system to be overhauled and put on a more sustainable trajectory. This was not a report that could be put on the shelf to gather dust.

For Hayne, that was something he agreed with in the opening pages of his final report. 'The time has come to decide what is to be done in response to what has happened,' he said. 'The financial services industry is too important to the economy of the nation to allow what has happened in the past to continue or to happen again.'

The central task given to Hayne had been to inquire into misconduct in the financial sector. Then, once misconduct was identified, he was to make recommendations to address its causes.

Across three volumes, each the size of a small-town phone book, he meticulously diagnosed wrongdoing that had taken place across decades, costing consumers untold fortunes while delivering outsized profits for the companies engaging in the misconduct. 'Very often, the conduct has broken the law,' he said. 'And if it has not broken the law, the conduct has fallen short of the kind of behaviour the community not only expects of financial services entities but is also entitled to expect of them.'

Hayne said most scandals could be boiled down to just four features of the financial system that had developed over decades and set the scene for the large-scale grifting of customers.

The first was the connection between behaviour and reward. Individual gain and the primacy of a company's bottom line had turned a services industry into a sales industry. Bankers had become sellers, advisers had become sellers, and sellers had become advisers. Rewarding misconduct is wrong, but bonus schemes and the way banks paid staff had done just that.

Second, there was a large imbalance in the relative power held by companies and by individual customers. Because customers were kept in the dark, purposely confused and trapped by banks that set the terms of engagement, financial companies could engage in misconduct as they had free rein to do so.

Third, the evolution of the financial system into one where the bank branch was no longer the sole point of contact for customers had led to a breakdown in responsibility throughout the system. Customers were now often dealing with a third actor when they engaged with a bank—a mortgage broker, a financial adviser, a car-yard dealer, an aggregation website. They would assume the intermediary was working in their interests, but in reality the intermediary was either working in the interests of themselves or in the interests of the company on whose behalf they were acting. While many of them had a duty to act in customers' best interests, often the reality was the pursuit of a 'good enough' outcome instead. 'Experience shows that conflicts between duty and interest can seldom be managed; self-interest will almost always trump duty,' Hayne said.

Lastly, misconduct was seldom punished. Wrongdoing would be deterred only if companies were investigated for poor behaviour, punished according to the severity of the crime, and publicly denounced to ensure faith the system was not rigged against the average Australian.

The royal commission in itself had already been a powerful denunciation of wrongdoing—to an extent no one had believed possible before the inquiry. But it needed to be not solely a process of public shame for companies and their senior management. There had to be a remedy. 'Saying sorry and promising not to do it again has not prevented recurrence,' Hayne said. A series of criminal and civil referrals had been issued relating to specific findings, and handed to ASIC and APRA months before the final report landed. Hayne wanted no time to be wasted in seeking retribution.

Specifically, there were three criminal prosecutions of AMP, Commonwealth Bank and NAB in train, relating to potential dishonesty offences with the corporate regulator. The alleged offences were all contraventions of section 1041G of the Corporations Act, concerning scandals in which AMP, CBA and NAB had charged customers fees but provided no services. In all three cases, money was being taken from the dead. Other referrals to the regulators included Suncorp, ANZ, IOOF, the insurance companies Allianz and Youi, and life insurer TAL. Hayne had made eleven specific referrals to ASIC of misconduct by eight companies or individuals, and another twelve referrals to APRA for possible breaches of the law in the superannuation sector.

ASIC was already attempting to prove it had turned itself into a more aggressive regulator. It announced in the wake of the final report that it had already launched twelve further investigations into case studies that had appeared before the banking inquiry but were not specific referrals from the former High Court justice. Another sixteen cases were then assessed for prosecution. This was on top of the cases already before the Federal Court against NAB over its $100 million fees-for-no-service scandal, and against rogue financial planning group Dover Financial and its former boss, Terry McMaster.

ASIC had set up a team of fifty staff to trawl through around 100 referrals, breach reports and case studies for potential enforcement action, including seven financial advisers who will likely be referred to the CDPP. Many targets of the referrals will remain a secret until ASIC has finished its investigations, so as to not prejudice the cases.

Hayne said there was 'one undeniable fact' coming out of the royal commission. 'There can be no doubt that the primary responsibility for misconduct in the financial services industry lies with the entities concerned and those who managed and controlled those entities: their boards and senior management. It is those who engaged in misconduct who are responsible for what they did and for the consequences that followed.'

Having found a few heads to put on stakes, it was now up to the commissioner to reshape the system into one where there wouldn't be such a need to hold another royal commission in the future. For this, there were four key goals.

First, the law had to be simplified to meet its intent. Next, conflicts of interest had to be removed. Then, once these conflicts were addressed, compliance with the law had to be improved and regulators had to become more effective at guarding against misconduct. Finally, there was an important question that Treasury had suggested be considered, and with which Hayne agreed: 'What more can be done to achieve effective leadership, good governance and appropriate culture within financial services firms so that firms obey the law, do not mislead or deceive, are fair, provide fit-for-purpose service with care and skill, and act in the best interests of their clients?'

To meet these goals, Hayne made seventy-six recommendations in total. Some closed loopholes in the law, some required no legislative change, and some were up to the industry to self-implement. All, however, revolved around six key principles: the law must be enforced; industry codes must be mandatory and adhered to; financial products should never be hawked to customers; intermediaries should only ever work in the interests of customers; conflicted remuneration should be banned; and the culture and governance of organisations should pay heed not only to financial risk but to the risk of misconduct.

As with any plan to reshape the financial industry, the most controversial recommendation was the one that would take the most money away from financial sector workers.

With more than half of all mortgages sold through a broker, Hayne had realised the mortgage broking sector had grown to become the new lifeblood of the banks—the source of much of their financial power. Ensuring brokers acted in the best interests of borrowers and not of the banks that paid them hefty bonuses was key to redirecting the rivers of gold running through the financial system.

While the mortgage broker sector had failed to generate headline-grabbing scandals during the commission, such as charging dead people fees or lying to regulators, it had grown to be one of the most important pieces in the puzzle of the financial system. In fact, nearly all the reforms targeted by Hayne at the business of banking related to mortgage brokers. Under the proposals, they would be subject to the same laws financial advisers must adhere to when advising clients. Borrowers, not lenders providing the product, would pay mortgage brokers a fee for the service of choosing a loan, and lenders would be forbidden to pay trail commissions to brokers. Then, brokers would be subjected to the same information-sharing and reporting procedures as financial advisers and to the same processes of inform-ing and remediating clients if misconduct was discovered.

'The present system of remunerating mortgage brokers is conflicted remuneration,' Hayne said. 'It can reasonably be expected to influ-ence the broker's recommendations about choice of lender, amount to be borrowed, and terms on which the amount is borrowed. And the influence is in favour of the party paying the commission—that is, the lender.'

The banning of trailing commissions charged to borrowers would cut off a stream of money that ran close to a $3 billion a year in total. The 'chief value of trail commissions to the recipient, to put it bluntly, is that they are money for nothing', said Hayne.

It was money for nothing, but the sector did not want to relinquish it so easily.

In order to tackle the causes of the fees-for-no-service scandal, Hayne suggested that financial advisers be forced to talk more routinely with their clients to make sure they knew what they were being charged and what actual services they were getting. Ongoing fee arrangements would have to be reviewed at least once a year by clients, with a written record of the service provided and what fees would be paid. At the same time, grandfathered trailing commissions, a legacy of the 2013 FOFA reforms, had to be banned as soon as possible.

'Even if the arguments relied on to justify the grandfathering exception were valid when that exception was introduced, it is now clear that they have outlived their validity,' Hayne said.

Advisers who sold life insurance products also faced a new reality under a proposal to reduce sales commissions to zero. Meanwhile, dodgy financial advisers would have to be reported to the corporate regulator on a quarterly basis, and all planners would have to be registered under a single, central disciplinary body.

To clean up the superannuation sector, Hayne recommended an overhaul of the current industrial-relations-linked process for creating super accounts. A 'default once' mechanism would end the system that had resulted in the proliferation of ten million fee-draining unintended multiple accounts. No consumer should be given more than a single superannuation account. This politically explosive recommendation was made without specifying the exact mechanism for doing so, saying only that a system to ensure Australians were only ever given one super account be created.

The adoption of the 'default once' recommendation put the government on a collision course with Labor, as the current industrial award process for nominating superannuation accounts for new workers overwhelmingly favours the union-and-employee-backed industry fund sector.

'The superannuation sector of the financial services industry is important, not only to the many individuals who participate in it as members of superannuation funds, but also to the nation,' Hayne said. 'Superannuation is important to individuals because it will affect, even determine, how they live after retiring from work.'

One of the most important proposals was to beef up the current superannuation laws with civil and criminal penalties, particularly by attaching fines to breaches of the duty to act in members' best interests. By doing so, the corporate regulator was put on notice to better stand guard over members' best interests, including being vigilant when super funds of any stripe appointed board directors. This potentially pushed the so-called 'equal representation model'—where unions and employer groups nominate officials to govern super funds—into the historical dustbin. Directors would have to be chosen for their skill set rather than because of their nominating body or the history of the super fund.

Hayne said the process of unions and employer groups, or for that matter a bank, appointing board directors to funds left open the risk that appointments would not be made in members' best interests. His proposal would give ASIC the all-clear to intervene in cases where funds appointed unskilled directors with ties to unions, employer groups or the parent banking organisation.

He said funds 'must also recognise and deal with conflicts between the interests of members and the interests of shareholders or nominating organisations ... Whatever the processes for the nomination or selection of directors, all directors must meet the best-interests obligation. As superannuation funds become larger and more complicated, the greater the need also grows for a skilled and efficient board of directors. The greater the need for board skills, the more pressing it is for nomination and appointment processes to recognise those needs expressly. Neither of those principles refers to the interests of those who stood behind the establishment of the fund or those who continue to stand behind it. Neither of those principles permits pursuit of any objective other than the best interests of members.'

Major vertically integrated banks would face legal action if they continued a practice of cross-selling services and kicking back lucrative contracts to their own related parties. Instead, they would be required to put out tenders to market for services that were in the best interests of members.

Hayne also recommended banning the deduction of any advice fees from a low-fee MySuper account and limiting the fees able to be charged on other superannuation products. Companies would be prohibited from hawking super products, and superannuation companies would be unable to offer cosy entertainment packages or special deals to employers to win 'default' status to manage worker savings.

In insurance, Hayne recommended a well-overdue redrafting of the law to ensure the sector no longer enjoyed the loopholes it had so thoroughly exploited. Hard sells of insurance products would be banned, and funeral expense insurance policies would be defined as a financial product to bring them under the remit of ASIC. Doing so would threaten the very existence of companies such as ACBF. Bonuses that could be paid to car sellers for add-on insurance products would be capped, and car sellers would be required to hold credit licences to ensure they were kept to the same standards as other lenders.

Other remuneration would also face a stiff overhaul. Under Hayne's plan, front-line bankers would be subjected to an annual review of their remuneration systems to ensure pay was focused not only on what staff did, but on how they did it.

For the punter on the street, there would be a new 'compensation scheme of last resort' for those unable to be remediated by a financial company. For the farmers, a national farm-debt mediation scheme would be set up to intervene in disputes between distressed farmers and banks. Hayne also recommended that lenders stop charging crippling rates of interest to agribusiness borrowers teetering on default. Liquidators and receivers would only be appointed to sell distressed farming land as 'a remedy of last resort', enshrining this provision in the industry's code of practice.

When it came to the entities guarding against misconduct, there was an obvious winner and an obvious loser. Despite the bludgeoning it had copped at the hands of the royal commission, ASIC had its remit specifically expanded by eleven recommendations. APRA, on the other hand, had its powers and remit hobbled.

Hayne relinquished more radical ideas that could have taken power away from both regulators. He retained the 'twin peaks' model of regulation, with ASIC keeping its responsibility as the primary watchdog against misconduct, and APRA continuing as a prudential regulator but handing over responsibility for clamping down on superannuation breaches of the law to its colleague. ASIC would also be brought into the administration and regulation of the Banking Executive Accountability Regime, which APRA currently had sole watch over.

The government immediately launched a capability review of APRA, a long-overdue examination that it had avoided for half a decade after the idea was first floated. As was the case when ASIC underwent its own capability review in 2015 led by former Treasury member Karen Chester, the APRA capability review, to be led by Graeme Samuel, would likely result in wholesale denunciation of the flaws that had contributed to APRA being asleep at the wheel. It was Samuel who had so thoroughly cut through the history of failures at CBA when he was given responsibility in mid-2017 for doing a prudential review of the bank in the wake of the money-laundering scandal. Now, the regulator that had given him the review job would be on the receiving end of his findings.

While ASIC was given a boost with new criminal and civil penalties at its disposal—laws it was more than keen to put to good use under new leadership—both regulators would now be overseen by a new authority to ensure they were doing their jobs. This would ensure the rest of Hayne's recommendations were being adhered to. ASIC would approach enforcement with a starting point of focusing on court action rather than infringement notices.

Under Hayne's plan, ASIC would expand its annual reporting of breaches to name companies as well as the type of breach, publicly denouncing bad behaviour. And, while there was separation of responsibilities for regulating the system, Hayne recommended that the law should be amended to oblige APRA and ASIC to cooperate with each other, share information, and notify each other of believed breaches of the law.

In the end, Hayne was willing to give ASIC, the watchdog that hadn't barked, a second chance.

The senior ranks of ASIC had already been bolstered. James Shipton had received Chester's capability review of the regulator when he joined as its new chairman. A few months later, Chester herself and Daniel Crennan, QC, would join as deputy chairmen, with Crennan, whose focus was on enforcement, immediately launching a review of ASIC to gear it up for more court actions. Sean Hughes, a senior regulator who had cleaned up New Zealand's financial sector, was also appointed, and superannuation veteran Danielle Press was recruited to tackle misconduct in the superannuation sector.

At every available point, ASIC stressed it was ready to change the country's perception of financial regulation.

It was a message Hayne was keen to hear. 'Importantly, ASIC has acknowledged that its enforcement culture must change,' he said. 'It should be given time to demonstrate that changes can be made and to demonstrate that, once made, the changes are durable.'

To coincide with the release of the royal commission final report, Frydenberg committed to reviewing funding for the financial regulators ahead of his federal budget. 'The findings and recommendations from the royal commission, along with more than twenty referrals, will require the regulators to take on new responsibilities and, in many cases, simply do more,' he said. It was a recommendation that in order to change the system, regulators had to be properly funded to enact change. If nothing else, the bollocking ASIC had received had shown the government the necessity of not starving the watchdog of vital resources.

Still, as Hayne remarked at the start of his report, senior management and boards were responsible for watching over the behaviour within their own institutions. It couldn't always be left to the regulators.

It would be fitting, then, that the comments he made about culture and governance were among the most important in the 1000-page report.

If the royal commission revealed how toxic culture and poor governance had led to a crisis at the heart of Australian finance, proposing solutions to a cultural problem would prove difficult.

Culture cannot be regulated. There is no way to instruct boards of directors and executives to have a good culture. This is not to say that culture cannot be changed—it is malleable and can be surprisingly quick to shift. However, it is also innate and stubborn.

Hayne described the culture of a bank as the shared values and norms that drive behaviour, as 'what people do when no one is watching'. At the same time, he said, governance is the structure and processes by which a company is run. 'By shaping how the business is run, governance shapes culture,' he said. In this way, governance and culture are determined by how decisions are made, and by whom they are made. 'It is rightly said that the tone of the entity is, and must be, set at the top,' said Hayne. 'That tone must also be echoed from the bottom and reinforced at every level of the entity's management and supervision. A culture that fosters poor leadership, poor decision-making or poor behaviour will undermine the governance framework of the entity.'

Over the decade following the GFC, banks on either side of the Atlantic had gone about ensuring there were clear lines of accountability when things went awry. In Australia, by contrast, the complex structure of management hierarchies had insulated senior executives from shouldering the blame when there were issues.

For example, when Commonwealth Bank broke anti-money-laundering laws, its board of directors remained largely clueless as to the extent of the wrongdoing for years after the breach was first identified. In the case of NAB's fees-for-no-service disaster, the company's board failed to press senior executives to resolve the issue in a timely manner.

According to APRA chairman Wayne Byres, the Australian banking industry by the end of the royal commission was only at the start of a long journey towards repairing its conduct and culture. One of the major problems in the sector was that there was no clear accountability for problems that arose. 'No one has actually taken responsibility for issues,' Byres told the commission. 'Boards have not known how to apply consequences because it's not clear who was responsible for things.'

The royal commission, Hayne said, had brought one kind of accountability on executives. By forcing bankers and companies onto the stand, there had been a public condemnation of the behaviour.

In the final round of hearings, Hayne said, most chief executives and chairmen professed to having learned something about the causes of misconduct, and many had ideas to respond to the revelations. 'But the nature and extent of their engagement with the issues differed rather more markedly than I had expected,' he said. 'It seemed to me that there remain elements of unwillingness to recognise, and to accept responsibility for, poor conduct of the kinds examined by this inquiry.'

As the final report was being hurriedly read by the hundred or so journalists in the media lock-up, who were given just three hours to consume the entirety of the documents before they were made public, there was one page that resonated: page 411. There, nestled unceremoniously at the tail end of Hayne's ruminations on culture and governance, were a few quick thoughts on the leadership of the big four banks.

CBA, perhaps the biggest contributor to the momentum for a royal commission, was unique among the major lenders, Hayne said. 'None of the other large banks have been confronted so directly with why each has had its own conduct and compliance issues.' With a lengthy and public inquiry into its governance and cultural failings already completed, along with the haste at which it indicated it wanted to implement change throughout the organisation and led by a contrite, young, ambitious and, importantly, sincere new chief executive in Matt Comyn, the bank appeared to have accepted its fate. 'I was persuaded that Mr Comyn, CEO of CBA, is well aware of the size and nature of the tasks that lie ahead of CBA,' Hayne said.

ANZ, led by an agent of cultural change, Shayne Elliott, was also endorsed by Hayne. 'I have little doubt that Mr Elliott, CEO of ANZ, is also well aware of the size and nature of the tasks that lie ahead of ANZ.'

There would be challenges for Westpac chief Brian Hartzer, Hayne said, pointing to that bank's decision to retain its scandal-prone wealth management unit, but the company appeared to be in capable hands: 'While I do not doubt Mr Hartzer, CEO of Westpac, when he says that Westpac has sought to reset its relationship with ASIC, only time will tell whether that proves to be right.'

Lastly—and there was no mistake that it had been left to last—Hayne delivered his verdict on NAB.

NAB 'stands apart from the other three major banks,' he said. 'Having heard from both the CEO, Mr Thorburn, and the chair, Dr Henry, I am not as confident as I would wish to be that the lessons of the past have been learned. More particularly, I was not persuaded that NAB is willing to accept the necessary responsibility for deciding, for itself, what is the right thing to do, and then having its staff act accordingly.

'I thought it telling that Dr Henry seemed unwilling to accept any criticism of how the board had dealt with some issues. I thought it telling that Mr Thorburn treated all issues of fees for no service as nothing more than carelessness combined with system deficiencies. I thought it telling that in the very week that NAB's CEO and chair were to give evidence before the commission, one of its staff should be emailing bankers urging them to sell at least five mortgages each before Christmas.

'Overall, my fear—that there may be a wide gap between the public face NAB seeks to show and what it does in practice—remains.'

Thorburn cancelled the rest of his planned long-service leave. For a second time in six months, the bank boss hastily arranged a video message to send out to staff and customers. It went live at 6.48 a.m. the day after the royal commission report was published.

At times stumbling over his words, Thorburn stressed that NAB would be embracing the 'ambition and the recommendations' contained in the report. 'There is clearly more work for us to do at NAB. We are taking steps to earn your trust. We want to earn your trust. We want to get better,' he said. It was a message for his customers, but clearly it was also a message for his board colleagues who were, like him, dwelling on the comments made on page 411. Thorburn was in the fight of his life to salvage his job.

Henry also set about protecting his reputation and his job. 'In his final report Commissioner Hayne said I seemed unwilling to accept criticism of how the board had dealt with some of the issues raised by the commission,' he said. 'I am disappointed that the commissioner formed this view. I know that it is not so.'

To most observers, the imminent departure of the duo seemed inevitable. Piling on the pressure was Prime Minister Scott Morrison, who instructed the bankers to 'reflect on' their positions.

The atmosphere was only compounded when the head of the RBA, Philip Lowe, was asked a day later whether chief executives and chairmen should take responsibility for the Hayne findings. In a Press Club address on Sydney Harbour, hosted by Westpac bankers with ABA boss Anna Bligh in tow, Dr Lowe's message could not be misunderstood.

'Should the leaders take responsibility? Of course they should take responsibility' he said. 'Cultural change really starts at the top in organisations. Leaders in organisations really need to be focused on delivering the right culture. It's something that at the Reserve Bank we talk about. There has to be accountability and it starts at the top.'

Institutional NAB shareholders were also circling. They had already shown their dissatisfaction with the bank's leadership just two months earlier, delivering a stunning 88 per cent vote against NAB's remuneration report—the highest ever recorded.

The country's sovereign wealth fund, the Future Fund, was likewise in on the act. Fund chairman Peter Costello revealed it had voted against NAB at the bank's AGM to send a 'pretty clear message' that the way it was paying its executives was not appropriate, and questioning how Henry had let shareholder discontent get so out of hand. 'I don't think any sensible director would ignore that. Most wouldn't let it get to that stage. You've got to ask what they were thinking,' Costello said.

The NAB board, based in Sydney, held two crisis meetings in the bank's George Street tower in the days after the Hayne report was released. Thorburn was stuck in Melbourne. It was only a matter of time before the board came to the same view as everyone else. An external adviser was brought in to convince some of the old guard to move on the chairman and the chief executive.

Just three days after the release of Hayne's final report, Thorburn and Henry reluctantly agreed on the need for them to resign. A statement was drawn up and sent out. There would finally be accountability for the bank's behaviour.

To explain the decision, a conference call was set up and the nation's business journalists dialled in for the historic moment. As the panic of the previous days subsided into acceptance, the mood of the moment changed too. While they had been shocked at Hayne's remarks, after forty-eight hours of 'deep reflection' the duo had decided it was best to go. There was no anger on the call, only resignation. Thorburn even thanked reporters for the tone of their questions.

When he was asked whether there was anything in particular in the final report that had convinced him of the need to resign, there was only one possible answer. 'Have you seen page four hundred and eleven?' he said, laughing ruefully. A few paragraphs nestled in the 1000-page document had been enough to seal the fate of two of the country's most senior bankers.

Henry and Thorburn were both sad to be leaving the business, and the manner in which it had to happen. 'While today is primarily a sad day, I accept that it's an important one,' Thorburn told the dozens of reporters hooked up on the phone call. 'I look forward to this company going on and being great into the future.'

Despite convincing the reluctant big four banks to establish the royal commission, Henry had become one of its most high-profile victims. 'I wasn't anticipating something of that nature,' he said of page 411. However, for many who had observed his gruff performance on the commission witness stand in November, such a slap-down wasn't entirely unexpected.

Henry said his decision to leave NAB couldn't be attributed to one newspaper article, one single event or one night of restless sleep before taking the stand. 'Have you lost your job because you woke up on the wrong side of the bed?' one journalist asked him.

'Maybe I did hop out of the bed on the wrong side,' Henry said. 'I've relived that performance many times in my mind. I really wish I had performed much better … I'm quite upset about that. I do not believe that the views [Hayne] formed about NAB could be explained simply by the claim that I got out of the wrong side of the bed.'

Until that day, sixteen senior executives across the Australian financial services sector had lost their jobs as a direct result of the royal commission. Now, two more scalps had been added to the pile. Hayne had come, seen and conquered.

Personal accountability was a new feature of Australia's financial system, and Henry and Thorburn wanted to show that the most senior executives at the biggest companies could no longer avoid it.

16

ILL FARES THE LAND

There is always more to the story.

The royal commission created its own narrative, which was carried by the nation's media and regurgitated in everyday discussion in a familiar, self-reinforcing process that ends up creating a single agreed version of reality. The same narrative has worked its way into the pages of this book.

However, the first draft of history often shows just a fraction of the whole story. Often, there are stories that remain untold.

In April 2016, when Kelly O'Dwyer was assistant treasurer, she visited the United States. In Washington, DC, she struck up a number of conversations at the G20 finance ministers and central bank governors meeting and at the International Monetary Fund and World Bank spring meetings.

Her talks with some of the world's most powerful financial regulators and government figures came a month after Commonwealth Bank had been hit by the CommInsure life insurance scandal. Just before she hopped on the plane to the US, Labor had started openly considering its support for a royal commission into the banking sector, a position it would soon officially adopt.

As O'Dwyer met leading international figures over the next fortnight, she was stunned at the questions she received. Many of the global central bank representatives who chatted to her only wanted to discuss one thing: was there a systemic misconduct problem in the Australian financial sector that warranted a royal commission?

As the assistant treasurer—who was responsible for the financial services and superannuation sector—flew back to Australia, she became convinced of the need to restore confidence in the country's banking sector. If it was going to face calls for a royal commission, the government needed to have a plan.

O'Dwyer started meeting with Peter Costello, a former treasurer and her predecessor in the federal seat of Higgins. She was not entirely opposed to a royal commission, but as she discussed with Costello what was needed to diagnose and fix the issues in the finance sector, she decided it would not be a bad idea to proceed with caution.

The government needed to be clear on what problems were afflicting the banking, insurance and superannuation sectors. It would also need to ensure there was no further contagion of scandals in the sector, in order to keep the system stable for customers, for overseas investors and for the banks' own operations.

Under Prime Minister Malcolm Turnbull, the government started considering the creation of a compensation scheme for victims of financial misconduct. It wasn't a royal commission, but it was hoped it would soothe the deteriorating public sentiment.

As O'Dwyer worked on pulling a scheme together with the help of commercial law professor Ian Ramsay and consumer advocate Alan Kirkland, she became weary of the types of people who were seeking redress through her office. While she received numerous reports of horrible treatment of consumers by super funds and life insurers, she was also inundated by spivs and businesspeople who wanted compensation for their own poor business decisions.

There were property developers who wanted the bank to pay for their losses after their projects fell over. She had no sympathy for small businesspeople whose poor handling of company finances resulted in the bank foreclosing on their loans. One was a parliamentary colleague: One Nation senator Rod Culleton. Senator Culleton, whose term ultimately ended after only six months, was a cereal and sheep farmer until he lost his farm in 2013, after which he took to fighting ANZ in the courts and in the media.

O'Dwyer spent countless hours arguing with Culleton, who once presented her with a drawn-up document purporting to show evidence that the existence of Commonwealth Bank was not in accordance with Magna Carta.

Culleton was pushing for a royal commission, but his party's leader, Pauline Hanson, struck a deal with the government to back down from that proposal in return for a parliamentary committee inquiry into foreclosed farming loans. Hanson chaired the committee, which was established in early 2017, in a momentary slip-up by Turnbull, who didn't at the time realise he had given the minor party the power to chair the inquiry during the discussions with Hanson and her senators over their support for various pieces of government legislation during the horsetrading.

Soon after, O'Dwyer went on maternity leave and gave birth to her second child. By the time she returned to work a few weeks later, she was thoroughly convinced of the need to hold a royal commission into the banks.

It was July 2017, and O'Dwyer had been holding discussions with banks and superannuation funds. She knew where many of the bodies were buried. Having also asked the Productivity Commission to conduct a wholesale review of the superannuation sector, she was more than aware of the need to launch a much more powerful examination of the nation's retirement savings managers, who were frustrating the PC's review. Senior members of the industry fund sector laughing at her suggestion that a royal commission needed to happen only firmed her resolve.

When, not even a month later, the anti-money-laundering regulator AUSTRAC launched a Federal Court action against CBA alleging more than 50,000 breaches of the law, she urged the government to launch a commission. O'Dwyer had even drawn up draft terms of reference for a royal commission into the banking, insurance and superannuation industries. Her office had drafted notes on how such an inquiry could be conducted and how the government could sell it. The royal commission was ready to be announced.

Despite the AUSTRAC claims implicating CBA in frustrating the authorities' attempts to clamp down on terrorism financing, giving the government a clear reason to launch a royal commission, O'Dwyer was blocked by internal resistance. Turnbull and his treasurer, Scott Morrison, couldn't find common ground. Sources say Turnbull was wracked by indecision, at times open to the government launching a commission and at others swinging back against the idea. When Morrison was open to the idea, he lacked the support of his prime minister. The two never seemed to want a royal commission at the same point.

Instead, the government opted to give APRA the job of doing a wholesale review of CBA's culture when Morrison was not satisfied with the bank's explanations for its failings.

The failure to launch a commission only strengthened Nationals senator Barry O'Sullivan's plans to introduce a private member's bill for a commission of inquiry into the banks. O'Dwyer believed this could be an option the government should pursue, and went about giving oversight to O'Sullivan as he drafted the terms of reference, as I detailed at the start of this book.

However, she was disheartened by O'Sullivan's lack of nous and had to insist that such an inquiry include a proper examination of the super sector. She attempted to get O'Sullivan to fashion a sensible and targeted royal commission, urging him to take a step back and work with the government to arrange a workable outcome. It was of no use. O'Sullivan wasn't open to being shepherded through the process.

During this time, NAB chairman Ken Henry and NAB senior executive Mike Baird were stalking the ministerial wing at Parliament House. Baird, a former NSW premier who had joined NAB after retiring from politics, was close with Turnbull, and Henry had long-standing government contacts due to his time as Treasury secretary.

The duo came down to Canberra to meet with Turnbull and Morrison frequently in the months leading up to the royal commission, presenting the government with a plan where the banks could formally ask the government to establish a properly constituted inquiry. The idea was divisive among Turnbull, Morrison and O'Dwyer. Why would the government want to look like it was doing the banks' work?

However, in the end this was the plan Turnbull and Morrison ended up choosing. The night before the major banks released their calls for a sensible royal commission in a statement to the ASX, Henry emailed a copy of the draft statement to Morrison. The rest is now history—or a fraction of it.

A little over a year later, a few weeks after the publication of Kenneth Hayne's final report, O'Dwyer stood up in parliament to give her valedictory speech. She was leaving politics after ten years as an MP. 'I am glad we called the royal commission into the banking and financial services sector,' she said. 'It was the right thing to do. We were so keen to address the issues we had already identified that we underestimated just how strong a disinfectant the sunlight from a royal commission would be.'

Most of the time, governments will take the most expedient course of action. Ideology plays an important part in determining the path taken, but expediency often dominates the choice of routes available.

The story above shows that the public face of a government can mask a great number of alternative directions being considered by competing ministers. That competition will now largely play out between the Coalition and the Labor Party. While Hayne has provided a road map for reform, it is up to each side of politics to decide how to implement it. The early indicators are that reforming the financial sector will sometimes be a dirty business.

Just a few weeks after pledging to implement all the recommendations, both sides of politics ditched the plan to clamp down on the bonuses being paid to mortgage brokers. With $3 billion a year at stake, the mortgage broker sector had instantly wedged the government and Labor with a massive campaign against the measures.

Of course, some of the concerns about the reshaping of the mortgage broker sector were legitimate. More than half of all loans in Australia are bought through a mortgage broker, and the sector has grown to be a vital part of the country's financial infrastructure. The banning of upfront and trailing commissions would likely put many brokers out of business—either that, or the salaries they enjoyed would become significantly smaller. If the sector was hobbled, it could reduce the access many smaller lenders had in reaching borrowers. Smaller banks don't have the branch network the big four banks enjoy.

The failure to adopt ideal reforms in favour of second-best regulations is a recurring problem in the financial sector. Because the big four banks have grown to be so large, any changes to laws governing the financial system can inadvertently hand them even more power.

Indeed, despite losing about $80 billion in share-market value over the course of the royal commission, the failure of Hayne to recommend any major structural changes to the big banks resulted in a $19 billion stock-price rally the day after his report was released. Bank stocks each rose about 5 per cent in one day. That compared to shares in the two largest Australian brokers, Mortgage Choice and Australian Finance Group, which crashed more than 25 per cent on the day Hayne's report was released.

Global ratings agency Moody's said the fact the royal commission had not recommended breaking up the banking oligopoly supported the sector's 'strong and stable profitability'.

As soon as the recommendations were made public, the mortgage broking industry began contacting MPs and senators, complaining the sky would fall in if the rivers of gold flowing into their pockets were stopped. Electoral offices were inundated with claims that the big four banks would be anointed with renewed power, crushing the benefits of competition in the market.

Hayne had known that forces would mobilise against his recommendations. 'In their submissions, some entities used the undoubted need for care in recommending change as a basis for saying that there should be no change,' he wrote in his final report. 'The "Caution" sign was read as if it said "Do Not Enter". "Disruption" and similar terms can be used, and in some submissions to the commission were used, as little more than pejorative synonyms for "change".'

Other nations, such as Denmark in particular, grappled with the same transition for mortgage brokers years ago. A fee-for-service approach was adopted, and borrowers in Denmark are still able to buy a mortgage.

As the sector in Australia quickly formulated a response to the attack on its remuneration model, consumer advocate groups quit en masse from a forum aimed at improving governance and remuneration practices in the sector, accusing brokers of being 'disingenuous'. This means that the Combined Industry Forum, established in the wake of a review of the sector by ASIC and following the recommendations of the Sedgwick review of banker bonuses, now lacks any members interested specifically in consumer outcomes. Choice, the Consumer Action Law Centre, Financial Counselling Australia and the Financial Rights Legal Centre left the forum, arguing that the sector 'cannot be trusted' to stand up for customers.

'We have been locked in discussions with them for years, with no progress on introducing a best-interests duty for brokers or removing conflicts from the sector,' Choice chief executive Alan Kirkland said. 'With many members of the forum now backing the mortgage broking lobby's political campaign against the royal commission reforms, it is clear that they are only interested in blocking meaningful change.'

Taking power away from the financial industry is tough.

While the banking and wealth management sector has incredible amounts of financial power, much of that influence is channelled through another powerful sector: the lobbying industry. In Australia, there are sixty-eight industry associations representing banks, super-annuation funds, insurers, financial planners, accountants, and so on. For a country with a small population, that is an enormous number of lobby groups representing a globally small economic industry. Is it any wonder that the financial sector maintains a 10 per cent share of all Australian economic output? Only Switzerland, a global centre for banking, has a financial sector with more domestic power than Australia—which, for all its self-promotion, lacks the regional stature of the Hong Kong and Singaporean financial centres in Asia.

Public policy think tank the Grattan Institute has found that after retiring from parliament, more than one in four federal ministers since 1990 have gone on to work for a lobbyist firm, peak body or other special interest. The revolving door between government and industry has whittled away the ability for MPs to take decisive action on vested interests, distorting the democratic process.

After analysing the industries most represented by the roughly 500 commercial lobbyists working in parliament, the Grattan found that almost 80 per cent of businesses who had hired lobbyists were operating in highly regulated industries. This meant that the design of the law had an unusually large impact on how those industries generated and maintained profits and revenue. Making the issue worse, the public service has over recent decades grown weak in terms of shaping laws. Many Treasury staff members now see their main role as shaving off the rough edges of policies that may harm the economy, instead of advocating for sound laws and regulations that operate on a principled basis.

With many industry organisations also becoming more partisan and wedded to current business models, the field of public debate has been vacated by sensible voices. It is increasingly left to statutory bodies to run silent campaigns against bad government policy. This puts government departments in a tricky position where they must develop strong policy positions while avoiding accusations of bias or politicisation.

Another problem arises when senior members of those departments, or of the regulators, look to the industry they are supposed to regulate as a golden parachute scheme. The boards of Australian financial institutions are littered with former heads of Treasury, the RBA and other government departments.

Of course, NAB was once lucky enough to count a former Treasury secretary as its chairman, and halfway through the royal commission another former Treasury secretary, John Fraser, joined AMP. Westpac was previously chaired by former Treasury boss Ted Evans.

When Glenn Stevens stepped down as head of the Reserve Bank, he hopped across the road at Macquarie Place to Macquarie Bank, on whose board also sits former Productivity Commission chairman Gary Banks. ANZ employed former RBA boss Ian Macfarlane as a board director. Former ASIC senior executives and APRA members sit on numerous financial company boards.

These men and women are some of the most patriotic Australians, with independent minds and independent behaviour, and it would be silly to think they have simply sold out to the companies they once regulated. But perception matters to many Australians. If the person on the street can't believe regulators will use their time in office to enforce the law or drive better standards that might threaten company bottom lines, then there is an issue. Maintaining trust in the financial system must be a primary motivator for senior regulators.

It was refreshing, two days after the release of Hayne's report, when RBA governor Philip Lowe questioned the profitability of the banks. Speaking in Sydney, he said that while banking sectors in many other developed English-speaking nations had registered a fall in profitability in the wake of the GFC, the profitability of Australian banks remained high by international standards.

'At the moment the Australian banks are earning roughly 13 per cent return on equity,' Lowe said. 'When I talk to overseas bankers and ask them what return on equity they're targeting, a number around 10 is common. The Australian banks still have higher returns on equity than many international banks. I don't know how long that's sustainable, whether extra competition in the system will drive that or whether they have low credit losses at the moment so high returns on equity. It is a good question to ask or contemplate: why it is that the Australian banks can earn, on average, higher rates on return on equity than similar banks overseas? I'm not sure of the answer to that.'

While Lowe rightly questioned the profitability of the major lenders, his offsider on the other side of the ditch went one further.

In a strange twist of fate, New Zealand lacks its own banks. Its major banking players are all subsidiaries of the major Australian banks. In the same week Lowe made his comments, Reserve Bank of New Zealand governor Adrian Orr attacked the four major banks for making supersized profits at a time he was attempting to force them to hold more capital to insulate them from economic shocks.

'We have to remember that the return on equity should be related to the risks they are taking,' Governor Orr said. 'At the moment, the return on equity for banking is incredibly strong and we would even hazard to say over and above the risks they are holding themselves as private banks, because there is an aspect in most OECD countries of the ability to free ride—where returns can be privatised and losses can be socialised.'

An optimistic interpretation of Hayne's central recommendations would be to say that, once conflicts of interest are banished from the system, true competition between financial companies will result in diminishing margins of profitability. A proposal that the ACCC conduct five-yearly studies of vertical and horizontal integration in the financial system—where companies cross-sell products owned by arms of their own conglomerations—could, over time, reduce the market domination of the oligopoly.

While Hayne's recommendations received harsh criticism for opting against wholesale structural separation of banks and wealth management businesses, and against a tearing-up of the main regulatory frameworks that guide the system, he was also considerate of the economic costs of doing so. When the government drew up the terms of reference for the royal commission, it specifically asked him to be mindful of the economic impacts of any recommendation that he made.

In many cases, it is more prudent to allow companies to slowly restructure over time rather than force immediate revolution. If slow changes of legislation are exhausting to guide through parliament, wholesale change would be dead on arrival.

If there can be no doubt that the primary cause of the misconduct in the financial system is the companies themselves, then the primary responsibility for restructuring their behaviour also rests with the banks. If bank culture and governance change, it will result in better outcomes for consumers.

When independent consultants were first brought in to investigate the failures in the banks' wealth management operations, what they found were recurring references to 'toxic revenue'. In banker parlance, this refers to product streams that produce such high rates of profitability that it is thought there must be an issue with the product.

Take the case of consumer credit insurance, where expensive policies were sold to unsuspecting customers and rarely claimed upon. Profits on the products were so lucrative that investigating the reasons why they were delivering such revenue for the company would only reveal that it was due to the toxic nature of the products. Bankers believed any product line delivering toxic revenue was best left unexamined.

During the royal commission, Westpac reviewed each and every financial product the bank offered. As it carried out the review, loans sold by financial advisers to self-managed super funds were shut down. Commonwealth Bank soon followed Westpac, and now no major bank will offer the so-called limited recourse borrowing arrangements.

If bankers hold themselves accountable, consumers will be better off.

In 1770, in his poem 'The Deserted Village', Oliver Goldsmith recorded his thoughts after surveying some of the unintended consequences of the Industrial Revolution and the pursuit of wealth at any cost. One line continues to resonate with me: 'Ill fares the land, to hastening ills a prey, where wealth accumulates, and men decay.'

Wherever enormous financial power amasses, so too does political and social power. Power has a tendency to corrupt. The narrative of the royal commission has forced the banking sector to accept that change is necessary. However, into any power vacuum will soon step another force. The risk of the royal commission is that while the banking sector has been thoroughly shamed by the process, the not-for-profit industry superannuation sector has come out without so much as a scratch. If the banks have been dethroned, there is a danger that another sector has been anointed to take the crown. This means the future of the superannuation sector needs to be more closely examined.

By 2035, there will be $10 trillion in the nation's retirement savings pool, and the lion's share will be managed by industry funds. It will be one of the most powerful sectors in the world.

As the royal commission revealed untold rates of criminality in the bank-run retail fund sector, the industry funds were shown to be beacons of sound, consumer-friendly financial management. Savers have already begun voting with their feet: Australia's largest industry fund, AustralianSuper, had received nearly $4 billion in savings directly from the retail sector by the time Hayne handed down his final report, and Hostplus said its rate of joining members jumped 350 per cent during 2018.

But the shift, and the growth of the sector, present new and different dilemmas.

With only a year to trawl through all misconduct in the financial system, Hayne had little time to conduct a thorough review of the mechanics of the industry fund sector. Multiple notices to produce information were sent to industry funds, but it was beholden to the funds themselves to nominate what they believed was misconduct. In the industry fund sector, outright misconduct wasn't necessarily the problem to be examined.

Rather, the sector's structure is evolving into one that closely mirrors the interconnected, vertically and horizontally integrated nature of the bank-run wealth management industry. Cross-subsidisation is rife throughout the sector, and the money guaranteed to the funds through enterprise bargaining deals represents a key sustaining life force that allows complacency to develop.

While there are a host of diligent, thoughtful companies, there is also an underbelly of mismanagement and deleterious consumer outcomes. A series of small industry funds governed by union and employer groups have presided over funds with sky-high rates of 'zombie' inactive accounts, made up of savings that are lost or forgotten and that have failed to be reunited with their members, and this has allowed small funds to exist where they otherwise would not be able to.

These include the CFMEU-backed $3 billion First Super, where 44 per cent of members are inactive, and the $3 billion Club Super, which is backed by United Voice and the Australian Workers Union and has 42 per cent of its members considered inactive. The $1 billion Meat Industry Employees Superannuation Fund has 36 per cent of its membership inactive, as does the $3 billion United Voice–backed Intrust Super Fund.

Several funds in the system, including First Super, are reluctant to leave the industry or merge, even under pressure from APRA. The $3 billion fund, which is co-chaired by Michael O'Connor, the brother of Labor workplace relations spokesman Brendan O'Connor, manages the retirement savings of more than 60,000 workers in the timber, pulping and furniture industries. Despite its top-quartile investment performance, its relatively small membership base is ageing and drawn from shrinking industries. While every other union-and-employee-backed industry fund has signed up to the Insurance in Superannuation Voluntary Code of Practice along with major retail funds run by the big four banks and wealth managers, First Super has not. It is the only one not to have done so.

There seems no good reason for many funds to be controlled by the same union. If the funds are concerned about accusations that they are taking members' money and handing it over to unions, then it would make sense to consolidate funds controlled by the same union. But this does not happen.

The superannuation system is beset by consumer apathy and disengagement. While some funds work tirelessly to put members' interests first, others are, at best, complacent. Public policy can be the first line of defence for consumers in these funds.

The PC's central recommendation—that prospective employees should be provided with a list of the ten top-performing super funds for them to choose from—is vital to force funds to operate in members' best interests. On its face, it seems like an entirely uncontroversial idea: simple, useful information provided to consumers that would have the effect of kicking super funds into gear. The PC reckons it will deliver a $165,000 boost to the average retirement balance. Underperforming funds will also be policed under the so-called 'elevated outcomes test' to ensure laggards are punished, which will further help savers. Consumers wouldn't even be forced into one of the top ten funds.

However, the proposal sparked sustained condemnation from the industry fund sector that was then filtered through the Labor Party.

There are more than 100 sub-scale funds in the system, where funds are too small to keep fees low. Many of these are small industry funds. Should the best-in-show list put pressure on these small funds to merge, many of their union appointees would lose their postings, limiting their ability to direct where capital is invested and influence how big companies behave.

I'm a proud member of the Media, Entertainment & Arts Alliance, the union for journalists, actors, photographers and others who work in media, the arts and sport. The $5.6 billion Media Super, which takes board directors from the MEAA, has top-quartile performance, but it lost 6 per cent of its membership in 2018, and $80 million of its savings in rollovers. The media is under pressure, and as people leave the industry, most take their savings with them.

When the government proposed consolidating lost and idle accounts through the Australian Tax Office, Media Super, along with other small industry funds, was worried. With many inactive accounts, it would have to convince members to consolidate into Media Super rather than risk losing the assets that were subsidising those left in the fund. Gerard Noonan has been the fund's chairman for almost thirty years. One has to wonder how he plans to avert its looming liquidity shortfall.

The problem is that many directors don't want to give up the influence they can wield. Having, in early 2019, almost a trillion dollars to invest gives these funds a power to shape the economy in ways they favour. This is not de facto a bad thing, but it isn't ideal, either.

As industry funds are under intense pressure to deliver high rates of returns on the investments they make, the more pressure companies they invest in will be under to deliver high rates of profit. Replacing one set of institutional investors that seek to drive supersized profits in the firms they own with another set of institutional investors seeking to drive outperformance raises the risk that everyday consumers and workers will lose out.

On top of this, the cosiness among industry funds raises very real concerns about the concentration in ownership of companies and assets. Most Australians would not know it, but the jointly owned IFM Investors, an asset manager owned by the industry fund sector, controls nearly all the major airports in Australia. It is slowly gobbling up more infrastructure assets across the country, on which it expects to generate a significant investment return.

For the Labor Party, the situation in the industry fund sector represents its biggest challenge. It is likely that when the next financial crisis arrives, there will be some damage caused by the interconnectedness and interdependence of the industry fund sector. Then, Labor's pledge to increase the current rate of wages flowing into the super sector, rising from 9.5 per cent to 12 per cent, will only serve to make the industry more powerful and will be done at a significant cost to the average worker, and to the federal budget.

The funds management sector has been begging for the superannuation rate to increase for years, complaining that retirees could be left in the lurch if more of their wages aren't handed over. The Grattan Institute study found that the average retiree can already expect to receive an income of at least 91 per cent of their pre-retirement salary under current savings rates—well above the 70 per cent benchmark recommended by developed economies. Putting more wages away in super will mainly boost the retirement incomes of already-wealthy Australians, at a significant cost to the budget.

Low-income Australians who don't own their homes—a growing cohort who are failed by the way the current super system is set up— would be best served by a 40 per cent increase in rent assistance rather than sidelining even more of their salary into super, where meagre contributions are swallowed up by fees.

While more money going into super funds would be a huge windfall for wealth managers, the government would lose significantly more revenue due to the generous tax breaks built into the super system. Treasury modelling in 2013 found the government would continue to lose more revenue through concessional tax breaks than it saved in keeping self-funded retirees off the pension. Increasing the super guarantee rate to 12 per cent will result in the total super tax breaks adding more than 10 per cent to the nation's debt by 2050. This means the government will have less money to spend on programs such as aged care, education and hospitals—all to satiate a questionable claim from the superannuation industry.

As the royal commission drew to a close, the close relationship between the Labor Party and the Greens was on show when the two parties refused to vote for the 'Protecting Your Super' bill, first announced by O'Dwyer a year earlier. Labor and the Greens demanded the government agree to amendments that would carve out entire funds from the measures.

More than forty groups had swarmed parliament to lobby against the bills, which were expected to slice $3 billion in revenue out of the scandal-plagued life insurance industry. These included odd bedfellows such as Australia's largest insurer, the Hong Kong–based AIA Group, the ACTU and Industry Super Australia. In some cases, insurance sold in super—where 70 per cent of Australians obtain life insurance— has been found to potentially short-change workers by as much as $600,000 by the time they reach retirement, according to a report by actuarial firm Rice Warner.

If it remains impossible to legislate modest, sensible changes to policy affecting the industry fund sector, then it will be everyday Australians who end up paying for it. And with every Australian forced to engage with the super sector, which is already perhaps more financially powerful than the banking industry ever was, it could be a recipe for disaster.

The day Hayne was due to hand down his report, I called Nationals senator John 'Wacka' Williams again.

This time, he was on his property and livid because the new John Deere Gator he had just bought for his farm had dodgy wheels. His last Gator had run for more than a decade without any problems, and he'd put it to good use on his land. The wheels on his brand-new machine were already starting to fall apart.

'I thought you'd have enough stories over the last year, Michael,' Wacka said. It was true. While the royal commission had been great for the legal fraternity, it had also been great for journalists. Each day that the counsels assisting brought a new witness onto the stand, it was explosive. For the companies, it was a rolling catastrophe as they stumbled from one disaster to the next, but for the reporters, it was a rich vein of complex, stimulating stories, with the best headlines you could ask for.

The man who had first stood up in the Senate nearly a decade earlier and called for a royal commission into white-collar crime believed the royal commission had done a superb job. As he drove around regional communities, he had already sensed a change in the air. The banks were now dealing with drought-affected customers with some level of compassion. Sentiments had changed. It was important that this cultural change was made permanent.

Wacka reminded me that it was now just a week until he was due to give his valedictory speech in parliament. Like O'Dwyer, he had chosen to leave at the federal election after a decade in politics. To celebrate his time on Capital Circle, he had organised a party. 'It's Wacka's shout,' he said.

And so, on 13 February, Senator Williams stood up to the speaker's podium to give his final speech.

The gallery was packed. Watching from the seats open to the public was Commonwealth Bank's Matt Comyn, who had struck up a relationship with the senator after rising to the role of chief executive. Comyn had even visited the farm. A few seats to his left was whistleblower Jeff Morris, who had exposed the financial planning scandal at

CBA. A few benches over from Morris sat ASIC deputy chair Daniel Crennan, the man now tasked with taking companies to court. Adele Ferguson, responsible for much of the groundbreaking reporting into financial sector misconduct, was sitting close by.

'People might think I am the banks' enemy,' Wacka said. 'No, I am not. Often I say the bank has got it wrong but many, many times I say the customer has got it wrong as well. I have worked closely with the banks.'

The crowning achievement of his time in parliament was the Royal Commission into Misconduct in the Banking, Superannuation and Financial Services Industry. 'It is a bit sad to see the politics being played but if both sides of the chamber had listened to that recommendation in those days in 2014 we would have achieved a lot more a lot sooner,' he said. 'However, as they say, better late than never.'

While Wacka was never right on every issue, he carried himself in a manner that showed he fundamentally respected the work of those on the opposite side of the fence to him. 'The one sad thing about the Senate is that it works a lot better than the public thinks. When the public looks at the TV they see hand grenades being thrown around the chamber, a bitter atmosphere,' he said. 'It is not like that at all. We work close together on committee work and have achieved so much.'

Standing in the Senate courtyard after he had received a standing ovation for his time in parliament, Wacka was surrounded by bankers he had pushed onto the witness stand, regulators he had shamed into action through his dogged pursuit of accountability, and members of each parliamentary party who admired his honest, matter-of-fact approach to solving issues.

It was easy to feel that sometimes things do work out for the best. Perhaps, yes, things have changed.

ACKNOWLEDGEMENTS

No one expected what the royal commission would eventually produce. I expected, even less, by the end that I would be producing a book on the topic.

But these pages would not have been possible if it were not for the kind support and generosity of a few people to whom I must give my sincere thanks.

First, I am indebted to Louise Adler, who took on this project with enthusiasm, when she needn't have. I thank my publisher, Sally Heath, for providing honest and helpful feedback in the early stages of writing, and for not withdrawing the project after meeting for breakfast when I showed up late and, admittedly, heavily mentally scattered. The marketing and editing team, Emma Rusher, Tessa Connolly and Katie Purvis, were patient, thorough and professional.

Thanks must also go to my senior editors at *The Australian*, Paul Whittaker and John Lehmann, for instantly backing me when I told them about the book, and to Helen Trinca for her continued support and advice.

This book would have never come into existence if it were not for Alan Kohler, Robert Gottliebsen and Stephen Bartholomeusz at the now-defunct *Business Spectator*. Alan must be credited for, perhaps unwisely, agreeing to give me my first experience of gainful employment as a journalist, for which I am eternally grateful. I cherish Robert's enthusiasm and energy, which never cease to amaze me, and Stephen deserves a sainthood not only for withstanding my endless stream of cheeky questions, but for engaging with them carefully without any sense of pretence.

Also, I would be nowhere without the wise counsel and friendship of my university professors Margaret Simons, Simon Mann and David Nolan, who all taught me how to write, how to listen and how to think.

I count myself among the luckiest journalists in Australia to have the privilege of being wrangled for yarns each day by Eric Johnston, the country's foremost business editor. Eric has had to deal with my intransigence, my frustrations and my troublemaking more than anyone else, and has always managed to stop me from blowing myself up at the same time as cultivating my work more than I'd have thought possible. Likewise for his deputy, Amber Plum, whose tirelessness in herding cats week in and week out is a daily miracle.

Special thanks must go to my friends and colleagues in the Sydney pod. Whether it's bouncing arguments or jokes off Adam Creighton, laughing with Scott Murdoch, or rolling my eyes at the other boys with Sarah-Jane Tasker, I have gained so much by sharing the same space with these fantastic journalists. The same goes for Andrew White, whose arguments and humour have helped shape my knowledge of the business world and life at large.

My former bureau chief in Melbourne, John Ferguson, also rates a mention for making me feel right at home whenever I visit the bleak city. The same can be said of James Kirby, who took me on early to write for him.

I couldn't have written this book without the company and friendship of those stuck in Courtroom 4A of Melbourne's Federal Court. Elizabeth Redman, Dan Ziffer, Annelise Nielsen, Misa Han, Sarah Danckert, James Frost, and special mention to James Thomson, who gave me my first internship, and in doing so, opened up the world of journalism to me.

And, most importantly, my mate Ben Butler, who is, and remains, one of the country's most indelible characters. The time I spent with Ben, the jokes we swapped during the royal commission, the articles we wrote together, and the pub-driven conversations afterwards provided not only the foundation for many of the anecdotes carried in this book, but also the keystone to the way I see the world. Ben is the country's best journalist, and I am lucky to count him not only as a mentor—which he is to many—but also as one of my best mates.

Of course, even considering pitching the idea for a book would be a figment if it were not for my friendship with Rick Morton, whose motivation, advice and willingness to answer each and every question I had about writing a book was met with heartfelt sincerity.

The book would also not have come into being if it were not for the warm and enlightening conversation of Ryan Cropp, who encouraged me to share my thoughts in a more formal setting, after discussing the idea over a walk through Tunks Park, with Derrick Krusche, a living legend who was also there. I must also credit Rose Piper for her constant friendship, humour and encouragement, but who was probably hungover that day.

Writing this book was made exceedingly easier thanks to the expertise of Mark Lawrence, who taught me about financial risk, the hard work of senior members of ASIC who always kept up the fight, the Productivity Commission's meticulous studies carried about by Karen Chester and Peter Harris, and the many banking-sector analysts who have spared their time in talking to me over the years. It would also be remiss of me not to thank those in the major financial organisations and sector groups who have talked frankly and helpfully to me. There are so many good people in those organisations who seek to only do what is best, but who are mostly invisible to the public.

Last, but certainly not least, I thank the solicitors and lawyers working on the royal commission, the consumer groups and legal advocacy workers assembling the case studies and continually lobbying for better outcomes, and the witnesses who submitted their stories and who built up the courage to tell their tale on the stand at the royal commission. The nation is indebted to you.